Indian Classical Music and the Gramophone, 1900–1930

In 1902 The Gramophone Company in London sent out recording experts on "expeditions" across the world to record voices from different cultures and backgrounds. All over India, it was women who embraced the challenge of overcoming numerous social taboos and aesthetic handicaps that came along with this nascent technology. Women who took the plunge and recorded largely belonged to the courtesan community, called *tawaifs* and *devadasis*, in North and South India, respectively. Recording brought with it great fame, brand recognition, freedom from exploitative patrons, and monetary benefits to the women singers. They were to become pioneers of the music industry in the Indian sub-continent. However, despite the pioneering role played by these women, their stories have largely been forgotten. Contemporaneous with the courtesan women adapting to recording technology was the anti-nautch campaign that sought to ban these women from the performing space and brand them as common prostitutes. A vigorous renaissance and arts revival movement followed, leading to the creation of a new classical paradigm in both North Indian (Hindustani) and South Indian (Carnatic) classical music. This resulted in the standardisation, universalisation, and institutionalisation of Indian classical music. This newly created classical paradigm impacted future recordings of The Gramophone Company in terms of a shift in genres and styles. Vikram Sampath sheds light on the role and impact of The Gramophone Company's early recording expeditions on Indian classical music by examining the phenomenon through a sociocultural, historical, and musical lens. The book features the indefatigable stories of the women and their experiences in adapting to recording technology. The artists from across India featured are: Gauhar Jaan of Calcutta, Janki Bai of Allahabad, Zohra Bai of Agra, Malka Jaan of Agra, Salem Godavari, Bangalore Nagarathnamma, Coimbatore Thayi, Dhanakoti of Kanchipuram, Bai Sundarabai of Pune, and Husna Jaan of Banaras.

Vikram Sampath is a Bangalore-based historian who has authored six acclaimed books on Indian history and classical music. He is a Fellow of the Royal Historical Society (UK), recipient of several awards such as the Sahitya Akademi's Yuva Puraskar for English literature, and the ARSC Award for Excellence in Historical Research in Music. He has founded India's first online digital sound archive for vintage gramophone recordings called Archive of Indian Music.

SEMPRE Studies in The Psychology of Music
Series Editors

Graham F. Welch, *UCL Institute of Education, University College London, UK*
Adam Ockelford, *University of Roehampton, UK*
Ian Cross, *University of Cambridge, UK*

The theme for the series is the psychology of music, broadly defined. Topics include (i) musical development at different ages, (ii) exceptional musical development in the context of special educational needs, (iii) musical cognition and context, (iv) culture, mind and music, (v) micro to macro perspectives on the impact of music on the individual (from neurological studies through to social psychology), (vi) the development of advanced performance skills and (vii) affective perspectives on musical learning. The series presents the implications of research findings for a wide readership, including user-groups (music teachers, policy makers, parents) as well as the international academic and research communities. This expansive embrace, in terms of both subject matter and intended audience (drawing on basic and applied research from across the globe), is the distinguishing feature of the series, and it serves SEMPRE's distinctive mission, which is to promote and ensure coherent and symbiotic links between education, music and psychology research.

The Artist and Academia
Edited by Helen Phelan and Graham F. Welch

Expanding Professionalism in Music and Higher Music Education
A Changing Game
Edited by Helena Gaunt and Heidi Westerlund

Indian Classical Music and the Gramophone, 1900–1930
Vikram Sampath

Body and Force in Music
Metaphoric Constructions in Music Psychology
Youn Kim

For more information about this series, please visit:
https://www.routledge.com/music/series/SEMPRE

Indian Classical Music and the Gramophone, 1900–1930

Vikram Sampath

Routledge
Taylor & Francis Group

LONDON AND NEW YORK

Cover image: Historic Images / Alamy Stock Photo

First published 2023
by Routledge
4 Park Square, Milton Park, Abingdon, Oxon OX14 4RN

and by Routledge
605 Third Avenue, New York, NY 10158

Routledge is an imprint of the Taylor & Francis Group,
an informa business

British Library Cataloguing-in-Publication Data
A catalogue record for this book is available from the British Library

Library of Congress Cataloging-in-Publication Data
A catalog record has been requested for this book

ISBN: 978-0-367-42132-8 (hbk)
ISBN: 978-1-032-27016-6 (pbk)
ISBN: 978-0-367-82202-6 (ebk)

DOI: 10.4324/9780367822026

Typeset in Times New Roman
by KnowledgeWorks Global Ltd.

For Margaret Barrett, my supervisor, who has
been a friend, philosopher and guide; the driving
force behind this work.

Contents

Figures

Tables

Acknowledgements

To my principal supervisor, Prof. Margaret Barrett, I owe so much for her patience, insightful research guidance, and constant assistance at every stage of the study. Thank you so much Margaret for being such a fascinating role model who, while managing multiple projects, still dedicates time for her research students and their scholastic growth. Your intervention has helped me grow immensely as a researcher and your kindness has taught me what an ideal mentor ought to be like. I owe this thesis entirely to you.

I am deeply indebted to The University of Queensland for considering my work as part of the Doctoral programme and, in particular, to the School of Music and the School of History, Philosophy, Religion and Classics and its faculty and staff for their immense support during the entire course of my study. I am extremely grateful to the Australian Government and the University for granting me the highly prestigious International Post Graduate Research Scholarship (IPRS), Australian Postgraduate Award (APA) and the Prof. Singhal bequest from the School of History, Philosophy, Religion and Classics for making this journey financially viable for me.

To my associate supervisors, Dr. Robert Davidson (School of Music) and Dr. Adam Bowles (School of History, Philosophy, Religion and Classics) I owe many thanks for their constant guidance and critical perceptions that have shaped the work and its course. My sincere thanks are due to Dr. Simon Perry and Dr. Eve Klein of the School of Music for their invaluable feedback and to Elizabeth Farrington, Research and RHD Administrative Officer of the School for her constant support.

I am very thankful to Prof. Graham F Welch, Chair of Music Education, University College, London and to the Trustees of Society for Education, Music and Psychology Research (SEMPRE) for awarding the prestigious Gerry Farrell Travelling Scholarship to facilitate my travel, stay, and archival study in London for the research.

All the participants and respondents – senior and contemporary musicians, musicologists and record collectors in this study have my deepest gratitude for generously sharing their time, stories, and insights. Many of the senior musicians and musicologists were of advanced age and deteriorating health and some of them have sadly passed on and will be unable to see this work upon completion. Their kindness, insights, and blessings have helped make this project a unique one in the field of Indian musicological research. Special thanks to T.V. Mohandas Pai, Sudha Murthy and the Infosys Foundation, Dr. Suresh Chandvankar, Kushal Gopalka, R. Natarajan, Christian Liebl (Vienna Phonogrammarchiv), Reinhart Meyer Kalkus and the Wissenschaftskolleg zu Berlin, Dr. Raghavendra Gadagkar and Geeta Gadagkar for their immense support in various capacities in this project.

I am very thankful to the several institutions in India and London where I conducted extensive field research – the archives, libraries, governmental and private institutions that welcomed me openly and provided every possible assistance.

My stay in Australia was made comfortable and hassle free, and for this I owe a big thanks to the Hebbani family: Aparna, Girish, Neha and Aditya. They ensured I never felt homesick or craved traditional Indian vegetarian cuisine in Brisbane!

Finally, to all my teachers in music for instilling the love and passion for this divine art form since childhood and to my parents Nagamani Sampath and Sampath Srinivasan, maternal grandmother Kantha Bai, and aunt Roopa Madhusudan for their unwavering belief in me and their patience, support and love.

Preface

She was the stuff of fairy tales: a flamboyant singer much sought after by British India's nobility; a socialite who threw lavish parties; a hedonist who went about town in expensive horse buggies; a fashion icon whose image appeared on matchboxes made in Austria. And then, the inevitable end for someone leading a life as feisty as this: self-destruction, betrayals, penury and a lonely death. She was Gauhar Jaan – the Indian subcontinent's first musician to record commercially on the gramophone when the technology was introduced in 1902. Despite the cult status she achieved in her lifetime, Gauhar Jaan has been a forgotten figure in the world of Indian classical music today. She does have a few admirers though – old-timers and record collectors who treasure her shellac discs and speak about her heydays in superlative terms. But none of this is commensurate either with her pioneering contribution to the world of classical music or with the dramatic life she led.

Gauhar Jaan entered my life in the most serendipitous way. It was in 2007, while sifting through the musty, yet meticulously catalogued, Palace Divisional Archives of Mysore in Southern India when researching my first book, "*Splendours of Royal Mysore: the Untold story of the Wodeyars,*" that Gauhar Jaan first caught my attention. The name had a certain ring to it that led me to peruse the slim file containing the exchange of letters from her short stay in Mysore. The heading on the file: "The first dancing girl and Gramophone celebrity of India who moved from Calcutta and died in Mysore" instantly caught my attention. Why did a celebrity of her stature move from Calcutta in Eastern India to distant Mysore in the South, only to die in anonymity? I wondered. Letters that she had written between 1927 and 1930 to the Maharaja of Mysore's government and to lawyers from various cities where she was still battling legal cases portrayed the image of an ageing diva in the last days of her life, desperately beseeching help from every quarter. Her letters were screaming to be read and retold.

To the Prime Minister of Mysore State, Sir Mirza Ismail she wrote pleadingly on 6 March 1929: "Respected Sir, I beg first of all to state that there is no benefactor of mine in this world after God the Almighty and the Holy Prophet, save and except the Maharaja Bahadur of Mysore and your goodselves, his *Vazier*...Considering the fact that your honour has saved me already from total destruction, I may again ... request you to be kind enough to help me at this juncture."[1] There were entreaties to increase the measly pension sum of Rs. 500 per month that was paid for her and her accompanists with a deduction of income tax on it as well. Then there were hospital bills, money she owed to the baker, washerman, pharmacist, tailor, milkman and others, after her sudden and mysterious death on 17 January 1930. The Krishnarajendra Hospital where she died, lonely and forlorn with none by her bedside to shed tears for her, provided no information on the cause of death of this renowned artist and gramophone celebrity of the sub-continent who was once Mysore's State guest. It was intriguing that a star like Gauhar had had to leave her hometown Calcutta, in Eastern India, and die in anonymity and under such pitiable conditions.

I decided then, almost on an impulse, to set forth on a journey to unearth more details about this long-lost musician. This story deserved to be told. Just as all good biographies begin as a love affair or an instance of "transference," my work on Gauhar Jaan did too. But I was entering an unknown and dark tunnel, given the difficulties of exploring the world of courtesans (*tawaifs*) and *nautch* girls who existed mostly in the romanticised versions of colonial writers and were viewed retrospectively with much nostalgia. To make matters more complicated, Gauhar Jaan had died decades ago, in 1930, and had no legal heirs, no family members or friends who were alive and who could be spoken to. But it was this aura of mystery surrounding her that made this exploration so exciting.

From Mysore, I went on to trace Gauhar's life across the length and breadth of India – Azamgarh, Varanasi, Allahabad, Rampur, Darbhanga, Kolkata, Lucknow, Mumbai, Patna, and Chennai. Every city, every town that she spent time in, threw up leads to other places and people. These connections were crucial, since documenting the arts in India is a difficult task for a researcher. There might be several musical treatises of the past that have survived, but we know little about the nature and content of early performances, and more importantly about the lives of musicians of yesteryears. The self-effacing world of artists of those times ensured that the art was always bigger than the artist, and the latter seldom merited detailed documentation. The problem gets more complicated when it comes to women musicians and their stories, especially those of the courtesan community. Starting in the 1890s, a nationwide campaign known as the "Anti-Nautch campaign" was unleashed, to demonise women performing artists and to brand them as common prostitutes. In the wake of this, their life stories have evanesced completely from all records.

When it comes to the issue of documenting music and musicians, it is quite a commentary on the Indian psyche, which allows music to permeate every sphere, phase and event of life – from birth to death, marriages, festivals, and change of seasons – but considers its documentation unimportant. The ephemerality of music is celebrated and eulogised. Music is to be heard, understood, and enjoyed; "What is there to write about it?" is the common refrain. It does require tremendous patience and perseverance to chronicle the performing arts in the Indian sub-continent, as sources are so scanty. The passion of an investigative journalist, who tenaciously puts together the parts to paint a portrait, is not something that everyone would be interested in enduring. Spicy gossip – which seldom touches upon the persona of the musician and concentrates instead on flimsy, superficial hearsay – is generally all that remains. And rumour and legend was, of course, rife when it came to Gauhar Jaan. Music in India rarely seems to have a written history and survives largely through anecdotal memory. And anecdotes being what they are tend to be specious many times. The one I heard a zillion times from several old timers was that being a *firang* (foreigner) she was so fair that each time she ate betel leaves (*paan*), one could see the red juice going down her throat – almost making her less of a human and more of a water lizard!

Since Calcutta (now Kolkata) was home for Gauhar and made her the legend that she was, my numerous visits to that city began. Visiting archives there and meeting the remnants of the *zamindar* (aristocratic landed gentry) culture that patronised singers like Gauhar, was literally like looking for a needle in a haystack. The city had come a long way since the time Gauhar left it for Mysore. Its name had changed, generations had passed, and new musical interests, icons and patrons had taken over. Accidentally, I came across an obscure Bengali journal that referenced two stormy cases she fought – one to prove her parentage in court, and another against her lover and secretary Ghulam Abbas Subzwari, who cheated on her and embezzled her money and property, leading to her eventual downfall. When the Calcutta High Court changed its premises a few decades ago, in its supreme wisdom it decided to make a bonfire of all old and unwanted civil papers. Thus, Gauhar's seemingly unimportant papers were reduced to ashes. But being possessed by the idea of resurrecting her, I tried to trace the author of that Bengali journal who was a retired scribe at the High Court. It was quite a stroke of luck and immense perseverance to find copies of these case papers in his house. They were to become irrefutable documentary evidence to balance the apocryphal legends and myths that musicians loved to relate about her.

Trying to locate Gauhar's house in Kolkata was another expedition. What was famously called "Gauhar Buildings" and was once a venue for her countless soirees was now a garish pink building named "*Salim Manzil*" along the crowded lanes of the street named Rabindra Sarani ("Chitpur Road" during her lifetime). The three-storied building had clothes hung out to dry on the parapet grills, and had shops on the ground floor that ranged from a dealer of nuts and bolts to a foreign currency exchange. Interestingly, all the shopkeepers and vendors in the vicinity knew that this was the famed "Gauhar Buildings" that Gauhar had had to sell off to fight her legal cases. While memory of her is completely lost in most other parts of the city she called her home, Gauhar seemed to live on in this narrow lane where people have forgotten neither her life nor her exquisite music. She might still be the topic of discussion over tea for many old timers in the vicinity.

As a musician myself, analysing Gauhar's music was as important for me as reconstructing the rubric of her life. In her illustrious career Gauhar recorded close to 600 gramophone records in nearly 20 languages. Her repertoire was vast and covered a wide range of North Indian classical (Hindustani) music. They ranged from the supposedly weighty and "classical" genre named *khayal*, to the seemingly vast set of "semi-classical" genres that were associated with women such as Gauhar – *thumri, dadra, kajri, chaiti, hori, bhajan*, and *tarana*. Many of these celebrated erotic and sensuous love and the change of seasons and festivals. Thus began another journey, of looking for her old 78-RPM shellac discs which I purchased in their hundreds from record collectors and scrap shops, bargaining for a reasonable price. The early recordings were from the acoustic era, when there were no microphones to amplify one's voice. Singers literally screaming in high-pitched voices, that one now hears even as the sound struggles through the heavy surface noise of the 78-RPMs.

My search for the story of Gauhar led me to Berlin, and to the British Library and the EMI Music Archives in London. The memoirs of the German recording expert of The Gramophone Company – Frederick William Gaisberg, gave vivid descriptions of Gauhar Jaan and his interactions with her. The British Library had an entire collection of Urdu poems by Gauhar's mother, Badi Malka Jaan, titled *Makhzan-e-Ulfat-e-Malka*, or the "Treasure trove of Malka's Love," published in the 1880s in Kolkata. The book had over 500 exquisite Urdu poems, with a foreword from Gauhar in chaste Urdu and brief biographies of both mother and daughter.

The roller coaster journey that began in Mysore ended in the same city. Masquerading as her grandson, I managed to trace her hospital records and death certificate. But it was disappointing to not find her final resting place even after making several rounds of all the Muslim cemeteries in Mysore. The first recording celebrity of the Indian sub-continent thus lies in an unmarked grave, completely unsung and anonymous.

After four long years of painstaking research, collecting authentic documentation on Gauhar Jaan and having been consumed by the idea of her, putting it all together into an interesting story was easy. As much as I could, I had lived her life all over again, and I believe every true biographer dies multiple deaths while navigating the highs and lows of the subject's life. Gauhar narrated her life's tale through me, and so I felt it apt to name the book on her that came out in 2010, in the same way she signed off on her recordings: "*My name is Gauhar Jaan!*"

But the fascinating discovery that I made during my research on Gauhar Jaan was that when recording was introduced in India in the early decades of the twentieth century, it was women who belonged to the courtesan communities and called *tawaif* and *devadasi* in Northern and Southern India respectively, who accepted and adapted to the challenges of this new technology. The courtesan had a dichotomous role in Indian society. On the one hand, they were venerated as the sacred keepers of art, music, dance, and culture, but on the other they were stigmatised for their sexually dubious existence. Although not all courtesans were prostitutes, they had the license to lead liberated lives and take on male patrons, sometimes multiple numbers of them. Many courtesans owned vast properties, thanks to the grants of royalties, aristocracies and their wealthy patrons. In Northern India, young sons of aristocrats were sent to the salons of a courtesan to be trained in courtly etiquette. *Tawaifs* and *Devadasis* were the only women taxpayers of British India. While women from "respectable" households were often kept in *purdah* (veil) and deprived of education, several courtesans were highly accomplished poets and writers of their times. However, despite their many talents and successes, they were never fully accepted by the same society that idolised them.

Between the first three recording expeditions of The Gramophone Company in India, in 1902, 1904–05 and 1906–07, the women's recordings of commercial Indian classical music accounted for 80.95%, 83.51%, and 85.36% of the total recorded catalogue of Indian classical music.[2] There were few male classical musicians who recorded. Disregarding several superstitions floated around by the menfolk, these women went ahead and recorded. Gauhar Jaan was the pioneer who led the way for other women musicians to follow.

While Gauhar Jaan's story was fascinating as was the journey of resurrecting her, I soon realised that the numerous other anonymous contemporary women singers were not as lucky as she was to even be remembered. Alongside, there was also a huge treasure trove of recordings of the early decades of the twentieth century on shellac, which were in danger of being lost forever. The search for Gauhar's 78-RPM records led me to shanties and flea markets across India. This is unfortunately where the valuable cultural heritage of India, in the form of vintage records, lies scattered and unattended. While I was looking then only for records of Gauhar Jaan, it was shocking to note that thousands of records of several musicians right from 1902 to the 1940s and 1950s were found in flea markets in each city or town in India. At the same time, it was disconcerting to realise that they were in a precarious condition and in the absence of a National Sound Archive in India they had not been catalogued, digitised and preserved. With the passing of years this entire treasure would be completely destroyed and unavailable for posterity. That would make India a culturally much poorer nation.

After the publication of the biography of Gauhar Jaan, in 2010 I was invited to be a visiting fellow at the *Wissenschaftskolleg* (Institute for Advanced Study) in Berlin. During my stay in Berlin, I made an extensive field trip to look for early gramophone recordings of India in sound archives across Europe in Vienna, Paris, Berlin and London. I was pleasantly surprised to find that these archives had sizeable holdings of early Indian gramophone recordings, not all of which were of Indian music alone. For instance, the Lautarchiv of Berlin, which is part of the Humboldt University, had a fascinating collection of recordings. In 1915, the Berlin phonetician

Wilhelm Doegen initiated the Royal Prussian Phonographic Commission, one of the most systematic enterprises in early sound archiving. Using the phonograph and gramophone he recorded a wide range of languages, music, and natural sounds. Contributors to the initiative included researchers based in disciplines such as phonetics, linguistics, Oriental and African studies, musicology and anthropology, zoology, medicine, and criminology. Between 1915 and 1918, over 1,030 Edison cylinders with musical recordings and over 1,650 shellac recordings of the languages of prisoners of war (including of the First World War) were produced. It was with a sense of utter disbelief and excitement that I heard the voices of several Indian prisoners of the First World War telling their stories in their native languages.

The constant question I was asked everywhere in the European archives was whether India had a national sound repository. It was embarrassing to admit that we did not have such an institution in India. The music is so "alive" that an archive of it is usually visualised as a museum for dead objects. The oral pedagogical tradition of Indian classical music through the *Guru-Shishya* method of "Teacher-to-Taught" without writing down or notating the music but internalising it as a way of life also makes the idea of documentation and archiving a somewhat Western construct for many Indians, musicians in particular. In my opinion, this explains the lack of a body like a National Sound Archive in India.

A small step forward that I took in this regard after being exposed to the beauty of gramophone records was the establishment of a public charitable trust called The Archive of Indian Music (AIM) with the support of philanthropist and corporate leader T.V. Mohandas Pai. AIM seeks to digitise, restore, preserve and disseminate old gramophone recordings of India in a variety of Indian languages and genres ranging from classical Hindustani and Carnatic classical music to folk music, theatre recordings, early cinema, and also voices of national leaders. AIM has to date collected nearly 15,000 gramophone discs from across the country and is the first open source digital sound library of its kind in India. The digitised tracks are uploaded for free dissemination through SoundCloud. It also curates online audio exhibitions in collaboration with the Google Cultural Institute (GCI) where people, particularly the youth, can access this music through various modern multimedia technologies.

Gramophone records remained a popular medium for consumption of music in India from 1902, until the 1970s when their production was reduced and ultimately stopped. Given this popularity of the gramophone, it might be speculated that the records played a vital role in determining whose music was preserved and whose stories were told. The agency of the gramophone changed Indian classical music since recording enabled the processes of transmission and commodification of music. Also, it facilitated the possibility of the music being assimilated into a global market and subjected to transcultural preferences and changing modes of ownership and exchange. The gramophone hence not only provides us today with a link to the musical aesthetics and consumption patterns of the past, but also a means to understand the power hierarchies in the creative economy of the past and the musical, artistic and aesthetic sensibilities of the times when it was a popular medium.

This book is crucial for the evaluation of music as history for a number of reasons. Firstly, it illuminates whose narratives were preserved on the gramophone record; secondly it tracks the shifting socio-cultural mobilities of the practitioners and the communities that made and consumed the music and, thirdly it reveals how recording technology altered conventional structures of social, political, musical, and cultural equity in such societies. It also examines the trajectory of Indian music in the early twentieth century and attempts to locate and identify when and why the notions of the "traditional" and the "classical" were constructed in Indian music history.

Despite the developments described above, the important role of the gramophone in Indian music history has been largely ignored. There have been very few systematic and scholarly interventions on this subject that evaluate both the musical and the social impact of the gramophone in India and the interplay between these factors. While the historical journey of the gramophone in India has been well-documented by Kinnear (1994), Gaisberg (1943; 1947), Gronow (1996; 1981), Farrell (1997), Sampath (2010), and Sharma (2012) among others, its impact on the musical sensibilities of artists and listeners, on social reforms, and on the political discourse that came to determine what was recorded and disseminated, have not been dealt with. Hence, an in-depth and critical study based on significant archival material, such as this work, addresses a major gap in Indian musical historiography.

Scholarly literature dealing with a sociocultural, historical, and musical analysis of the gramophone in India appears to be scant. One of the few pioneering works on the history of gramophone recording in India was Michael Kinnear's *"Early Gramophone Recordings of India: 1899–1908."* Kinnear compiled catalogues of the Gramophone Company with details of the recorded artists, matrix number of each recording, raga and language of the composition, etc., for Indian recordings made in the period from 1899–1908. The study, however, did not include an analysis of the music or the sociocultural context of the recordings or the recorded artists, especially the courtesans.

This book builds on the foundations laid by my earlier work *"My name is Gauhar Jaan"* by expanding the scope to analyse the larger impact of the gramophone on Indian classical music from three perspectives: the sociocultural, historical, and musical. It addresses important issues for consideration in the study: the advent of recording in India and the role that women played in the development of the early recording industry; the impact that recording had on their lives and on the music; the abolition of these women thereafter from the performance space and its impact on the art form and how the gramophone shaped musical outcomes as a carrier of the "new normal" in the Indian classical paradigm.

Given the complexity of the research questions raised above, a multi-method research approach was adopted. This included semi-structured individual interviews with key stakeholders, extensive archival research, and musical analysis of the gramophone recordings sourced from the Archive of Indian Music and other archives across India.

While several first-hand voices of the beginnings of the recording industry in India have sadly passed on, some contemporaries of that era were still alive during the time of my research. To access this rich source of first-hand experience of the phenomenon, in-depth, semi-structured interviews were conducted with eight musicians of the era when the gramophone was extremely popular in India. Further interviews were undertaken with contemporary performing classical musicians of India, musicologists, record collectors, and students and family members of the gramophone-era artists, to contextualise and triangulate the perspectives offered by the senior musicians. Secondary research was conducted at several archives and libraries both in India and abroad. This included the EMI archive and the British Library in London, High Court archives of Madras, Bombay and Calcutta,[3] and newspaper archives in Chennai and Kolkata. This research informed the questions related to the historical journey of the gramophone in India and the reasons that led to the establishment of The Gramophone Company as a monopoly player in the Indian market. It also informed the evaluation of the role of these women who pioneered the recording story in India, the impact it had on their lives and on music, the social debates around the abolition of women from the performing space, and its impact on future recordings.

Notes

1 Courtesy Mysore Divisional Archives.
2 Calculation based on the catalogues of The Gramophone Company of these expeditions.
3 The names of the cities of Calcutta, Madras, and Bombay have changed to Kolkata, Chennai, and Mumbai, respectively. However the High Courts and Universities still retain the old names.

1   THE EXOTIC EAST

Prior to sunset on an auspicious day, chosen carefully by the temple priest after consulting the almanac, the little girl, aged seven, was brought into the temple sanctum by her mother. Earlier in the day, the older women of the household had gone to the temple and brought with them the golden pendant (*pottu*), a wedding sari, blouse, and other items for worship. Dressed like a bride, the little girl was brought to the temple in a grand procession with accompanying music. After circumambulating the sanctum, she sat near the deity, watching in silence as the priest conducted elaborate rituals. At the end of the rituals, he tied a sacred yellow thread with the same golden pendant (*pottu*) – hitherto placed at the feet of the deity for worship – around her neck. This marked her formal "marriage" to the deity of the temple. She was then led to the outer precincts of the temple (*mandapam*) where her teacher (*nattuvanar*) began the formal training of the little girl in dance and music. With this formal "dedication" she had now become a vassal of the temple, a bride of the deity, the "ever-auspicious" one who was free from the scourge of widowhood. She was the *"Devadasi"* – literally meaning the slave of the God.

The Rituals of "Dedication" of a *Devadasi*

The subject of the Indian courtesans only recently began attracting the attention of scholars of gender studies and women's rights activists. Until the early 1980s, this topic was virtually proscribed in both the academic and artistic fields due to the moralistic attitude (both in colonial and post-colonial India) towards the behaviour, freedom, and agency of these women. Building on the pioneering works of some Indian and Western feminist historians and anthropologists (Srinivasan 1985; Marglin 1985a,b; and Kersenboom 1987), followed by other scholars (Tharu & Lalita 1993; Jordan 1993; Nair 1994; Parker 1998; Kannabiran and Kannabiran 2003; Soneji 2012; Leucci 2005; and Vishwanathan 2008), several publications have emerged in the field that have now caught the attention of scholars of gender studies worldwide. The outcome of all this scholarship has resulted in a more holistic study of the artistic and socio-religious institutions of Indian courtesans

DOI: 10.4324/9780367822026-1

and resurrected this marginalised community from being viewed as a mere sub-category or footnote of the larger prostitution phenomena. Notably, these works have either omitted or addressed only in passing the important role that was played by courtesans in recording for the gramophone.

In 1901, Edgar Thurston (1855–1935), a scholar with a medical background, was appointed by the British government as the Superintendent of Ethnography for the Madras Presidency. By 1909, he published a comprehensive seven-volume account *Castes and Tribes of Southern India* with several pages dedicated to the *devadasi*. He brought together numerous anthropological studies, census reports, and legal cases involving the *devadasi* in this publication. His account becomes important for the study since he gives a first-hand account of the social traditions and customs of *devadasis* across various provinces of southern India, and includes citations from court cases that address issues around inheritance rights of the *devadasi* community and also the sale and adoption of girls by *devadasis* and temple dedications.

Thurston and Rangachari (1909) mentioned in the third volume that in large parts of the southern districts of the present-day Indian state of Tamil Nadu, the community of traditional weavers were known as Kaikolans. By the time of Thurston's survey in the first decade of the twentieth century, the Kaikolans had been impoverished enough to abandon their hereditary occupation of weaving in favour of agriculture and even took to being cart-drivers and coolies. But interestingly, Thurston mentioned that, despite these difficulties, it was compulsory for every Kaikolan family to set apart and dedicate at least one girl of the family to ritual temple service as a *devadasi*. As long as she or her female progeny lived, there was no need to dedicate another girl. Despite this close linkage between the Kaikolan community and the *devadasis*, in public the former always denied any connections with the latter, though they shared meals together and *devadasis* also had relationships with rich Kaikolan patrons (36–37). Thurston gives an indication of the social inhibitions against the *devadasi* that had already begun creeping in by the first decade of the twentieth century when he wrote:

> Kaikolan girls are made *Dasis* either by regular dedication to a temple, or by the headman tying the *tali* (*nattu pottu*). The latter method is at the present day adopted because it is considered a sin to dedicate a girl to the god after she has reached puberty, and because the securing of the requisite official certificate for a girl to become a *Dasi* involves considerable trouble. (37)

Thurston gave an elaborate description of the rituals of dedication of a girl to the temple as a *devadasi*. He gathered this through his interviews with Kaikolans of Coimbatore. Young girls born in the community would be dedicated to the profession when they were between five and nine years of age, much before the onset of puberty. On the day of the dedication, the girl was decked with jewels and made to stand on a heap of paddy. Two other *devadasis* (or *dasis*) stood beside her on similar heaps of paddy and held a folded cloth before the girl. A man who would take on the role of her future dance teacher would move the girl's legs up and down in rhythm with the music that was played, indicating a formal initiation into the art. A big feast was organised with relatives and friends being invited. The girl was seated on a pony and taken to the temple, where the *tali* or *pottu* – the chain that would be tied around her neck as a symbol of her dedication to the deity of the temple – was kept ready. This process of dedication was called *Pottukkattutal* or the tying of the *pottu/tali* or pendant around the girl's neck. The girl entered the sanctum of the temple and sat facing the deity while the officiating Brahmin priest tied the *tali* that had been kept at the feet of the deity around her neck. The *tali* was a chain with a golden disc or pendant with black beads around it. Betel and flowers were distributed to all present in an atmosphere of great joy and enthusiasm and the girl was taken in a procession across the principal streets of the town. She then got back to her training, which was conducted by a *Nattuvan*, or a dancing master of the Kaikolan caste, and learnt music under a teacher known as *Bhagavathan* who belonged to the Brahmin caste (38–39).

Almost every scholar, from Srinivasan (1985) to Soneji (2012), who has worked on the sociocultural history of the *devadasi* begins with an invocation to Thurston's important work as an authoritative study on the *devadasi* history and tradition, which shaped scholarly perceptions on how the *devadasi* community operated, its traditions and arbitrage.

Like Thurston, both Kersenboom (1987) and Vishwanathan (2008) elaborately describe the process through which a young girl born into the *devadasi* community would be "dedicated" to the deity of a temple. This dedication took place when the girl was between six and nine years of age. She would be married to God, and the priest of the temple would officiate as the intermediary by conducting the rituals on behalf of the deity. This rite of passage was known as the *pottukkattutal* ritual or the tying of the sacred emblem or *pottu* around the girl's neck. Her formal training in dance and music would follow immediately thereafter. A major milestone in a *devadasi's* life was attained when she was fully trained and also attained the age of puberty. She would then be publicly proclaimed as a skilled artist and a woman dedicated to serve the deity of the temple. Her first performance would be arranged with much fanfare, and several wealthy men of the town would be invited to witness it. The "wedding" with God would be consummated through a wealthy patron who would be selected by the girl.[1]

But several women of the *devadasi* community did not undergo such rituals and still participated in the aesthetic practices and non-conjugal sexual lifestyles associated with the community (Soneji 2012). The dedicated women would be invited to perform at the royal courts on festive occasions and, much later, for entertaining British government officials as well.

Vishwanathan (2008) argues that from the Vedic times (c.1500–500 BCE) the dancing and singing girl held an exalted position in society. She was

known as the *Pumschali*, a role far more complex than that of a mere courtesan or a prostitute (7–9). The Epics Ramayana and Mahabharata too
refer to her presence in all courtly duties. Kautilya in his *Arthashastra* mentions her variously as a *ganika, pratiganika, rupajiva, vesya, dasi, devadasi,
pumschali, shilpakarika, kausikastri,* and *rupadasi.* She was the expert in
love-making in the *Kama Sutra* of Vatsyayana and the enchanting seduc-
tress, Madhavi in the *Silappadikaram* of the Sangam literary era of Tamil
Nadu. Vishwanathan (2008) further argues that in the entire history of
Indian performing traditions, the *devadasi* traversed three major domains:
first, as a *dasi* or ritual singer-dancer in temples; second, as a part of the
king's royal entourage with suitable accompanying repertoire; and third, as
a salon performer independent of the king or temple (8). The third domain
became more prominent with the decline of royal court patronage by the
end of the nineteenth century.

In South India, the *devadasi* was also given the adjective *Nityasumangali*,
meaning ever auspicious. Being married to the deity of a temple, she was
free from the scourge of widowhood and hence gained the connotation
of eternal auspiciousness (Kersenboom 1987). The *devadasi* in traditional
South Indian temple and royal settings was not despised but looked on as
an important component of the cultural ecosystem.

Vishwanathan (2008) documents that once trained, the girl gave her
full-fledged public performance and was then led into a mock nuptial ceremony with the deity by her maternal uncle. Her coming of age and onset
of puberty was celebrated for nearly 20 days. A rich Brahmin or a landlord
was the patron who actually got "married" to her as a representative of the
deity. Thurston and Rangachari (1909) add that "when the man who is to
receive her first favours, joins the girl, a sword must be placed, at least for a
few minutes beside her" (39).

As Vishwanathan (2008) postulates:

> The ritual consummation was followed by a ceremony to mark the
> actual taking on of a sexual partner. A patron was usually waiting…a
> number of prospective men were invited and their offers received. The
> final selection was with the consent of the girl. The verbal contract
> between the man and the dasi's family stipulated the amount to be paid
> as also the duration of their relationship. Some dasis had 'steady' hus-
> bands. Following the agreement, an announcement was made to the
> community giving the name of the patron. It was after this that the girl
> was known as a *sumangali*[2]. (63–64)

Soneji (2012) argues that the *pottukkattutal* ceremony was not understood
as a religious marriage but as a "transaction that secured a girl's commitment to local economies of land and guaranteed her sexual and aesthetic
labour" (42). The ceremony assured the girl and her family of stipulated
amounts of grains and food items, and also gifts of land, jewellery, and

clothes (39–42). Similarly, Srinivasan (1985) argues that the *pottu*-tying ceremony was increasingly being led by "conscious economic motivations" as it became a kind of a passport to social mobility and economic advantages. Huge grants of land (*manniyam*) or jewels and garments and other riches were the motivational factor here and the *pottu*, far from being a religious ceremony, was more a kind of a commercial transaction that was necessary for sustenance for members of the community. Russell (1916) reports:

> When a dancing girl attains adolescence, her mother makes a bargain with some rich man to be her first consort. Oil and turmeric are rubbed on her body for five days as in the case of a bride. A feast is given to the caste and the girl is married to a dagger walking seven times round the sacred post with it. Her human consort then marks her head with vermillion and covers her head-cloth seven times. In the evening she goes to live with him for as long as he likes to maintain her, and afterwards takes up the practice of her profession. (380)

In her seminal work, Kersenboom (1987) tries to recover the *devadasi* system from the charge of sacred prostitution that came to be levelled against it during the colonial period and makes a case for the *devadasi* tradition to be seen from the Hindu cultural and ritual view of the world as a "sacred play" of which the living, functioning temple "drama" was an inextricable part. It was the disintegration of this cosmology under the changed political conditions of modern times, which according to Kersenboom (1987) led to the gradual decay and disintegration of the *devadasi* system (156).

In my interview with her, Lakshmi Vishwanathan (born in 1944), herself a trained and eminent dancer and musician, mentioned that as a student one of the first compositions she was taught to dance on was a *padam*[3] in the language Telugu and set to raga *Sahana*. It was a love-poem of the eighteenth century composed by Sarangapani. She translated it for me thus:

> My husband beckons me,
> I must go, my beloved.
> Forget you, I never shall.
> Beautiful, benevolent Venugopala,
> When I was an unknowing child
> He tied a *pottu* around my neck.
> Like a lotus that blooms at sunrise
> The distance between us matters not.
> I place my devotion at your feet.

Lakshmi Vishwanathan mentioned in my interview with her:

> As a young girl, I was unable to comprehend the purport of the *padam* and thought it referred to child marriage that was widely prevalent in India. It was much later that I realized that the song was the *devadasi*'s

plea to the deity she was dedicated to: Venugopala in this case. While she was 'married' to the deity, she also had to fulfil her contract with the 'husband' who had tied the *pottu* or the marriage pendant around her neck and was thus torn between her love for the deity and the worldly duties of so-called 'marital life'. As a woman, I could deeply empathize with her pain![4]

The *devadasis* were part of a well-knit community of dance teachers and musicians. Soneji (2012: 145–147) mentions that the male relatives of the *devadasis* identified themselves using a range of caste names and occupational titles, the broadest of which was the *melakkaarar* or one who plays in the *melam* or the artistic guild of performers. Under this large umbrella of artists came the dance masters or *nattuvaanars* for *devadasis* and the professional ritual musicians in temples who, by and large, played the reed pipe the *nagaswaram* and its percussion accompaniment, the drum called *thavil*. At the bottom of the hierarchy came men who were barbers by the day and also performed at night as semi-professional *nagaswaram* and *thavil* musicians. The group of musicians who performed on a professional basis on the *nagaswaram* and *thavil* comprised the *periya melam* or large band, while those *nattuvanars* who accompanied the *devadasis* in their performance were the *chinna melam*, referring perhaps to the small drum or the *muttu* that accompanied the performance. Soneji (2012: 145–147) contends that the status of these men of the *chinna melam* who lived off the performances of the women-folk was considered "contentious at best" (147) and always a source of embarrassment within the community itself.

Shifting Patronage

Subramanian (2006) and Soneji (2012) illustrate how, with the collapse of the royal courts of patronage such as Tanjore by the middle of the nineteenth century and the emergence of urban centres such as Madras (now Chennai), the *devadasis* had to quickly reinvent themselves and their repertoire. While one does not have recorded versions of the *devadasi* repertoire prior to 1904, colonial accounts give us a glimpse into what these new performances might have been like in a salon setting, where they were to entertain an urban audience or the colonial British master rather than a traditional patron, such as the king.

Wheeler (1878) provided an account of one such performance in 1878 that Prince Albert Edward was grudgingly "obliged" to witness, in which he eventually "seemed to have become thoroughly tired of the stupid spectacle" (176–178). He elaborates:

These ladies and their male accompanists with tom-toms, fiddles and zithers, sang songs and shared in grotesque dances...In the nautch dances there are sometimes two or three performers, sometimes, as on this occasion, only one. They are always young, and frequently beautiful. The dancer clashes together the silver bands worn on the feet above the ankles, and raises her arms, jingling the bangles, in alternate movements above her head, to a droning accompaniment from the musicians; now and again she bursts into a twangy song with apparently no distinct air or meaning, and which always ends abruptly...There is nothing lively, graceful or attractive about it. No one cares to see a nautch twice unless the dancers have very pretty faces and very pretty dresses. (176–178)

It was this community of singers-dancers or *devadasis* who were the pioneers of the gramophone recording in South India.

The Tradition and History of the *Tawaifs*

While there has been considerable scholarly investigation of the social history of the *devadasis*, for reasons unknown, a commensurate effort has not gone into that of their North Indian counterparts, the *tawaifs*. With the advent of Muslim invasions and their subsequent rule in North India from the eleventh and twelfth centuries, dancing and singing girls from Persia and Central Asia made their way to India. Etymologically, the word *tawaif* itself is from the Persian root, *tauf*, which describes both a category of roaming merchants and also a category of women who lead nomadic lives (Jafa 1998: 18). The *tawaifs* traditionally migrated from place to place in mobile nautch parties; hence, the word seems appropriate.

Jafa (1998) mentions that the *Lonis* were a sub-class of *tawaifs* who descended from courtesans of Persia and sang only in Persian, and a second sub-class, the *Domnis*, sang in Hindustani. The *tawaifs* were entertainers whether in terms of music, dance, theatrical arts, poetry, or even sex (24). Jafa (1998) also describes the various social categories within the community of *tawaifs*. Highest in the hierarchy were *Deredar tawaifs* who were descendants of the dancing and singing girls who were originally tent owners and moved from town to town and fair to fair entertaining people. These women were highly accomplished and were well versed in music, dance, and also poetry. They usually kept one or two patrons all their lives and remained committed to their patron(s). It was the patron's duty to maintain the *deredar tawaif* and provide for her expenses and livelihood, and also the children she bore him. They were allowed to invite other patrons to their salons to watch their performances, but physical relationships or commitments were kept up only with their chosen patron, who was the only man allowed to stay back in a salon after the performance while the rest of the guests had to leave.

Jafa (1998) illustrates that the various classes of women performers who came after these *deredars* in the hierarchy included the *Kanchans, Nats, Domnis, Patars, Ramjanis,* and *Bedins* (27–30). Some of them sang, others danced, and some did both singing and dancing. But most of them, unlike the *deredars*, were not given access to the best of classical music and dance traditions. At the bottom of the social pyramid, Jafa elaborates, came the *Thakahis*, *Randis*, and *Khangis*, who were common prostitutes and who had absolutely no access to the classical arts (27–30).

Schofield (2012), however, argues that the term tawaif, to indicate a "unitary meta-community of elite female performing artists in North India," came into circulation much later, somewhere around the 1800s (152). She mentions that right through the reign of the Mughal Empire (1526–1858), which saw an Indo-Persian courtly culture in India, many communities of female performers existed. These included *paturs*, *daruni-parastars*, *lulis*, *kancanis*, *kamacanis*, *hurukanis*, *domnis*, *dhadhinis*, *ramjanis*, *kalawantis*, and so on (152). These women are referenced in the royal chronicles of the various emperors of the Mughal dynasty, written by commissioned court-historians. Schofield (2012) categorises these women into those who strictly performed within the harem; those who performed in both male and female spaces; and, finally, those who strictly performed only under the gaze of men (153–154). Schofield characterises the first two categories of liminal performers in the Mughal era as "auspicious singers" and separates a sexual dimension (though with a few notable exceptions) from their functions in the royal court (154). Even though *tawaifs* were considered to be the domestic and sexual property of Mughal noblemen, to have sexual relationships with them was the discretion of the patron. These liminal performers were not considered common property of the men in society at large. Schofield quotes the Mughal etiquette manual of the c.1660 to substantiate this point, where a courtier is barred "from giving a chance to his male friends and companions to listen to the singing of his private concubines; otherwise it would amount to pandering, and may lead to him being cuckolded" (156). While the *domnis* were the liminal performers, the *lulis* were exclusively performers of the male space in the Mughal India. The latter were trained in courtly etiquette just like the former, but, in addition, also possessed wealth, property, and the sanction to interact with unrelated men and even pursue sexual relationships. Schofield states that their sanction to promiscuity located them outside the bounds of "respectability" of the Mughal harems and households of nobility. The collapse of the Mughal Empire and the shift of patronage to smaller principalities (such as Awadh) and the nobility, slowly diminished the role of the "domestic" singer. The courtesan had to make a transition to colonial modernity that became further complicated by political events such as the 1857 uprising and the social movements of purity.

Several *tawaifs* were highly educated, unlike most women of their times. Jha (2010) explains that many of the tawaifs wrote extensive poetry collections in Urdu called *divans*. Two such *tawaifs* were Mahalaqa Bai Chanda of Hyderabad (c. 1767–c. 1824) and *Memsahib Tawaif* Malka Jaan of Banaras (c. 1858–c. 1906) (n.pag.). The former had a royal patron and lived a courtly life, while the latter was Gauhar Jaan's mother. According to Sampath (2010), Badi Malka Jaan was of Anglo-Indian origins and migrated from small towns of the United Provinces, specifically Azamgarh and Banaras, to the cosmopolitan city of then Calcutta (now Kolkata), giving her daughter Gauhar Jaan access to the latest pedagogy as well as concert and economic opportunities that a medium such as the gramophone brought to these women. Through a study of their poetry styles and the production and circulation of their *divans*, Jha (2010) deconstructs how these women negotiated their status as performers and entertainers in their respective settings and thereby locates women performers and their compositions within larger gender debates of women and their role in shaping the worlds of vernacular modernity.

It is through such poetry collections and biographies that one deconstructs the social history of the *tawaifs*. Ruswa (1970) translated by Khushwant Singh and M.A. Husaini (of the 1905 novel *Umrao Jaan Ada*) is one such example. The fictional protagonist, Umrao Jaan, is supposedly a famed courtesan of Lucknow. But the novel gives us valuable insights into the social hierarchies of the *tawaif* society, their lifestyles, the matriarchal system of control and succession within a *kotha* or salon, ceremonies of initiation into the professional life of a *tawaif*, her training, and her relationship with her teachers and musicians. Ruswa (1970) feels the need to include lengthy passages in the first voice of Umrao, describing herself as "an unhappy wretch who has drifted through life without any mooring; a homeless vagrant who has brought shame upon her family; a woman whose name will be as disgraced in the world to come as it is in the world today" (17). Ironically, her prophecy hardly came true, as Umrao Jaan became a cult figure in the imagination of popular culture in India with two successful Bollywood films made on her life.[5]

In the novel, Umrao's life is set around 1857, which was when the First War of Indian Independence occurred in various parts of India against the oppressive rule and tactics of the British East India Company. The collapse of the mighty Mughal Empire in Delhi led to the consolidation of power in the hitherto smaller principalities that were subservient to the Emperor in Delhi. One such locale was the principality of Awadh (or Oudh as the British called it) with its princely capital Lucknow, whose court and aristocracy attracted many *tawaifs* to the state. The *tawaifs* soon became a firmly entrenched part of urban life during the nineteenth century. As urban centres started expanding in various parts of Awadh, they presented an increasingly expanding circle of patrons for these *tawaifs*, bringing in newer opportunities of wealth, fame, and power. Oldenburg (1990b) mentions that *tawaifs* are listed as property owners and the only women taxpayers in princely Awadh, in "civic tax ledgers of 1858–77 and in the related official correspondence preserved in the Municipal Corporation records..." (259.). Sampath (2010) also describes how while they migrated from place to place in search of opportunities, their permanent establishment was the *kotha* or salon controlled under the sharp gaze of a matron called *chaudhrayan* (20–22). This matronly head of the house supervised the education and training of younger wards, many of who were also kidnapped girls, as was Umrao. The performance space was usually the first floor of the house while the male musicians who accompanied the women performers on the instruments, *sarangi* and *tabla*, taught them and also fathered their illegitimate children occupied the ground floors (Sampath 2010: 20).

Sampath (2010) mentions that while talented female progeny would be trained to be successors, the male children grew up to become pimps and agents or took to musical accompaniment (21). Oldenburg (1990) quotes her assistant (who wished to remain anonymous and is named Chhote Miyaan) who helped her in translation of Persian texts, accompanied her to the *kothas* of Lucknow, and was himself born at a *kotha*. Chhote Miyaan, literally translating to "Mister Small," was the son of a courtesan, and Oldenburg (1990) narrates that his mother never revealed the identity of the father to him. Chhote Miyaan tells Oldenburg (1990b):

> While I love and respect my mother and all my "aunts" (other courtesans of the salon) and my grandmother, my misfortune is that I was born a son and not a daughter in their house. When a boy is born in the *kotha*, the day is without moment, even one of quiet sadness. When my sister was born, there was a joyous celebration that was unforgettable. Everyone received new clothes, there was singing, dancing and feasting. My aunts went from door to door distributing sweets. (262)

This is ironically the plight of a male in a salon, in a country such as India, where the social evil of female foeticide is rampant to this date because a girl child is treated as unwelcome.[6]

Sampath (2010) mentions that the *kotha* itself had unwritten rules of conduct. The performing space had walls with end-to-end mirrors implying the visitors were under strict surveillance for misconduct or unethical behaviour. Only the members of the *kotha* served liquor to the wealthy visitors who came each evening. Monetary offerings were never discussed publicly and were quietly slipped under a mattress by the visitors after watching the performance (*mujra*). Wealthy patrons who were enchanted by a particular *tawaif* had to pay extra money to the matron to be able to spend private time with her after the performance. Aristocrats, poets, wealthy patrons, and the rich and famous men of the city congregated at the *kothas* every evening for their daily entertainment (20–21).

Some of the *kothas* of affluent *tawaifs*, such as Gauhar Jaan, did not have an open-door policy where anyone could walk in to witness her perform. The patron had to belong to a certain social class and hierarchy to gain access. It is precisely this closeted patronage that the gramophone industry broke by making the performances and music of such *tawaifs* easily accessible to people at large.

Sampath (2010) describes that the *kothas* became the centres of conspiracy and rebellion during the 1857 War of Independence (30). Oldenburg (1990) and Sharar (2000) detail how, after the British crushed the uprising of 1857, they dealt with the *tawaifs* and their *kothas* with a ferocious retribution, as they believed that many *tawaifs* had lent their covert support to the sepoys. *Tawaif* properties were appropriated, new zoning laws created, public health regulations forbid men –particularly British soldiers – from visiting *kothas* or indulging in dalliances with the *tawaifs*, and the salons came under strict government surveillance. With the fall of Awadh and its aristocratic set-up after 1857, the *tawaifs* began migrating to new urban centres, looking for patronage and opportunities. Banaras and Calcutta (now Kolkata) were such centres where they had to reinvent themselves to appeal to the sensibilities of a completely new set of urban patrons. Ruswa (1970), Nevile (2009), and Sampath (2010) portray this transitional sociocultural condition that the *tawaifs* found themselves in towards the end of the nineteenth century, between the revolt of 1857 and just before the *tawaifs* took to gramophone recording in 1902.

Similar to the *devadasi's* rituals of passage, the *tawaifs* too had their own ceremonies related to the initiation into the professional world of performance. This was called *missi* or *nath uthaarna*. The literal meaning of *nath uthaarna* is removal of the nose ring, which actually symbolised the loss of virginity. Jafa (1998) describes that the female matron of the *kotha*, who was known as *chaudhrayan*, would formally advertise for the *nath babu* or the man who would undertake to pay a sizeable dowry and maintain the girl. It was a kind of contract-based union. Jafa (1998) states that the ceremony was accompanied by a lot of gaiety, music, dance, and merriment (23–24).

Maciszewski (2007) mentions that numerous songs sung by the *tawaifs* had subtle references to the *nath uthaarna* ceremony. She cites a song recorded by a renowned *tawaif* of Banaras, Rasoolan Bai:

> *Eri thaiya, mothiya hiraye gaile Ram*
> *Na koi aila, na koi jaila*
> *Chor batahu ghar se bahar na jaila*
> *Eri saiyya mothiya hiraye gaile Ram.*

> Alas, the pearls have been lost O Ram!
> None entered nor left the house
> Neither did a thief break into the house
> Yet, I lost the pearls O Ram, I lost them all! (135)

The lyrics subtly speak of the young *tawaif's* grief and pain at the loss of her virginity (denoted here by "pearls") and her helplessness in the situation that she can barely comprehend or control. The ceremony was a manner of proclaiming to the world that the *tawaif* now had the sanction to settle down with a benefactor and was to provide him conjugal bliss.

Shah (1992) mentions that several contenders would come to lay claims on the girl by bidding, and the girl would be given to the highest bidder. On the day of the ceremony, the girl would be dressed up like a bride. The patron would then approach the waiting girl and remove her nose ring (again a symbol of loss of virginity). The patron would give gifts to all the members of the *kotha* or salon. It was understood that he would provide for the girl's upkeep and maintenance. Sometimes this even lasted for an entire lifetime and the girl remained devoted to him though she was allowed to perform for other men. If the relationship broke, she would then be free to be bid for by another patron (23–24).

Learning dance, music, and poetry would begin at an early age for the *tawaifs*. The relationship between the teacher and the *tawaif* was not always a happy one. Sampath (2010) talks about how Gauhar's teacher Kale Khan tried to molest her and impose himself on her in the midst of his training (159–160). Ganguly (2008) refers to similar accounts of other women singers, including the legendary musician Begum Akhtar, which have been spoken about as casual misdemeanours of the male teachers and expectations of sexual favours in return for teaching music (158–160). This was considered a normal thing to do. Many teachers wilfully taught the women students half-heartedly as they did not want the women to be better than them in musical virtuosity. *Ustad* Abdul Rashid Khan makes the same point that teachers were wary of imparting complete knowledge of music to women, in the course of my interview with him. He narrated an anecdote that he had heard several decades ago:

> In those days (*he was unclear about the years, but it is assumed within the first two decades of the twentieth- century*), Munnibai, a *tawaif*, was a famous student of the celebrated *Ustad*, Abdul Karim Khan Sahib. Her rendition of ragas such as *Bilaskhani Thodi* would go on for a minimum of one to one and a half hours with no repetitive sounding musical phrases. On one occasion another eminent musician *Ustad* Alladiya Khan heard her in concert and was stunned by her virtuosity. He is said to have chided Abdul Karim Khan saying: 'What are you doing? Just teach her as much as is required. If she starts singing so well and for one and a half hours, who will come to listen to us?'[7]

Sampath (2010) mentions that with the collapse of the royal Mughal court of Delhi and the Nawabs of Awadh after the Uprising of 1857,[8] the patronage of music and dance shifted to wealthy landlords and thereafter to urban centres, including Banaras and Calcutta (now Kolkata). This was akin to the situation in South India, where the courtesan had to reinvent herself in a modern urban setting such as Madras; a very different circumstance from the hitherto royal patronage in courts such as Tanjore and Mysore. Like the *devadasis* down South, these *tawaifs* were the ones who readily embraced the gramophone recording technology when it was first introduced in India.

Notes

1 See Vishwanathan (2008, pp. 58–71) for details of all the rituals associated with the dedication of girls to temples as *devadasis*.
2 Sumangali means Auspicious or married/non-widowed.
3 A genre within Carnatic music widely identified with the *devadasi* and identified as erotic. Although extinct in Carnatic music performances today, it is still used as the song to dance on in contemporary Bharatanatyam performances.
4 Excerpt of interview of Smt. Lakshmi Vishwanathan by the author.
5 The first cinematic adaptation of the 1905 novel was the Hindi film 'Umrao Jaan' in 1981. It was directed by Muzaffar Ali and had the glamorous Bollywood actress Rekha playing the lead protagonist. A remake of the same story was undertaken in 2006, titled 'Umrao Jaan,' directed by J.P. Dutta and starring the Bollywood actress and Miss World of 1994, Aishwarya Rai in the lead.
6 See Census of India 2011 report and UNICEF Press release 2015, which reported an increase in female foeticide in India, and estimate more than 50 million girls as 'missing' as killed at birth or as a foetus.
7 Interview excerpts of the author with *Ustad* Abdul Rashid Khan.
8 The Indian soldiers or sepoys who worked in the British army rose up in a nation-wide rebellion in 1857, which was also supported by several royal houses that were deposed by the British using the Doctrine of Lapse. This episode is famously called the First War of Indian Independence of 1857.

2 THE MECHANISED WEST

It was another day of trial and error for John Kruse, an expert technician who worked as Thomas Alva Edison's assistant at his "Invention Factory" in Menlo Park, which was approximately 25 miles from New York City. In early November 1877, Edison had given Kruse a detailed technical drawing and declared, "This should talk." Kruse's job was to assemble the contraption according to the directions of his master. What he was putting together was a device made up of brass and iron cylinders, diamond styluses and several other mechanical arrangements that would facilitate the rotation of these cylinders. Kruse's colleagues watched him at work with great scepticism and were positively amused by a strange horn-shaped metal cone that was fitted with a tiny needle at its end. Edison entered the laboratory after being told that the work was done. One look at it and he gave a pleased smile to convey his approval to his diligent assistant. First, he wrapped tin foil tightly around the curved surface of the foot-long cylinder. Then, he placed the diamond stylus carefully at one end of the foil and began to rotate the cylinder at a gentle and uniform speed, using the handle that was fitted on the right of the turntable box on which the cylinder was mounted. All the while, he ensured that the needle cut a uniform groove in the tin foil. He then shouted into the horn, reciting the famous nursery rhyme,

> Mary had a little lamb; its fleece was white as snow,
> And everywhere that Mary went, the lamb was sure to go.

The sound of his voice created vibrations in the needle, thereby producing zigzag patterns on the tin foil. He then brought the horn and needle to its original starting position, changed the stylus, placed the needle in the newly formed grooves, and began to rotate the cylinder as before. The people who had crowded around had stopped blinking and breathing and many hearts must have skipped a beat. When the entire contraption began to move, a terrible noise started emanating from the horn, drawing stifled laughter from the onlookers. Suddenly, as the needle began to pass through the zigzag groove that had been cut by Edison's shouting, the nursery rhyme echoed back distinctly from the device, though feebly. Edison froze with excitement even as the crowd clapped and cheered.

DOI: 10.4324/9780367822026-2

Mechanical Reproduction of the Human Voice

Thomas Alva Edison invented the phonograph in 1877. It was the first device that recorded and reproduced the human voice (Sampath 2010: 69–70). On 22 December 1877, Edison proudly displayed his machine in the office of the *Scientific American*, which announced the invention of his "Phonograph" to the rest of the world. Edison was hailed as the "Wizard of Menlo Park." Finally, on 19 January 1878, Edison received the patent for his invention of the cylinder phonograph.

Ironically, Edison had never intended the phonograph for music. He had written that his invention would "annihilate time and space, and bottle up for posterity the mere utterance of man" (Edison 1878: 529). Prior to the invention of the phonograph, Karl Marx had observed what had then seemed to be an unchangeable truth about music: "The service a singer provides for me, satisfies my aesthetic need, but what I consume exists only in action, inseparable from the singer, and as soon as the singing is over, so too is my consumption" (Blaukopf 1992: 176).

But Edison realised that though the device was an important breakthrough in the field of recording and production of sound, it had little value except as a talking toy. So he shelved the project for over ten years, during which time he continued to think hard and work harder to find ways to make the device better and more useful.

By June 1888 Edison was ready with a new model of the phonograph, with a battery-operated motor for maintaining uniform speed. However, the experimentation and improvements continued until 1911 under the aegis of the Edison Phonograph Company. But frankly, no one – including Edison – realised the commercial potential of this invention and how it could revolutionise the entertainment industry. They had merely thought of it as a scientific experiment that worked at times and failed at others. It was the gramophone that was to become an agent for propagation of music through the recordings.

The Phonograph in India

The Record News (1999) states that the Bengali periodical *Samachar Chandrika* was the first to report the arrival of this "wondrous Talking Machine" in India in its issue dated 9 January 1878:

> By the help of this machine, words can be stored in its bottle and whenever one prefers, he can open the cork and hear the words. Even after hundred or thousand years, by reopening the cork one could hear the same words. (76–77)

Live demonstrations of the talking machine were held in various parts of India, much to the amazement of the people and the amusement of children who could hear their voices back from the machine (Sampath 2010: 70).

Figure 2.1 Felix Exner conducting field-recordings of local priests and the librarian at the Adyar Library, Madras (1905).

Source: Picture courtesy The Vienna Phonogrammarchiv.

Many European scholars and anthropologists travelled across the world undertaking non-commercial field recordings of various communities to create an ethnographic archive. Between 1904 and 1905, Felix Exner (1876–1930), son of the Vienna Phonogrammarchiv's founder Sigmund Exner and later director of Vienna's Central Institution for Meteorology and Geodynamics, led a field recording expedition to India (Figure 2.1). He made over sixty sound recordings of recitations in Sanskrit, Tamil and other Indian languages in Madras (now Chennai), Banaras, Jaipur, and other towns of India.[1]

The Invention of the Gramophone

Edison had inspired a whole generation of young scientists to experiment in sound recording. It was almost a fad those days to be seen sitting poring over a tin foil in some shanty laboratory. Everyone wanted to come up with some new discovery like Edison had. Twenty-one-year-old Emile Berliner of Washington was no different. He was a migrant from Hanover, Germany, and earned his living as a draper's clerk. He was obsessed with solving electrical problems connected with telephones and phonographs. In the early days of his research efforts Berliner was staying in a rented room on the third floor of a dingy house run by a widow and her three children. He frequently tried to simulate long-distance communication, much to the excitement of the children. He would place a soapbox, which had been converted into a transmitter circuit on the ground floor where the landlady and the kids would be asked to speak. He would then try and receive these messages in his third floor room, which was littered with odd bits of string, wire, and batteries.

Around this time, Alexander Graham Bell and Charles Sumner Tainter, the winners of the Volta Prize for the invention of the telephone, came to Washington. With the prize money they had established the Volta Laboratory from which was issued the master-patent for "cutting a sound line in a solid body." In this laboratory Bell and Tainter further developed the gramophone.

Meanwhile Berliner's experiments continued. Hearing about the encouragement that the Bell Telephone Company was providing to talented scientists, Berliner decided to submit the idea of his telephone transmitter to the Company. He managed to get it patented and also received a cash prize of $75,000 from the Company. He used this to set up a makeshift laboratory on New York Avenue, where he further experimented with the phonographs of Edison.

One fine morning, to this laboratory came a young man of sixteen, Frederick William Gaisberg, accompanied by his friend Billy Golden. Gaisberg was a pianist of sorts and made some small money by displaying his musical skills. The most common public entertainment those days were amateur singers accompanied by pianists like him performing along the pavement with Edison's phonograph. For a payment of just five cents the listener would be shown the marvel of human achievement —the machine that could faithfully reproduce the music created by the musicians. Children would clap with delight and believe that one of the musicians had hidden himself inside that cylinder! Apart from such amateur ventures, Gaisberg had also had some formal training in sound production at the Volta Laboratory and the American Graphophone Company at Bridgeport, Connecticut.

The day Gaisberg made his entry into Berliner's laboratory, he had been coaxed to make a visit by his friend Billy, who promised to show him a clown. The outlandish dress sense and queer mannerisms of Berliner had earned him the tag of "clown" from many people. That day, too, Berliner was dressed in a monkish frock and was pacing up and down the room. He was buzzing test messages of "Hello, Hello" on a diaphragm and repeating the famous English rhyme with his distinct German accent "Tvinkle Tvinkle little star, how I vonder vot you are." Concealing his laughter, Gaisberg watched on. After the formal introductions were done, Berliner enquired if the two visitors would participate in his experiment, being amateur musicians themselves. Without waiting for any answer, Berliner quickly placed a muzzle over Billy's mouth and connected this up by a rubber hose to a diaphragm. He pushed Gaisberg towards a piano and asked him to play. The piano's sounding board was also boxed up and connected to the diaphragm by a hose resembling an elephant's trunk. "Are you ready?" he asked. Upon receiving the affirmation, he began to crank the recording device as one would a barrel organ and said "Go." Billy was to sing a little song to the accompaniment of Gaisberg's piano. In a few minutes the song finished. Berliner stopped cranking, took a bright zinc disc from the machine, and plunged it into an acid bath for a while. Taking it out, he washed the disc and placed it on a reproducing machine, which was hand-operated like most coffee-grinders. Much to the astonishment of the visitors, Billy's song and Gaisberg's piano played back from the etched grooves. Berliner went hysterical with excitement. He had made the first "gramophone record." He claimed that his technology was far superior to that of Edison's cylinder. This was because when the recording stylus was vibrated laterally on a flat surface it encountered an even resistance – unlike on the cylindrical surface – and that accounted for the clarity of tone. Thus was created the first gramophone zinc-disc "record" in 1891.

Gaisberg's initial amusement turned into awe and respect for the funny man. He begged Berliner to allow him to work with him in his lab. Over the next few months, Berliner and Gaisberg conducted several experiments to record a variety of sounds on this new marvel. Until 1897, Berliner used 7-inch zinc discs for the etching process. Ebonite was employed for pressing these zinc records. Because ebonite withstood a lot of pressure, it would not retain the impression permanently.

Soon a new substance known as "shellac" began to replace the original zinc as the material for making the discs. Lac was hardened resin secreted by the tiny lac insects, which settled on twigs and sucked the plant's sap. These insects were scraped from the twigs, crushed, dried, sieved, winnowed, washed and again dried. The mangled mass was then passed through a hot melting system, filtered and stretched into thin sheets, which were known as "shellac." This was a non-toxic substance and began to be used as the base material for gramophone records.

Despite all the improvements made to the original model of the gramophone, sales were sluggish. Berliner and Gaisberg realised that unless the gramophone was fitted with a clock-driven motor, it would never become a serious commercial proposition and merely remains a toy for the curious. The clock-motor had to perform the task of rotating a turntable at a uniform speed for two minutes continuously against the resistance of a heavy sound-box, and thereby produce consistent sound. By chance, Gaisberg's eyes caught sight of an advertisement in a newspaper of a sewing machine firm that had made an innovation with the usage of their indigenously developed clockwork motors for their machines. This gave him the answer to the problem they were trying to fix. Gaisberg then utilised the services of a young mechanic in New Jersey, Eldridge R. Johnson, to work on the clockwork gramophone motor which was simple, practical, and cheap.

The popularity of the gramophone now began to swell. From popular and comic songs to marches and dialogues, it could play for 1 ½ to 2 minutes anything that the people wished to hear, through its circular records that were 5-inch and 7-inch in diameter. The singers were paid a fee of $3 for each song.

Sampath (2010) notes that the invention of the talking machine remained merely a marvellous scientific discovery of the nineteenth century; nobody realised the commercial potential of the discovery and its ability to revolutionise the music industry until 1887, when the gramophone was invented

(70–71). Emile Berliner, the inventor of the gramophone, founded The Gramophone Company in London as a syndicate in April 1898. The gramophone was an improvement over the wax cylinder phonograph invented by Thomas Alva Edison. Morton (2014) notes that the gramophone offered marginally better quality, better portability, and the ability to stamp multiple copies from a master recording. This ability of mass production was an essential prerequisite for commercialisation and sales, and it is here that the gramophone scored over the phonograph whose popularity began flagging.

The gramophone had an impact on oral histories and cultural identity transformations and created new paradigms for creative economies worldwide. As O'Connell (2013) argues, mechanical forms of recording made Irish music popular across the world, even while traditional oral methods of teaching and learning of music continued. Mechanical recording gave many immigrant Irish musicians, who had fled to the North American urban centres of Boston, New York, Philadelphia, and Chicago towards the end of the nineteenth century following the widespread economic devastation of Ireland, an opportunity to immortalize themselves and their music. The gramophone created a substantial catalogue of Jewish, Turkish, Greek, and Russian music in the early decades of the twentieth century.

Seroussi (1990) argues that the gramophone revolutionised the learning and transmission of Ladino folk music throughout the Sephardic world. The traditional songs were not only standardised and learnt by many more people, they also spurred an interest in the creation of new songs (175). Ross (2005) notes how recording made popular stars of some of the best of Western classical musicians, including Dame Nellie Melba, Feodor Ivanovich Chaliapin, Enrico Caruso, Adelina Patti, Francesco Tamagno, Nikolai Figner, Medea Mei-Figner, Mattia Battistini, and others. Ross (2005) mentions that contemporaries of these musicians, including American composer and conductor of the late Romantic era, John Philip Sousa, frowned upon the recording device and predicted that it would bring about the eventual demise of music, erode the finer instincts of the ear, and render professional musicians unemployed. Ross (2005) quotes Sousa: "The time is coming when no one will be ready to submit himself to the ennobling discipline of learning music, everyone will have their readymade or ready pirated music in their cupboards. Something is irretrievably lost when we are no longer in the presence of bodies making music. The nightingale's song is delightful because the nightingale herself gives it forth" (n.pag.).

Such criticisms and apprehensions aside, the gramophone made listening to music a personal experience as compared to a community one where music was consumed in concerts. The living room now replaced the concert halls and clubs where bands played. The music of popular musicians could be obtained on demand, repeatedly heard and more incisively analysed.

Starting in 1902, The Gramophone Company sent recording experts from England to India on "expeditions" to record "native voices" and to create a viable business proposition (Sampath 2010: 77–78).

The Early Beginnings of The Gramophone Company

Jones (1985) documents that The Gramophone Company was founded as a syndicate in April 1898, as the result of a licensing agreement between Trevor Lloyd Williams, a London solicitor, and Emile Berliner, the inventor of the gramophone, signed on 23 February 1898. While the mechanical components for the gramophone were to be made in the United States of America and then assembled in England, The Gramophone Company would make its own recordings wherever the recording experts, as they were termed, happened to be located. The discs reproduced from these matrices were to be manufactured at a factory in Hanover, Germany (80).

Jones (1985) argues that many aspects of The Gramophone Company's business model were akin to a typical British multinational firm. The establishment of foreign factories was the first wave of British multinational foreign direct investment that occurred in the last two decades of the nineteenth century. The Gramophone Company was headquartered in Britain, and was formed with British capital. But no manufacturing and production happened in Britain. All its products and technology and most of its senior management came from the United States of America. This was facilitated through an extensive licensing and marketing agreement with the Victor Talking Machine Company of the USA. This was again a unique relationship the two companies shared, and in the first 20 years of its existence The Gramophone Company's growth hinged on this partnership with The Victor Talking Machine Company (77–78). Jones (1985) describes how the two companies were financially and managerially independent of one another but linked to each other through marketing agreements, share of trademarks and logos, technology transfer from The Victor Talking Machine Company, and a clear division of world markets, where each of them was supposed to operate. The Gramophone Company was not a subsidiary of The Victor Talking Machine.

Jones (1985) writes:

> Similarly, the Gramophone Company's wide network of foreign factories, which by 1914 included ventures in Austria, France, Germany, India, Russia and Spain, was not uncommon among early British multinationals...The preference of British companies for investing in the British Empire began only in the interwar years. Before World War I many British multinationals found Continental markets at least as attractive as those of the empire. (77)

In July 1898, Emile Berliner's assistant, Frederick William Gaisberg, was appointed as the first recording expert for the fledgling Gramophone Company. He was sent on what The Gramophone Company called expeditions to different continents to record native voices. He conducted several successful recording trips to Germany, Hungary, Spain, Italy and Russia between 1898 and 1902. By 1902, most of Europe was covered by the recording team. Racy (1976) states that unlike Thomas Alva Edison's phonograph, which had little commercial potential, the gramophone was revolutionising the world of music production and consumption. The phenomenon of the gramophone, according to Racy (1976):

> ...had an unmistakable ethnomusicological implication; it signified the gradual transformation of the phonograph from a curious toy into a serious musical mass medium that involved the performer, the audience, and the businessman. It evidenced a significant change in musical life represented by the emergence of the recording artist and by a musical market sustained by a record consuming audience. (25–26)

The purpose of his expeditions, according to Gaisberg (1942), was to "open up new markets, establish agencies and acquire a catalogue of native records" (48). Thanks to the work of John Perkins, Alan Kelly, and John Ward (1976), we now have an almost complete reconstruction of The Gramophone Company's recording activities up to 1910.

Kinnear (1994: 3–69), Sampath (2010: 69–99), and Sharma (2012) describe in detail the foundation of The Gramophone Company and its early expeditions to different parts of the world. The recorded masters were sent to Hanover where they were reproduced as 7-inch single sided E-Berliner gramophone discs. The company initially did not have printed labels and the information on the contents of the record were etched or handwritten into the centre of the disc. The company adopted the "Recording Angel" trademark which was later replaced by the iconic picture of a dog called Nipper listening to a gramophone and the legendary image of "His Master's Voice" was born.

The Gramophone Company devised a very elaborate system of cataloguing the records and maintaining the lists. Kinnear (1994) explains how the first recordings of languages with non-Roman scripts were allocated to a 10000 series for Oriental recordings and a Russian series beginning at 11000 was also introduced, along with one recording in Chinese at 10500. He also describes that the Oriental series first appeared in the May 1899 "Foreign" catalogue of the Gramophone Company, giving a basic listing of twenty records in Persian, fifteen in Hindi, five in Urdu (Hindustani), five in Sikh (Gurumukhi) and two in Arabic. "Their commercial potential," Kinnear writes, "could not have been too great" (3–4). It was in London that technically the first Indian voices were etched on the shellac discs. There were 47 numbered recordings of Captain Bholanath, Dr. Harnaamdas, and Ahmed, who sang, recited, and spoke in several languages. The musical content was not as important for the company as building up a vast and multi-ethnic, multi-lingual repertoire.

Gronow (1981) mentions that in the early decades of the twentieth century half a dozen companies of the recording industry created an oligopolistic market. All of them followed very similar business models and strategies (253). He writes:

> They manufactured both recordings (discs or cylinders) and record-play-ing equipment (gramophones, phonographs) and tried to market them worldwide. Directly-owned subsidiaries were established in the most important markets; in smaller countries, their products were marketed through local agents. Regional factories served several countries. (253)

Kenwood and Lougheed (1971) state that although Europe and North America were the mainstay of recording, Asia and Latin America repre-sented almost one-fifth of the total world trade and also distributed and sold the factory produced goods from the industrialised countries (93).

On 15 August 1899, the syndicate was transformed into a limited liability company called the Gramophone Company Limited. Naming procedures were further standardised. The expeditions across the United Kingdom, Russia, and other parts of Europe were hugely successful, and the Company saw brisk business and sales. Exports of gramophones to Africa, China, India, and Australia were steadily on the rise, and about 500 recordings in European and Oriental languages were catalogued. But, despite the success, the new managing director William Barry Owen felt that the gramophone alone was insufficient to run a profitable business and that the Company needed to diversify and bundle its product offerings. The Lambert type-writer was chosen as the odd partner. Thus, the unusual marriage of the Lambert Typewriter Company based out of Broadway in New York and the Gramophone Company Ltd, took place on 10 December 1900, resulting in the Gramophone and Typewriter Ltd or GTL. Ironically, years later, it was the typewriter that failed to attract customers. So, by 1905, the typewriter portion of the business was sold off to Sidney Herbert of France, though the Company continued to be called GTL until 1907. "His Master's Voice" or HMV (the label curiously appeared only by 1916), which was the cap-tion that accompanied the Company's trademark popular logo of the dog listening to the record, represented the earliest ventures that aimed at the globalisation of a cultural commodity.

The marvellous gramophone had arrived on the world music scene and there was no stopping it. It was just a matter of time before it was to enter the Indian sub-continent, which was to become its most lucrative and viable musical market in the decades to come.

Note

1 Interview of author with Mr. Christian Liebl, Centre for Linguistics and Audiovisual Documentation, Austrian Academy of Sciences, Vienna Phongrammarchiv.

3 WHEN THE TWAIN MET

The Gramophone Company Comes to India

Sampath (2010) writes that prior to Gaisberg's expedition to India, The Gramophone Company sent its agent John Watson Hawd to survey the Indian market and conduct market research on the business potential that it offered. In a letter dated 13 January 1900, Berliner wrote to Hawd acknowledging the vast musical potential of India that was waiting to be recorded on gramophone discs. He stated that in the city of Calcutta (now known as Kolkata) alone, with a population of about half a million inhabitants "there is scarcely any city in the world which contains so many people who are able to spend a fair amount of money for an article like ours."[1] Berliner wanted to start his business in India and solicited the "wisdom" of Hawd, given his good past track record at Hanover, for this. He suggested that within a few weeks Hawd leave for India by steamer

> with at least 500 machines and say, 30,000 records and go and stay long enough in Calcutta and Bombay to prove the possibility of making a business there and then after that has been done, in 3, 4 or 5 months turn the business over to some large House on the basis of wishing to start the work in different localities of that region.[2]

Berliner advised him to go prepared with advertising collaterals of the company and strongly believed that Hawd would emerge immensely successful in this venture.[3]

Hawd accordingly left for India and made an elaborate survey of the Indian market. In a letter to the Head Office in London dated 29 August 1901 he wrote:

> This is a large country and a stock of less than 20,000 is little to no good…I am absolutely dying to …get things going. Can you by any means have some Bengali and other songs made for us in London? I am sure you should be able to find someone to make 25 or 50 numbers until you can find it convenient to send someone out here for with native songs, 1000 should be sold.[4]

DOI: 10.4324/9780367822026-3

A lot of these early correspondences are primarily concerned with establishing markets, trademarks and franchises through lawsuits. The musical or musicological worth of the potential recordings are neither discussed nor mentioned and the agents' knowledge or interest in Indian music appears to be completely unknown or considered unimportant and at best on a purely transactional level.

In January 1902, the London office wrote to Hawd confirming the trip of the recording expert Frederick William Gaisberg to India for the recordings. An extract of a letter to this effect, dated 1 January 1902 states:

> I am planning to send out Gaisberg to you on the first of February to make records in your vicinity...I am going to have him make haste to go there direct and to do work thoroughly and well, and I predict as a result getting a very large business. We will now take up the Indian business on thoroughly business lines and put it on a firm and good foundation.[5]

However for reasons best known to it, the Company did not send Gaisberg on the expedition to India as scheduled. This frustrated Hawd, who had by then spent more than a year in India making preparations for the maiden expedition. In a letter dated 3 June 1902, he expressed his frustration to the London office:

> Is he [Gaisberg] really coming?... Of course I don't care only I had made arrangements with artists which are now cancelled and I am not going to trouble again until he has really landed for by the time he arrives the *pooja* [religious feast, devotion] will have commenced and nothing can be done till after December...about 12 to 14,000 people are dying in this territory weekly now of plague.[6]

Gaisberg finally arrived in Calcutta by the end of October 1902. In his memoirs, Gaisberg (1942: 54–55) documents his maiden visit to India, the logistical challenges, and the cultural shock that he experienced while he was there. He wrote that it took them three days to unload thirty heavy cases they had brought in from London and pass the customs office. Jack Hawd had arranged a location and had assembled a collection of artists who watched curiously as they prepared their makeshift studio for recording. Gaisberg (1942) wrote:

> It was the first time that the talking machine had come into their lives and they regarded it with awe and wonderment. We entered a new world of musical and artistic values. One had to erase all memories of European opera houses and concert halls: the very foundations of my musical training were undermined. (55)

Through local interlocutors and agents, The Gramophone Company managed to source the first artists whom they decided to record. Kinnear (1994) mentions two such local proprietors of Calcutta theatres, Amarendra Nath Dutt, and Jamshedji Framji Madan. Being unaware of Indian music, Gaisberg and his team had to rely on any artist that these proprietors suggested or took them to hear. Hence, some of the early recordings were musically arbitrary with everything from classical music to "Bengali Comic Talk" being recorded (9–20). Kinnear mentions that the first recordings of Indian artists were made on 8 November 1902. These were of Miss Soshi Mukhi and Miss Fani Bala, who Gaisberg (1942) mentions as "two little nautch girls aged fourteen and sixteen with miserable voices" (56). The recording catalogues mention these recordings in the E-series ranging from E1001 to E1012. They are Bengali and Hindustani songs.[7] They include folk and theatre melodies such as *Aami Ki Sanjani Kasumeri* (Bengali, by Soshi Mukhi), *Jatana Ditey Amanar* and *Saral Maney Saral Praney* (Bengali, by Fani Bala), *Nime Ser Tore Sararme Bashilo* and *Hilmil Paniyan ko Jaari Nandiya* (Hindustani theatre duet by Soshi Mukhi and Fani Bala) and so on.

The consequences of such arbitrary visits to theatre shows and musical soirees are reflected in Gaisberg's (1942) exasperation after he heard a musical play:

> Our first visit was to the 'Classic Theatre' where a performance of Romeo and Juliet in a most unconventional form was being given. Quite arbitrarily, there was introduced a chorus of young Nautch girls heavily bleached with rice powder and dressed in transparent gauze. They sang 'And her golden hair was hanging down her back' accompanied by fourteen brass instruments all playing in unison. I had yet to learn that the oriental ear was unappreciative of chords and harmonic treatment, and only demanded the rhythmic beat of the accompaniment of the drums. At this point we left. (56)

The cross-cultural incompatibilities that the above paragraph highlights are important. To catch the European's attention, local artists were clamouring to present badly arranged English plays and Western songs while the recording experts, being unaware of Indian music, were keen on listening to its traditional forms. Gasiberg's disgust for Indian music in his earliest encounter is evident in his writings:

> Never again will I be able to summon up an equal enthusiasm for Indian music, for one indispensable accompaniment to most songs was a simple missionary's organ. The keys were played with one hand while the other worked a bellows. I found it produced a dull and uninspiring sound, and I soon came to loathe the instrument. Only one or two male singers were recommended to us and these had high-pitched effeminate

voices. There was absolutely no admiration or demand for the manly baritone or bass, and in the Orient vocalists in these categories would starve to death. (56)

Gaisberg's (1942) accounts, however, give us a glimpse into the performances, social hierarchies and connoisseurs of music of the times. He speaks of making their way through unsavoury alleys to be then ushered to a soiree hosted by a native. The women of the native household were never allowed to attend and the only women there were the nautch girls, who Gaisberg says, "have lost caste" (56). Europeans ate at separate tables where even the host did not join them. After dinner, they were led to a large salon and entertained by the music and dance of the nautch girls. The room, according to Gaisberg (1942):

> presented a most interesting sight. At one end were the native gentlemen in their white gowns; some wore strings of pearls and diamonds and valuable rings. At the other end was our small party of Europeans in evening dress. The Singing Girl advanced slowly around the room singing. Following her closely was her band of five musicians, consisting of two *esrag* or Hindustani violins, one tumble player with a right and left *tamboora* and two *mandieras* (bells) players. Bringing up the rear were attendants for preparing the betel nut and another holding a silver cuspidor. The singer was heavily laden with gold ornaments and bracelets, anklets and pearl necklaces, and to crown all these was a large diamond set in her nostril. She was a Mohammedan and very popular. She terminated each song with a cleverly executed muscle dance...She could lay considerable claim to a coloratura voice. She performed with some ease, very difficult vocalizing such as scales and a sort of guttural trill which drew our attention to herself. As a courtesy to the Europeans among the audience she sang an English song 'Silver threads among the gold' that received a thunderous applause. (55–56)

The artist whom Gaisberg mentions above was one of India's leading classical vocalists and a *tawaif* of the city of Calcutta, Gauhar Jaan (1873–1930). Speaking of Gauhar Jaan, Farrell (1993) describes her as being "multilingual, glamorous, flamboyant and fully aware of the potential of the new medium," and given her Anglo-Indian background, considers her an "appropriate figure to play a role which bridged tradition and modernity, India and the West" (35–36).

Sampath (2010) writes that Gaisberg realised that recording Gauhar Jaan would be commercially viable for the company as she was a popular artist (Figure 3.1). Gaisberg negotiated the commercial terms and she demanded Rs. 3000 for every recording session, which was agreed by Gaisberg (85).

On 11 November 1902 in a makeshift studio in Calcutta, the first commercial Indian recording was made of Gauhar Jaan. The EMI Music

Figure 3.1 Advertisement on The Gramophone Company catalogue featuring Gauhar Jaan posing with the gramophone.

Source: Picture Courtesy *My name is Gauhar Jaan!* By Vikram Sampath (2010).

Archive catalogues list several songs of this expedition, including *Dhagar Na Jaani Jabe Kaise* (Tune Dadrah, Mahomedan Song), *Bhalo Basibe Baley Bhalo Basiney* (Bengali), *My Love is Like a Little Bird* (English), *Jana Bali Champali* (Gujrati), and so on.[8] Sampath (2010) mentions that Gauhar Jaan cut close to 600 records in nearly 20 languages that included Hindustani, Bengali, Urdu, Persian, English, Arabic, Pushto, Tamil, Marathi, Peshawari, Gujrati, and French (99). In the very first recording expedition, Gauhar had sung songs in thirteen languages—Hindustani, Urdu, Sanskrit, Bengali, Arabic, Turkish, Madrasi (Tamil), Gujrati, Katchchi, Tailungi (Telugu), English, Peshwari, and Gurmes.

Sampath (2010) quotes Gaisberg's admiration for Gauhar Jaan's musicality and her flamboyance:

> Her flair for publicity is well illustrated by the feast she once provided for her cat when she produced a litter of kittens. This affair cost her twenty thousand rupees. There were hundreds of guests, so naturally this feline function became the talk of the bazaars. When she came to record, her suite of musicians and attendants appeared even more imposing than those who used to accompany Melba and Calve. As the proud heiress of immemorial folk-music traditions she bore herself with becoming dignity. She knew her own market value, as we found to our cost when we

negotiated with her...Every time she came to record she amazed us by appearing in a new gown, each one more elaborate than the last. She never wore the same jewels twice. Strikingly effective were her delicate black gauze draperies embroidered with real gold lace, arranged so as to present a tempting view of a bare leg and a naked navel. (56)

Kinnear (1994) states that during the six-week stay in Calcutta, Gaisberg, assisted by George Dillnutt, had taken some 216 of the 7-inch wax matrices and 336 of the 10-inch wax matrices, which were shipped to Hanover. These included recordings of Gauhar Jaan, nautch girls Soshi Mukhi and Fani Bala, theatre stars of Calcutta such as Miss Sushila, Miss Binodini, Miss Acheria, Miss Kiron, Miss Rani, Babu N C Bose and male classical vocalists Peara Saheb and Lal Chand Boral. Of the 550 odd matrices that Gaisberg recorded, only about half of these were used to make pressings for sale to the Indian public. The first stock of produced records started flooding the Indian market from April 1903. These single-sided recorded discs came to be known as "Gramophone Record" (7-inch ones) and "The Gramophone Concert Records" (10-inch ones) (12–14).

The early recording techniques on the gramophone were not easy for either the experts or the artists. Noble (1912), a recording expert and a British National working for the French recording company Pathe, writes that "the skill required to secure the natural tone quality of the artiste, the great amount of labour required to produce the multitudinous records which are sold in every corner of the globe, the fees paid to artistes, which alone runs into many thousands of pounds per month, and other similar incidentals" make it an arduous exercise (331–334). Initially, the experts conducted primary trials of several artists to secure a "recording voice." Not every accomplished concert artist managed to succeed in recording – much depended on the quality of the voice (weak/strong; nasal; soft) or the quality of enunciation.

Based on the trials, the musical director of the company would ascertain the key that suited each artist. On the day of the recording, the guidance of the recording expert was necessary for musicians who had no prior experience in recording.

The artists and their orchestra rehearsed and timed their presentation before the actual recording so that it fit within the limited duration of three minutes, which was all that a single side of a shellac disc could hold. The artist had to sing into the recording horn kept close to the face to ensure evenness in the strength of the voice. The sound waves of the artist's voice, Noble (1912) writes:

travels down the horn, through the special rubber attachment, through the trunnion [sic] supporting the diaphragm, on to the diaphragm itself, thereby vibrating the recording glass, which in turn vibrates the sapphire, cutting the indentations or sound-waves into the fast revolving disc or cylinder. (332)

The recording expert had to physically move the artists closer and farther from the recording horn into which they sang depending on the loudness or softness in a portion of the recording. Noble mentions that "during the singing...on a loud note it is sometimes necessary to take the artiste a few inches back from the horn, and on a subdued, or low note nearer to it." The completed recording was heard in the presence of the artist, expert, and music director and, if found faulty, re-takes were made. A satisfactory record was numbered and carefully packed away for transit to the factory.

The Second Recording Expedition

The South of India was not covered in the first tour of Gaisberg in 1902. Kinnear (1994) documents that a second expedition of The Gramophone Company was sent to India led by William Sinkler Darby, assisted by Max Hempe, in 1904–05. Starting in early December 1904 the expedition lasted until March 1905 and was held at multiple locations: Calcutta, Delhi, Lahore, Bombay and Madras. The 7-inch series were suffixed as "G" and 395 recordings of these were taken. The "H" suffixed 10-inch series had 821 recordings, and the "I" suffixed 12-inch series had 58 recordings. All these were single-sided recorded discs with paper labels (21–26).

Sampath (2010) notes that the second tour offered an opportunity for The Gramophone Company to work on issues with Indian artists such as cultural and musical sensitivity that they had possibly missed in the first expedition. The intervening period also gave them an opportunity to correct any mistakes that might have been committed in the recording process in the maiden edition. We, therefore, observe a better quality in recording and also a wider variety of performers engaged to record in the second expedition.

Thomas Addis who took over from Hawd as the local agent conducted elaborate research on the market conditions and opportunities for the company. In his correspondence to the London office dated 23 December 1903 he states:

> India is a peculiar country in regard to language as if you go 300 miles out of Calcutta you would find a different dialect altogether which would not be understood here and so on through every state and presidency. Each particular district has its own local and popular singers male and female, beside which there are a few amateur singers whose records would sell freely. Now it is this class of work that the better and middle class natives, who have the money enquire for and we are creditably informed the present sales are largely due to the excellent results obtained from the instruments alone, and that it is not the records themselves that are inducing the public to buy instruments.[9]

Addis' correspondence points to a vibrant and growing Indian market for the gramophones and to the Indian middle class and the elite who were enthusiastically buying the gramophones, often less for the music than as a status symbol. In another letter dated 23 December 1904 (accessed by me from the EMI Music Archives, London), Addis states:

> We have taken records in various vernaculars, but we have not, in my opinion gone far enough into this matter. Permit me to fall back on figures to show the immense field there is to be developed in India:
>
> India— Total Population [1901] 287,000,000
>
> There are 147 vernaculars of extraordinary variety.
>
> Hindi spoke by 60,000,000
> Bengali spoke by 44,000,000
> Bihari spoke by 47,000,000
> Telegu spoke by 20,000,000
> Mahrati spoke by 18,000,000
>
> After which come Rajastani, Kanarese, Gujarati, Oriya, Burmese, Tamil, Malayalam, Pustu, pure Urdu etc, etc. The above figures convey, no doubt the enormous diversity under the name 'India'.[10]

Gronow (1981) underscores this fact by explaining how the company considered the ethnic and linguistic sub-divisions of the country. From the very beginning, separate lists were published for Hindi, Bengali, Urdu, Sikh, Pashto, Gujarati, Punjabi, and South Indian (Tamil, Telugu, Malayalam and Kannada) records. Other languages were gradually introduced, and by the 1920s the company had made recordings in Assamese, Bengali, Chattisgarhi, Garhwali, Gujarati, Hindi, Kannada, Konkani, Kumauni, Malayalam, Marathi, Multani, Pashto, Punjabi, Oriya, Sindhi, Sinhalese, Tamil, Telugu, and Urdu. This was done with a view to tap all potential markets within the country (257).

Jones (1985) elucidates that from 1901 to 1914 there was a remarkable expansion in the activities of The Gramophone Company. Both the international manufacturing and the sales of its products increased. He details that when complaints came up about the quality of records pressed at Hanover, The Gramophone Company established a record factory in the United Kingdom at Hayes, Middlesex in 1908. By then similar factories had come up in a number of countries, including in India at Calcutta (now Kolkata) in March 1907. Jones argues that while overcoming tariff barriers on importing records could have been one motivation in establishing these record pressing factories locally, the overriding concern seems to be early availability of records in the local markets. There was approximately a six-month delay between recording and sales and distribution due to the fact that manufacture had to be undertaken in Hanover and shipped back to India. Local factories also implied lower inventory cost (87).

Table 3.1 Number of recordings of the Gramophone Company
in Asia and Africa between 1900 and 1910

Country	# of recordings	% of recordings
India	4410	31
Turkey	1925	14
Egypt	1192	8
Burma	508	4
China (1903 only)	476	3
Japan (1903 only)	276	2
Algeria	223	2
Iran	221	2
Tunisia	180	1
Syria	158	1
Malaya	121	1
Thailand	97	1
Java	93	1
Sri Lanka	44	0
Tibet	18	0
Far East	4265	30
TOTAL	**14207**	

Source: Gronow (1981).

Gronow (1981: 255) mentions that between 1900 and 1910, the Gramophone
Company made over 14,000 recordings in Asia and North Africa (of which
India accounted for the biggest share, accounting for about 31 percent; refer
Table 3.1).

By 1914 The Gramophone Company had established itself as a truly
multinational company. The geographical distribution of turnover (in
pounds) of The Gramophone Company between 1906 and 1914 is listed in
Table 3.2.

From the above table, one sees that the India market occupied a significant component of the percentage of profit share/turnover of the Company:
6 percent in 1906–1908, rising to 8 percent in 1909–1911 and to 10 percent by
1912–1914 (Table 3.3).

The data clearly show that while the total turnover of The Gramophone
Company between 1909–11 and 1906–08 showed a negative growth of −0.42
percent, the India profit share of grew by +16.70 percent and was close to the
British market share of +19.30 percent. When we compare the 1912–14 numbers with the base of 1909–11 numbers, we notice a decrease in the market
share; particularly in Europe, as it was the advent of the First World War.
But during the same period, the India market share jumped to +27.07 percent, even as the British market share sharply declined to a +9.20 percent.
The total turnover showed a positive growth of +11.41 percent, powered
mainly by the Indian market.

The problem that The Gramophone Company faced was the high cost of
its machines, which made consumers buy low-priced gramophones instead

Table 3.2 Geographical distribution of turnover of Gramophone Company
1906–1914

	1906–08		1909–11		1912–14	
	£	%	£	%	£	%
United Kingdom	670760	25	800200	29	873810	29
India	*176440*	*6*	*205900*	*8*	*261640*	*10*
Overseas*	165470		81520	3	257270	9
Scandinavia	96200	4	93230	3	157320	5
France	174370	6	131880	5	108540	4
Spain	62410	2	82180	3	81280	3
Belgium	38100	1	34200	1	35980	1
Germany	478540	18	517660	19	466140	14
Austria	161530	6	65380	2	62750	2
Hungary	33260	1	41480	2	41900	1
Russia	670910	25	662960	24	679720	22
TOTAL	**2727990**		**2716510**		**3026350**	

Source: "Report on Future Prospects of the Entire General Business of the Gramophone
Company, 1921," EMI Archives, London.

* Including Australasia, Holland, Italy, South Africa, Egypt, Ottoman Empire, North Africa
and Albania.

of the HMV ones. In India cheaper German and Swiss machines were more
popular than HMV gramophones. The issue relating to the high cost of
the machines persisted until the 1920s but was never seriously addressed
by The Gramophone Company. An official of The Gramophone Company
confirmed this to the head office in London in 1922:

> We are beaten out of the market by Swiss and German manufacturers.
> The Indian buyer thinks of money first, and quality second. He is quite
> content with Swiss quality.[11]

The Gramophone Company's main competitor Pathé produced cheaper
machines that did not play records of The Gramophone Company. Thereby
not only did Pathé try to kill competition when it came to sale of machines
but also of the records of The Gramophone Company, by rendering them to
be useless and redundant on Pathé machines.[12]

Table 3.3 India vs United Kingdom in terms of change of profit share:
Calculated from Table 3.1 figures

	1909–11 vs 1906–08	1912–14 vs 1909–11
Total	−0.421%	11.406%
India	16.697%	27.071%
United Kingdom	19.298%	9.199%

Gender Composition and Musical Forms in Early Recording Catalogues

So who were the main artists in India who came forward to record for the Company in its early expeditions? Was this new technology openly embraced by one and all? A closer investigation of the catalogues of the Company as compiled by Kinnear (1994), of the first three recording expeditions shows an interesting trend (Table 3.4).

In the first Indian recording expedition of 1902, The Gramophone Company made 516 recordings, about 46.51% of which were of women artists. If we include all categories such as classical music, theatre songs, recitations from religious texts, comic pieces, and other recitations that were recorded in the first expedition, there are about thirty male voices recorded and about sixteen female voices. The strictly classical pieces in this collection are only of Gauhar Jaan and the male artist Lal Chand Boral. The "Others" category in Table 3.4 above refers to orchestras and bands whose gender composition is unknown.

By the time of the second recording expedition led by William Sinkler Darby in 1904–05, Kinnear's (1994) catalogues show that not only had the number of recordings gone up but so had the number of women artists in the catalogue. Between December 1904 and March 1905, Darby and his assistant Max Hampe made 1280 recordings (23). Of these recordings, 579 (i.e. 45.23%) were recordings of women. The recordings of this expedition were of a more diverse range of artists across North and South India. Recordings were conducted at Calcutta (now Kolkata), Allahabad (now Prayagraj), Lucknow, Delhi, Lahore, Bombay (now Mumbai), and Madras (now Chennai) (Kinnear 1994: 22). The catalogues reveal that apart

Table 3.4 Number of recordings and number of women who recorded

	1902		1904–05		1906–07	
	Number	%	Number	%	Number	%
Number of recordings of women (non-classical)	189	36.63	118	9.22	41	3.09
Number of recordings of women (classical)	51	9.88	461	36.02	659	49.70
Total number of recordings of women	**240**	**46.51**	**579**	**45.23**	**700**	**52.79**
Number of recordings of men (non-classical)	192	37.21	596	46.56	474	35.75
Number of recordings of men (classical)	12	2.33	91	7.11	113	8.52
Total number of recordings of men	**204**	**39.53**	**687**	**53.67**	**587**	**44.27**
Others	72	13.95	14	1.09	39	2.94
Total number of recordings	**516**		**1280**		**1326**	

from Gauhar Jaan, Keeti Jaan of Meerut, Binodini Dasi of Calcutta, Kali Jaan of Delhi, Dhanakoti of Kanchipuram, Salem Godavari, Bangalore Nagarathnamma, and Salem Papa of Madras were the prolifically recorded women artists. The catalogues from the EMI Music Archive show that the bulk of the male recordings in classical music during this expedition are of the eminent Ustad Abdul Karim Khan, who was serving as court musician of the Gaekwad king of Baroda. The other prominent male musicians include Ustad Barkatulla Khan (Sitar), Ustad Imdad Khan (Sitar), vocalists Ustad Mauzuddin Khan, L C Boral, Peara Saheb, Ustad Ahmed Khan of Lahore, Ustad Kale Khan of Lahore, and Ustad Abdul Gafoor Khan of Calcutta. Relatively unknown male artists such as T. Narayanaswami Iyer (Vocal and Violin), P.S. Krishna Iyer (Vocal), and Vaidyanadha Iyer (Vocal) are part of the Carnatic music catalogues in this expedition. The "traditional" classical male musicians are scant.

The third recording expedition of The Gramophone Company to India was led by William Conrad Gaisberg in 1906–07 and was conducted in Calcutta (now Kolkata), Lucknow, Delhi, Lahore, Bombay (now Mumbai), Hyderabad and Madras (now Chennai). The catalogues reveal that of the 1326 recordings made in this expedition, 700 (i.e. 52.79%) were of women artists. Some of the prominent female artists who recorded in large numbers in this expedition were Wazir Jaan of Banaras, Jhandi of Jhelum, Bhavani of Kanchipuram, Gauhar Jaan, Salem Godavari, Malka Jaan of Agra and Janki Bai of Allahabad. Kinnear (1994) states that by mid-1907, The Gramophone Company had more than 3000 Indian titles, which made it by far the largest sound recording company operating in India (28).

Analysing the number of recordings of classical music only reveals the following (refer Table 3.5).

The trends seen from Table 3.5 indicate that in the first expedition, The Gramophone Company seems to have recorded only 12.21 percent classical music and the rest were all folk tunes, comic stories, religious chantings, theatre songs, and recitations. But by the time of the second and third expeditions, the number grew to 43.13 percent, and 58.22 percent indicating a clear inclination of the consumers towards the classical music segment. Women clearly formed the overwhelming majority of the classical music recordings of both Hindustani and Carnatic music in the catalogues. From 80.95 percent in the first expedition, the number grew to 83.51 percent, and

Table 3.5 Number of classical music recordings of men and women artists

	1902		1904–05		1906–07	
	Number	*%*	*Number*	*%*	*Number*	*%*
Women classical	51	80.95	461	83.51	659	85.36
Men classical	12	19.05	91	16.49	113	14.64
Total classical	**63**	**12.21**	**552**	**43.13**	**772**	**58.22**

85.36 percent in the second and third expeditions, respectively. Also, the number of women who recorded classical music was far greater than the number of men recording classical music.

And when we talk of the "classical," what sub-genres fell within this definition and was there a hierarchy or gender marker associated with these forms?

By and large, musical forms in Hindustani music categorised as being "higher" in the pyramid or more classical (*khayal, dhrupad*) fell into the male dominion and were strictly contained within the inherently patriarchal hereditary lineage of artists (the *gharana* system of Hindustani music). "Lighter" forms categorised again loosely as semi-classical (the romantic *thumri* and *dadra*, folk tunes of *hori, kajri, chaiti* or devotional *bhajan*) formed the preserve of the women artists. There were exceptions, such as Zohra Bai of Agra whose classical *khayal* recordings in a range of ragas display her immense musical virtuosity. But the above trend of gender in the forms of music that were recorded by the women and men is visible in the Hindustani catalogues. Given the large number of women who recorded in these early expeditions, the musical forms sung and popularised by the women naturally formed the mainstay of the catalogues. It can therefore be said that the number of recordings in the early Hindustani catalogues is inversely proportional to its place in the imagined hierarchy of musical forms (Figure 3.2).

Based on Kinnear's (1994) catalogue and the data collected from the sales catalogues at the EMI Music Archive in London, I compare below the recordings in the 1906–07 expedition of The Gramophone Company across some of the prominent women Hindustani singers (with greater than 10 recordings to identify the split across musical forms) (Table 3.6).

Other than the one *khayal* recording of Gauhar Jaan, evident in Table 3.6, most of the women recorded only semi-classical and light musical

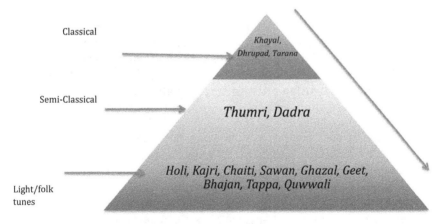

Figure 3.2 Imagined hierarchy of musical forms within Hindustani classical music.

Table 3.6 Number of recordings by musical forms recorded by some of the prominent women Hindustani musicians in the 1906–1907 recording expedition

# of recordings	Gauhar Jaan	Malka Jaan	Janki Bai	Wazir Jaan	Kali Jaan	Oomda Jaan
Khayal and Dhrupad (classical)	1					3
Tarana (classical)						3
Thumri (semi-classical)	4	6	3	6	4	1
Dadra (semi-classical)	3	5	11	5	3	
Holi (light/folk)	3	2	1	2	2	1
Kajri (light/folk)	2	1	1	2		
Chaiti (light/folk)	1					
Sawan (light/folk)	1					
Ghazal (semi-classical)	8		2	6	9	1
Bhajan (semi-classical)		1	1		1	
Geet (light/folk)						1
Tappa (semi-classical)					1	1
Quwwali (light/folk)	2	3	2		1	
Total number	**26**	**18**	**21**	**21**	**21**	**11**

forms. Oomda Jaan of Hyderabad, however, presents an interesting exception. While the total number of her recordings is less than that of the other women, the range encompasses all the three categories of the hierarchy and, notably, about three *khayals* and *dhrupads* each.

It might be speculated that recording offered the women artists the freedom to negotiate genres and explore those that normally were forbidden for them due to the social distinctions that determined musical hierarchies too. Recasting of musical identities thus became a possibility for the women artists; recording offered to them that space. The reverse was true as well. Due to the sale of records and their popularity, the lighter musical forms became well known and this prompted the male musicians to negotiate them as well. Thus, we have men such as Maujuddin Khan and Abdul Karim Khan and, by the 1930s, Bade Ghulam Khan, who were as popular for their soulful and erotic *thumris* as they were for classical renditions. The men also seemed to imitate the tonal quality and pitch of women in their recording. Whether this was due to the limitation of the technology of the time that necessitated the artist to sing at high pitches or the success of women in the recording field, the aesthetics of the feminine voice predominated is tough to deduce.

In Carnatic music there is no such demarcation mainly for two reasons. First, hardly any male musician of significant repute in Carnatic music recorded in the first decade of the twentieth century. Second, the women sung all kinds of forms, from the supposedly "heavy" classical compositions, or *kritis*, composed by the famed Carnatic music Trinity (Thyagaraja, Muthuswamy Dikshitar and Shyama Shastri), to devotional songs in Tamil and Sanskrit and erotic *padams* and *javalis*.

Sampath (2010) writes that there was reluctance on the part of the male artists to adapt to the new technology. He quotes an anecdote about a celebrated male classical vocalist Rahimat Khan Haddu Khan who was hailed as a celestial musician on earth to illustrate this point:

> Recording session lasted for two days. As it was done acoustically, two large horns were placed before him as microphones. He was very much disturbed by the recording atmosphere and talked too much during the singing. One large HMV emblem frame of dog looking and singing into the horn was placed to catch his attention. However, it irritated him even more and he asked them to remove the dog picture from his sight. When the sample was played back to him, he got angry since someone else like him was singing back through the horn. He got up to leave the hall immediately. With great difficulty, he was persuaded to stay and the recordings were taken. (95)

I speculate that this male reluctance was not determined only by aesthetic limitations of gramophone recording such as lack of sufficient time for exposition, unease with new technology, social taboos and superstitions, and a perception that it constituted a vulgarisation of the music and a compromise of its magnificence. A significant reason for male reluctance to record also seems to stem from the fear that the records would bring out into public realm the secrets of their musical system. This fear of losing control over traditional musical knowledge kept many male artists away from recording. Male musicians claimed descent to hereditary lineages of artists (called *gharana* in the Hindustani system and *bani* in Carnatic music). Within a strict patriarchal and closely bound *Guru-Shishya* tradition of teacher to the taught, the musical knowledge was orally transmitted. The gramophone, democratising this knowledge and making it easily accessible to everyone who could afford to buy it, was naturally seen with suspicion.

In my interview with him, Ustad Abdul Rashid Khan (aged approximately 110 years old during the interview in 2015), and who had witnessed some of these changes in the musical world, confirms this fear that several male musicians possibly shared:

> No doubt the gramophone records played an important role in popularizing music, but when you hear some of those records, do you even feel it is music? In three minutes could these women sing anything musical, that too of a musical system such as ours where ragas are treated with care and improvised for hours? These things seemed like gimmicks to us. May be it works for some foreign music, but not Indian classical music. My *abbu jaan* (father), who was also my *ustad* (teacher), would teach me just three notes: Ni, Ri, and Ga of the raga Yaman with which I started my musical training, for three long months. I had to sing the same notes over and over again till I got the perfect pitch and sound.

Once, when I got bored of singing the same thing and tried to make combinations of these notes, he suddenly appeared from somewhere and chided me saying if you feel you are a great *ustad* already and do not heed my advice, I will cease the training. So, this was how we learnt music. Three notes for three months, and later one raga for three hours! And here, in three minutes you are being asked to pack virtuosity. What kind of joke is that?[13]

Every *gharana* or school of music in the Hindustani system had a different way of exposition of a raga and this needed time. According to him:

Now, tell me, what distinguishes the *gaayaki* (singing style) of Agra to that of Gwalior or Jaipur? After all, you do know some music, don't you? It is the way the musical thoughts are processed and presented and this largely rests on improvisatory techniques. When there is no scope for expansion how can I show you in a recording what the distinctive feature of my *gharana* is? Is that not cheating the art and the audience, and more importantly my own conscience and my teacher? I find that in these three minute records the very definitions of and distinctions between various *gharanas* are redundant. This is not a good thing for classical music where distinctions were blurred and everything homogenized to one normal form. This is what we are hearing today due to all this Western influence; same type of music even in classical forms.[14]

When I tried pointing out that some of the recordings did show distinctive *gharana* features, such as those of Zohra Bai of Agra *gharana*, Abdul Karim Khan of Kirana *gharana* or Kesarbai Kerkar of Jaipur *gharana*, Ustad Khan seemed irritated and hence I did not continue with the line of argument. But Ustad Abdul Rashid Khan's observations encapsulate the reasons for the diffidence and initial reluctance on the part of the male musicians to adapt to recording. In contrast, the ease with which the women recorded is noteworthy. However Ustad Abdul Rashid Khan quipped:

They did it only for money. These women were *tawaifs*, music was a business. They were used to selling and so when this horned instrument came to India, they decided to make some money from the white man and sold the music to them. Of course, some of them were good musicians, but majority of them were purely below average as is evident in the *gaayaki* (singing). Even in live concerts they would try all kinds of tricks. Once in an overnight concert, I remember that a fantastic rendition was done by (forgets name) a famous *Ustad*, after which Gauhar Jaan was to perform. She knew that if she sang immediately after such a wonderful recital, the audience would know how shallow her music is! We could sense the tension on her face. She got on to the stage though and very cleverly tried to tune her *tanpura*[15] in a manner that she cut the string! Now, without the *tanpura*, obviously she could not sing. This concert was in some distant village and so by the time the poor organizers managed to get a new string in the middle of the night, it easily took an hour or so, by when the ambience created by the previous concert was lost and Gauhar Jaan managed to sing with more confidence. Such is the musical 'virtuosity'! But yes, she was indeed very fair and beautiful and half the people came to see this foreign woman.[16]

However, with time, it was the gramophone's reinforcement of the *gharana* styles in its three-minute formats that encouraged the wary male musicians to give up their inhibitions and record. Thus, while the gramophone and the fear of a new technology kept many musicians away, with time, once the medium and the format was understood, it was also seen as the best way to reach out to a larger audience and popularise the art form. Thus, it did bring many musicians to the recording fold.

The women who embraced recording early in its journey in India seemed to be comfortable with this new technology and the challenges it posed. This is illustrated by Noble's (1913: 48–49) account of one of South India's prolifically recorded artists Salem Godavari.[17] It seems from his account that by then, having recorded several times for The Gramophone Company Salem Godavari was an expert in negotiation skills as also in the whole experience of recording in a studio. Hence her directions seemed beneficial for the quality of the recording too, as Noble notes. There is a graphic account of the seductiveness of her home, her appearance in the studio in all her lavish glory, and the curious phenomenon of her taking all her jewels off when requested for a photograph. Another important observation is the presence of the "agent" who bargained fees and settled the deal, but also accompanied the artist to the studio and haggled for more money. In fact, in some of Godavari's recordings, we hear some male voices shouting in the middle or the end with loud exclamatory remarks of "*Bhale!*" or "*Shabhaash*" (literally meaning wonderful and excellent); these were perhaps the same agents who were trying to impress the European that the quality and classicism of the music was indeed so high that it deserved higher remuneration. Noble (1913) notes that the Pathé Company,

> secured her for 16 titles for the sum of 300 rupees per song. I may add that she held out consistently for 2 days for 900 rupees per record. The trouble we discovered was through the agents, who are a most arbitrary set of men. They persuade most of the artists to ask for large fees in order to swell their commission and at the same time advise us that such and such a price is usual for a particular artist. (48)

Like Gaisberg's (1942) accounts of Gauhar Jaan, Noble (1913) too notes with admiration that Godavari "came to the hotel to record, accompanied by a retinue of seven servants, including two accompanists" (48).

She was playing another instrument bejeweled in the most elaborate fashion. The instrument was valued at 12,000 rupees. She was covered with gold and precious stones of great value. It was for the express purpose of guarding these jewels that she possessed a guard of four men. An Indian artist by-the-by invariably dons her finest jewelry in the presence of a white. Round her throat she wore a necklace of English sovereigns, the clasps holding each to the other were studded with diamonds. There being in all fifty sovereigns and fifty clasps, the value can be appreciated. On the toes she wore platinum and gold rings. I secured a photograph but she insisted on removing from her person all jewels, for what reason I was never able to comprehend. In the photograph nevertheless, can be seen the rings on her toes and the large diamonds in the ears. (49)

Not only did Noble (1913) admire her costly jewellery but also her singing, which he thought was exceptional with loud, clear, and high cadenzas that become advantageous during recording. On the broker he says that the man was "so enraptured with the singing that he immediately ordered 3000 of each title" (49). This was possibly to give the recording agents an idea of how well the record would do commercially once it came to the market and hence the artist deserved better payments. Noble (1913) concludes:

Having made records before, (Godavari) was little troubled and in fact was a great assistance, for it was she who instructed the accompanists exactly what to do and where to sit, explaining to me that the position in which she placed the men was the best position, for the so-and-so company had already experimented with the placing and had lost two days before ultimately succeeding. I therefore left it to her and the result proved eminently satisfactory. (49)

In Mumbai, in 2015, I interviewed the nonagenarian musician, cine star, and film entrepreneur of her times Sushila Rani Baburao Patel (1918–2014) who had learnt under several gurus, two of whom were women musicians Moghubai Kurdikar and Bai Sundarabai of Pune. Sundarabai (1885–1955) was not a *tawaif*, but was among the early women musicians in Western India to record on the gramophone. Sushila Rani mentions:

Taai (elder sister, Sundarabai in this reference) would go on foot from door to door to her fellow women musicians campaigning in favour of the gramophone. She would chide those who had inhibitions about it. She would tell the other women and *tawaifs* that this instrument is your future laden with gold. If you want to escape poverty and these lecherous men who exploit you all the time, then forget your fears and go to the studio to record. This gramophone is a God-sent visa of our freedom from exploitation and you will only be foolish if you abstain.[18]

Incidentally, Sundarabai was among the few musicians who adapted to multiple media. Sushila Rani narrates:

> She was an inspiration and was way ahead of her times, and of all those men! She recorded on the gramophone; she acted and sang in plays with renowned Marathi theatre personality Bal Gandharva; she took to the radio when it began broadcasts and also acted in a Marathi film. She lived a luxurious life in Bombay owning several cars and an entire floor of an upscale luxury hotel before she lost all her wealth and was reduced to penury.[19]

The Indian Recording Industry and Competitions to The Gramophone Company

Kinnear (1994) mentions that between 1908 and 1910, several record labels of European origin had issued a large number of Indian recordings. Following the successes of The Gramophone Company, several European firms vied for a share in the Indian recording industry market. These included Beka Grand Record, Universal Record, Neophone Disc Phonograph Record, Royal Record, Pathé Record, Odeon Record, Nicole Record, Ram-A-Phone Disc Record, James Opera Record, Singer Record, Aldridge Salmon & Co. Ltd, Elephone Record, and the Sun Disc Record. There were local Indian players too such as H. Bose's Records, Binapani Record, and Kamala Record (36–59).

Kinnear (January 1991) documents that The Sun Disc Record caused an upheaval in the market in that their products were being offered for Rs. 2 per double-sided record, while all other makes were selling for Rs. 3 or more. The Gramophone Company responded to this challenge by introducing their own Rs. 2 priced double-sided disc under The Zonophone Record label. Zonophone was used to release new recordings that had been previously held in reserve and also to re-issue recordings that had been released previously under the Gramophone Concert Records label. By October 1914, The Zonophone Record label had become the major inexpensively-priced record in the Indian market and was given a double-letter prefix series beginning with N-1 for 10-inch series and V-1 for the few 12-inch issues (7–10).

Jones (1985) and Gronow (1996, 1997) suggest that The First World War disrupted the growth of The Gramophone Company. Before the War, Germany and Austria-Hungary had contributed 20 percent of The Gramophone Company's turnover. Russia, which had contributed 22 percent to the turnover, had its share of political turbulence with the Bolshevik Revolution in 1917. The well-crafted international production and distribution arrangements of the Company were thrown into disarray by these political upheavals. The Hanover factory was damaged during the War, and factories in Russia were shut down by the Bolshevik Government. In such a scenario, with an already strong market, and as a colonised country, which also abundantly provided shellac (the raw material for making the discs), India was to become the mainstay for the consolidation of The Gramophone Company's international fortunes.

By late 1915, the bestselling titles in the Indian repertoire of the Gramophone Company were issued with the "His Master's Voice" label. They were issued as E-1 series for 7-inch, P-1 for 10 inch, and K-1 for 12-inch discs. In 1912 and 1913 several disc records that had been available as single-side recorded discs were re-issued as double-sided discs, and in 1915 several of the best-selling discs were given violet-coloured labels. Violet label discs sold at Rs. 3 and 12 annas, whereas black label discs sold for only Rs. 3. Kinnear's catalogues (1994) suggest that all the recordings of the South Indian super star musician, Coimbatore Thayi, the *devadasi* from Madras, were issued exclusively on the violet-coloured label.

Kinnear (April 1991: 9–12) documents that The Nicole Record was the second label to be introduced in India by mid-1905 after The Gramophone Company. John Hawd of The Gramophone Company, who was its first agent in Calcutta, quit the company due to differences with the management in London, and joined the rival firm Nicole Freres Ltd. The recording expert Stephen Carl Porter took several recordings in Calcutta, Madras, Bombay and Rangoon. About seven hundred recordings of Indian songs and tunes in Bengali, Hindustani, Gujarati, Burmese, Kannada, Tamil, and Telugu were released in 1905. They were the first double-sided records of Indian repertoire to arrive in India. After conducting brisk business for a few years, the company was plagued by several legal tangles and by 1910–11 had folded its business in India.

Kinnear (1994) describes that in 1905, the Neophone Co. Ltd of London decided to send its agent Percy J. Packman for the Indian expedition. Their agents in India were Aldridge Salmon and Co. Ltd and had created a popular market for the Neophone machines. But very few records were released of Neophone, and these were limited mostly to the Gujrati language. Kinnear further writes that The Beka Record label name was derived from the surname initial of the founders of the label- Heinrich Bumb and Max Koenig, who began the business in Berlin in 1900. After working as agents for The Gramophone Company, by late 1904 they set out with their own recording expeditions. On 18 November 1905 Bumb and Koenig arrived in Bombay and engaged Valabhdas Runchordas and Lakhmidas R. Tairsee as brokers. During this tour they recorded some 330 single side disc records. In December 1906 a second expedition made recordings in Bombay, Lucknow, Banaras and Calcutta. The Beka Grand Record offered a great competition to The Gramophone Company catalogue (Figure 3.3). The Phon-O-Phon label was the low-priced version that offered a direct competition to the Zonophone of the Gramophone Company. Their Beka Record (8-inch) and Beka Grand Record (10-inch) were very popular in the Indian market. By 1911 there were about 3000 titles under this catalogue. However the outbreak of the First World War in 1914 severely impacted the business of many of these labels and also of brokers such as Runchordas (40–41).

Figure 3.3 Advertisement dated 1906 of The Gramophone Company catalogue; painting by G.N. Mukerjee depicting the Hindu Goddess of Music, Saraswathi.

Source: Picture courtesy EMI Music Archive, London.

Kinnear (July 1991: 11–19) argues that the losses that The Gramophone Company faced due to the First World War were much less than those faced by all the other companies from Europe. Also, the Gramophone Company had already entrenched themselves well in the Indian market with a wide catalogue by 1907 and a record pressing plant in Calcutta by 1908. The support it received from artists who were popular among the masses also contributed to its consolidation in the Indian market. The London-based Gramophone Company was naturally favoured by the British government that ruled India at that time. All these factors contributed to The Gramophone Company eliminating all the competition and eventually emerging as the market leader of the Indian recording business by the end of the second decade of the twentieth century.

Marketing and Advertising Campaigns of The Gramophone Company in India

To brand itself and also popularise its products, the Gramophone Company launched a massive marketing and advertising campaign. Unlike any other recording company, it was The Gramophone Company that made use of innovative ideas of advertising. Images from Indian mythology, religion, history and society were used in the advertisements. This was necessary because, as Farrell (2004) argues:

> The gramophone is an object, a possession that represents a bridge between two cultural domains, the West and India, and as such is a symbol of the aspirations of the burgeoning Indian middle classes at the turn of the century. It is also a technological innovation that crosses generations. (132)

Using Hindu Goddesses such as Saraswathi as consumers of the gramophone, and depicting the machine in use at a mythical court of Jahangir, the Mughal emperor of the seventeenth century was undertaken to appeal to Indian sensibilities. Farrell (2004) notes that these advertisements and images were meant to inspire Indians to buy the gramophone and the records (130–135).

Around the same time, one of India's iconic painters Raja Ravi Varma (1848–1906) was making portraits of Hindu Gods and Goddesses that were slowly beginning to have a pan-national recall. In c. 1896 he depicted the popular Hindu Goddess of music, the arts, and learning, Saraswathi. Chawla (2010) writes about the painting of Goddess Saraswathi by Raja Ravi Varma and describes it as being

> Iconic in their visualization...The religious texts and oral tradition that formed the basis for these paintings do not belong to any particular region of India as the entire country has always absorbed these goddesses into their midst. Despite such identification, Ravi Varma could not have realized the extent to which his images, given a new meaning through the medium of oil paint (and later through his lithographic press), were to endear themselves to the people of India. Similar to other artists and writers, Ravi Varma presented his goddesses in his own manner and with a specific intention in mind. He was seeking to convey their pan-national identity at a time when foreign rule was being questioned and dreams of a free nation were being voiced. (57)

It is sheer advertising genius on the part of The Gramophone Company to not only use an iconography that was so popular in the context of Indian music but, as Chawla mentions above, contributive to the idea of a pan-Indian identity, to create their own advertisement collaterals.

The "Gramophone Saraswathi" has the horn of the machine emerging from the instrument, Veena, which she plays. Just as Ravi Varma's painting depicts the peacock sitting by her side, looking possibly enraptured by her music, the advertisement depicts several animals such as a snake, a swan, a frog and a tortoise, and some other animals swimming close to where she sits, to listen to the records being played. These records are strewn in the lake over aquatic plants, which she seems to be lifting from her hand and playing on the turntable of her Veena. At once, the gramophone seems to enter the aural universe of Indian mythology and music, endearing it to a large section of people, who would possibly no longer view it as a foreign instrument, but one of their own, and one that has been accepted by their own Goddess of Music.

Farrell (1998) argues that the images of mythology and music were considered potent by The Gramophone Company to sell its products to the burgeoning Indian middle classes. He writes:

> Traditional images were clearly important as a bridge between the past and modernity, and musical images referred to ancient and complex aesthetic traditions in Indian culture connected with the magical power of sound. In 1906 no sound was more magical than that which emanated from mysterious small black discs - the complexity of the images do justice to that magic. (22)

Farrell (1993) describes another above iconic advertisement depicting the Hindu Goddess Durga. Durga is the Goddess of raw might and power, who is in a destructive mode of battle against the evil demons. The advertisement could possibly have meant that the gramophone music was so soothing that the Goddess forgets her battle and enjoys the music instead. With the rising tide of India's struggle of freedom and nationalistic sentiments, there was a popular literary and visual iconic representation of the Motherland India as *Hind Devi* or *Bharat Mata*, the benign maternal power, synonymously equated at times to Durga as well. Using the same iconography of the divine feminine that was also being equated to the country's spirit, appears to be yet another masterstroke by The Gramophone Company of exploiting the existing nationalistic sentiment in India, for freedom from British rule, to sell their products. Ironically, this was being done by a British company in a colony that was seeking liberation from that very country. Hence, possibly their advertisement could not make it very apparent with the usage of the Indian tricolour that was normally associated with Bharat Mata, because being a British firm and working in India with the aid of the British government this could jeopardise their business prospects. Yet, they used the iconography of the lady and the lion with her to appeal to the prevailing sentiments of the masses.

Farrell (1993) writes that The Gramophone Company utilised the "twin mediums of photography and recorded sound," to turn "Indian music and musicians into saleable commodities" (32). Not only were the photographs of popular artists such as Gauhar Jaan, Janki Bai, Coimbatore Thayi, Abdul Karim Khan and other artists used in catalogues and advertisements, The Gramophone Company named their needles after celebrated artists. Needles used to run the machines were called "Gauhar Jan needles,"

Figure 3.4 Advertisement dated 1907 featured in The Gramophone Company
       catalogue.

Source: Picture courtesy EMI Music Archive, London.

keeping in mind the cult status that she enjoyed across the country. This was
again an innovative idea that none of the other recording companies utilised
in India.

In Figure 3.4, the gramophone is seen placed on a majestic table right
in the middle of the drawing room, which appears to belong to a wealthy
man. The male head of the house, the lady of the house (standing there not
even in *purdah* or veil, as was customary in wealthy households for women),
the children, an old gentleman, and the servant of the house are all keenly
listening and appreciating the music emanating from the machine. The picture seemed to convey a strong message to the Indians that the gramophone
broke barriers of age, gender, and class and brought music right into the
drawing rooms of everybody. This was again important in the prevailing
socio-political situation in India, where the nationalistic movement was
addressing issues related to women's emancipation and inclusion of lower
castes into the mainstream society.

In all of the above cases, The Gramophone Company seems to have been
adept at understanding the pulse of the Indian consumer and tailoring its
advertising message to appeal to all the religious, historical, and emotional
sentiments of the Indians.

The Gramophone and Its Influence on Performers, Listeners, and Record Collectors

Given its wide reach and vibrant sales, the gramophone naturally played an important role in popularising classical music across India. I gathered data regarding this aspect of the gramophone in popularising Indian classical music through interviews with senior musicians and record collectors. My initial questions to the senior musicians were about their recollections of listening to the gramophone as a child or of recording on it themselves. Childhood memories and recollections of how they heard their favourite artists in a communal gathering evoked a sense of nostalgia and joy among all the respondents. They volunteered details about how the arrival of the gramophone machine to a community listening centre in the days of the British Raj in India created a sense of immense anticipation and excitement in the entire community. They also spoke about popular myths and suspicions that existed about recording. The most common superstition Ustad Abdul Rashid Khan cited was that "It was widely believed that recording on a gramophone would lead to a loss of voice and that the musical Gods would be angered. This is quite similar to suspicions that people had about photography where it was believed that getting photographed would reduce one's lifespan!"[20]

The senior musicians, such as Abdul Rashid Khan and Sushila Rani Patil, who had lived through the era of freedom struggle against British colonialism in India, recounted how the gramophone recordings of patriotic songs arousing nationalist sentiments and speeches of national leaders such as Mahatma Gandhi, Jawaharlal Nehru, Subhas Chandra Bose, and others were also heard secretly in many communities due to the fear of the police who would round up and brutalise anyone involved with the freedom movement or supporting it.

Some of the participants had not connected the two issues of the gramophone's advent and the courtesan's involvement with it. However, participants were reticent about discussing the lives of the musicians who recorded, particularly the courtesans. The participants narrated a few anecdotes and stories from the lives of the courtesans and/or experiences of listening to their live concerts.

Renowned Hindustani music stalwart Pandit Jasraj (born 1930) mentions:

> These 78-RPM gramophone discs or HMV records played a very important role in my life and supplemented the musical training I received from my father and elder brother. These records attracted so many of young people in our generation to our Indian classical music. I still remember how on my way to school as a little boy, I would stop by at teashops that played gramophone records and would be so mesmerized and lost in the music that many times I would end up even missing my classes! I vividly recall that I was particularly enamoured by the records

of the ghazal queen of Indian music Begum Akhtar (1914–1974) and her evergreen popular recording *Deewana bana de.*[21]

Begum Akhtar herself attributed her musical career to the records of Gauhar Jaan (1873–1930). Her student Rita Ganguly, mentions:

> Begum *sahiba* had once even contemplated shifting from music and taking to a career in theatre and films. But it was the gramophone records and live concerts of Gauhar Jaan that made her stick to music. She had told me that she even requested Gauhar Jaan's *sarangi* player Imdad Khan to be her teacher so that she could imbibe the same musical nuances as Gauhar. Such was the power and impact that these records created on young musical minds of the times.[22]

Another famous woman artist of her times who was mesmerised by the gramophone records was Siddheshwari Devi (1907–76) of Banaras. Her daughter and disciple Savita Devi narrated:

> *Maa* (Siddheshwari Devi) was denied music education by her aunt and stepmother who wanted her less talented daughter to outshine Maa. Maa would tell me that apart from sneaking into the music classes, she used to secretly listen to gramophone recordings of Gauhar Jaan, Malka Jaan, Zohra Bai, Maujuddin Khan, Abdul Karim Khan and Janki Bai, learn the compositions they recorded and imitate their singing styles and create a style of her own. Much later, in the 1930s when Maa sang at a famous conference in Calcutta she was overcome with emotion. She was after all singing in the same city where her icons such as Gauhar Jaan, Malka Jaan, Maujuddin Khan and others had sung. When she started singing the *thumri, Piya pardes mora man hara* the audience was reminded of all these yesteryear women singers who had popularized the song on the records and greatly applauded her. Maa concluded with a fine rendering of a *thumri* in *Bhairavi, Kahe ko dare gulaal.* Incidentally the doyenne of the Agra gharana *Ustad* Faiyyaz Khan was there in the audience and he came up on stage and said the young girl had reminded him of Gauhar Jaan and Malka Jaan and after them the crown of the queen of *thumris* rests on Siddheshwari's head.[23]

Despite the general derision for musical worth of the recordings or the women musicians who recorded on it, in my interview with him Ustad Abdul Rashid Khan mentions:[24]

> In our little village, Salaun, in Rae Bareily district of the then United Provinces (now the North Indian state of Uttar Pradesh), a local salesman would bring the gramophone with its gleaming horn to each locality for a community listening session. People had to pay him an amount

(*which he could not recollect*) to sit together at a corner of the street. The gramophone with its gleaming horn would be welcomed with claps by little children and women in *purdah* assembled quietly as well. The men-folk triumphantly sat on couches waiting for the machine to start playing. The salesman would keep the gramophone on a little table right in the middle of the congregation, crank the machine, adjust the horn, rotate the disc, and place the needle on it. Excited faces would wait to hear the first strains of the song from the record. I still remember as a young boy of 10–15 years of age, hearing many of the *Bai jis* (female singers) such as Gauhar Jaan, Malka Jaan, Janki Bai, Zohra Bai and others on these records.[25] At the end of the record when the singers would scream out their names "My name is Gauhar Jaan!" or "I am Janki Bai of Allahabad", all of us, especially the kids, would giggle and clap raucously with excitement.[26] The Gramophone Company's logo of Nipper the dog also attracted a lot of attention, especially of the kids who wondered why the dog was looking into the horn of the gramophone and whether it was contributing to the singing as well. With time, owning a gramophone was seen, as a matter of prestige and the economically prosperous families would own their own machines that cost approximately Rs. 250–300 in those days. They would then invite the rest of the locality to their homes to show-off their new possession. Yes, I think I must admit that these records played a major role in popularizing music and making people want to listen to it. But once better versions of the three-minute shellac discs came, such as the Long Playing Records, Spools and Magnetic Tapes, people lost all interest in shellac discs and took to the new media that provided better quality music. However these records created awareness about classical music and made people interested in attending live performances more.[27]

In my interview with senior musician Pandit Jasraj, I asked him what in his view recording in a studio meant for an artist, as compared to a live performance:

In our classical music the audience or *rasika* as they are called are as important as the artist. The very word *rasika* means someone who can taste and appreciate the *rasa*[28] of the music and in the process also inspire the artist to improvise better. As you know, concerts would not be in these large prosceniums that we see today but in intimate settings where the artist and audience were in close contact with each other. At every turn and twist of the raga, the audience would exclaim in appreciation and that inspires and stimulates us to sing even better. In a studio this important component is absent. In the gramophone era, I think many artists would ask for planting some enthusiastic listeners in the studio, just to get a feel of a live performance! I have heard records of Maujuddin Sahab where suddenly there are exclamations of *Wah!*

Wah! Maujuddin Khan! Subhan Allah! Masha Allah! I think these were
planted to inspire the artist![29]

Pandit Jasraj points to the important issue that recording eliminates a
vital channel of communication for artists to express themselves to their
audiences not only through the sound of their voices and instruments, but
also their faces and bodies, and to respond to the audience and thereby
shaping their music. Igor Stravinsky explains that: "The sight of the gestures and movements of the various parts of the body producing the music is
fundamentally necessary if it is to be grasped in all its fullness (Meyer 1956:
80)." When this aspect of the performance is removed, it could possibly be a
daunting task for many musicians who therefore shied away from recording.
As French soprano Régine Crespin (1997) writes in her memoirs:

> Fear of an audience is healthy; it stimulates you. The people are there
> in front of you. With them there can be mutual love-fests. But how can
> you fall in love with a microphone? First of all, a microphone is ugly. It's
> cold, steel, impersonal thing, suspended above your head or resting on a
> pole just in front of your nose. And it defies you, like HAL the computer
> in Stanley Kubrick's film 2001: A Space Odyssey, although at least he
> talked. No, the microphone waits, unpitying, insensitive and ultrasen-
> sitive at the same time, and when it speaks, it's to repeat everything
> you've said word for word. The beast! (153)

For some artists the seclusion of a studio bereft of distractions was wel-
come. As Violinist Yehudi Menuhin (1997) writes that recording allowed
him "a monastic dedication, which is oblivious of audience" (371). Thus
recording presented challenges that the performers had to adapt to.
Senior musician Girija Devi points to another aspect of recording:

> I used to hear my own records several times. A concert is a live occur-
> rence. Recording is something that not only audiences, but we artists
> can also hear. Not just other artists to get inspired or to learn and
> emulate what other great masters of the past have sung, but our own
> recordings. And then cringe: Oh God! Why did I sing this so badly! Or
> *Wah!* That was a nice exposition! This is not possible in the context of a
> concert. In the flurry of a concert, sometimes we may overlook certain
> nuances, be they of style or of interpretation.[30]

Girija Devi's insight into the ability of artists to assess their own recordings is similar to what Klein (1990) quotes of the celebrated opera singer
Adelina Patti who had said in 1905 about her own recording on hearing it:
"My God! Now I understand why I am Patti! What a voice! What an artist!"(589). As self-congratulatory as that might sound, it refers to a process
that Soprano Martina Arroyo elaborates about in her interview with John

Harvith and Susan Edwards Harwith on 1 May 1977, which Katz (2004) quotes:

> There are some...who say, 'Oh no, I do exactly the same thing in recording as in live performance.' But what happens is that...when you hear (yourself) you adjust without even knowing, because you say 'Ah, that's not exactly the way I want to sound.' And you adjust, perhaps without being aware that in a performance you wouldn't have made that adjustment." (33)

Recording parcels the performances into segments, sometimes connected and disconnected at other times, which can possibly prove to be disconcerting for both the performer and the listener. Gramophone records of Carnatic music have an *aalaapana* recorded in one raga on one disc and a composition based on the same raga recorded in a disc with the successive matrix number.

Senior musician Girija Devi mentions:

> Constantly what must have run in the minds of artists was that the time was ticking and we had to wrap up fast. At times, when an artist might get into a creative crescendo or artistic climax, it was time to wind up. That must be such a terrible experience and sometimes robbed the creativity. Many musicians would prefer to go to the studio well prepared, rehearsed and timed to the last second. No retakes were possible and so any mistake committed was left on the disc forever![31]

Nellie Melba, Australian Soprano, writes of a 1906 session citing similar concerns as articulated above by Girija Devi:

> I shall never forget that once after making what I believe would have been the most beautiful record, I stumbled backwards over a chair, and said 'Damn' in an all too audible voice. That 'damn' when the record was played over, came out with a terrible clarity, making me feel much as a sinner must on the Day of Judgment.
>
> (Melba 1971: 252–253)

The phenomenon of recording and thereby preserving the human voice ran counter to the fundamental philosophy of the ephemeral nature of Indian classical music. This transient nature of music was celebrated as the strength of the art form. Summing up this sentiment, the last King of Mysore, Jayachamaraja Wodeyar (1940–74), himself an accomplished Indian and Western Classical musician, Prabhakar (2005) quotes him from an unpublished work titled *The Aesthetic Philosophy of India*:

> Music has been called the finest of fine arts. In a sense it is also the most elusive and apparently unsubstantial of the fine arts. A musician

builds a palace of sound, which vanishes into nothingness, even as it is being raised. But need induce no feeling of frustration since the musician builds his structure right in the heart of his listeners. We may well say Wordsworth 'The music in my heart I bore long after it was heard no more'...In Indian music there is a clear emphasis on the resemblance between the joy of music and the joy of spiritual experience. The final purpose of music is to create a deep joy, similar to the joy that artists get out of the realization of God. An aesthetic experience lasts only a short time, no doubt it is temporal but it is none the less worth having, since it helps us even though temporarily to attain the highest plane. (41–42)

It was this fundamental idea of music and its purpose that the agency of the gramophone challenged, and eventually succeeded, in its advent in India.

Record Collectors

Katz (2004) describes that record collecting is an extension of the old practice of acquiring music related objects. The difference in this case is that the object being collected is the sound itself, and not the means to create music such as scores or instruments (13). The *New York Times* (1877) made a prophetic statement about the human fascination for record collection: "Whether a man has or has not a wine cellar, he will certainly, if he wishes to be regarded as a man of taste, have a well-stocked oratorical cellar" (4).

In a country such as India, where there is a disregard for records and the absence of a National Sound Archive, it is the passion of record collectors that has kept these valuable musical artefacts available for researchers, music lovers and for posterity. Suresh Chandvankar, a retired physicist and the Honorary Secretary of the Society for Indian Record Collectors (SIRC) recounts:

Since the early 1960s I have been collecting records. Slowly, this childhood fascination grew into an interest in reading the history of records and record players. I would scout around record shops and flea markets for buying old records. It was with fellow enthusiasts Krishnaraj Merchant and Narayan Mulani that we began SIRC to give a public face to our private passion. We wanted to bring together all persons and institutions interested in preserving, promoting and researching aspects of Indian music with respect to the 78-RPM records. It was Australian discographer Michael Kinnear whose association with us helped SIRC to become a structured body bringing out regular journals titled The Record News. We began conducting guided listening sessions, and had chapters in other cities and towns such as Bangalore, Pune, Nanded, and Solapur. I do not say it has been a very successful attempt. Some sessions have hardly three or four members attending. Still, it is our earnest desire to preserve this valuable heritage. The young generation is what I am very optimistic about and their fluency with technology to assist in this preservation and propagation.[32]

Another prominent record collector V.A.K. Ranga Rao mentions in his interview with me in his house stacked with records, in Chennai:

I have more than thirty five thousand 78-RPM records, about five thousand EP (Extended Play) and thousand LP (Long Playing) records. Gramophone records are a mirror to society. Music was not the only thing recorded. I have records ranging from medical therapy and linguistics to bird songs recorded in the twentieth-century. Records reflect evolution and development, be it in language or in music. I have records of speeches of national leaders such as Mahatma Gandhi, Rabindranath Tagore, Subhas Chandra Bose, Sarojini Naidu and, also international figures such as Churchill and Mussolini. The collection includes advertisements such as Lipton Tea, Anacin tablets, and Cavender cigarettes. From the time I was given pocket money as a teenager, I would spend them on buying records. They are my life; I have no family, spouse or children. I would buy any 78-RPM record that I could lay my hands on. Even now, through a network of friends and word of mouth, I buy an average of fifty records every month. All of them are neatly classified by genre and most of them are in a playing condition.[33]

As Chandvakar puts it:

There have been roughly about four lakh record releases in India so far, and about half of that number is in the hands of known collectors, as far as I know. So the search is on for the remainder![34]

Chandvankar also showed me a letter of a French aficionado and Indian music record enthusiast, Andre Brunel, written to him in 1996:

One day I had an opportunity to listen to some nice 78's of Indian music. The records were from South sung by Coimbatore Thayi...early 1905/10 recordings. That was something great to hear... The records of course were not for sale, but it did not matter. I realized that these 78's were very nice to look at and to listen to and I was fascinated with these old records. The sound is original and not trafficked! These first records have got something of magic. They represent and show the evidence of the past and most of the time these have not been reissued on LPs and some of them might appear on CDs I hope. But how many singers and musicians are forgotten or disappeared forever? ...Slowly my little collection of records began to grow. It is now of a reasonable size. My wish is not to become an important collector. I do not have the money for it. When you are collecting it is an history (sic.) without end![35]

The common themes of passion for collecting records, family resistance, lack of societal support, and investment of personal funds in the absence of any institutionalised or governmental mechanism for archiving and preservation is what possibly defines the record collectors of India. Against all odds, they have managed to preserve a very important component of India's musical heritage.

Notes

1 EMI Music Archives, London, Indian Correspondence, 13 January 1900.
2 Ibid.
3 Ibid.
4 EMI Music Archives, London, Indian Correspondence, 29 August 1901.
5 Ibid. 1 January 1902.
6 EMI Music Archives, London, Indian Correspondence, 3 June 1902.
7 EMI Music Archives, London, Indian Records Catalogues, 1902.
8 EMI Music Archives, London, Indian Records Catalogue, 1902.
9 EMI Music Archives, London, Indian Correspondence, 23 December 1903.
10 EMI Music Archives, London, Indian Correspondence, 23 December 1904.
11 EMI Music Archive, London: J. Muir, Report on 1922 Indian Tour.
12 Compagnie Frangaise du Gramophone Past History, 7 Feb. 1921; File: France, Portugal, Switzerland, Algeria, EMI Music Archive, London.
13 Excerpts of interview of author with *Ustad* Abdul Rashid Khan in Kolkata.
14 Ibid.
15 The drone instrument or *tanpura* is an essential component of an Indian classical performance as it gives the basic tonic for every artist and their accompaniments. Each artist tunes the tanpura to his/her pitch and so do the accompanists.
16 Excerpts of interview of author with *Ustad* Abdul Rashid Khan in Kolkata.
17 This seems to be his experience in India prior to 1911 as Salem Godavari's obituary in the Hindu newspaper indicates her death in the year 1911. But this article was published in the *Talking Machine World*, 15 May 1913. I accessed a microfilm of this at the British Library, London.
18 Interview of author with Sushila Rani Baburao Patel.
19 Ibid.
20 Interview excerpts of author with *Ustad* Abdul Rashid Khan.
21 Interview of author with *Pandit* Jasraj in Mumbai.
22 Interview of author with Rita Ganguly in Delhi.
23 Interview of author with Savita Devi in Gurgaon.
24 Interview of author with Abdul Rashid Khan in Kolkata.
25 Given the current age of *Ustad* Abdul Rashid Khan is about 107, we can assume the time period of this anecdote relates to 1918–1925. At that time, the records of the musicians he mentions did make brisk business as is borne out by records by Kinnear(1994) and the EMI Archives catalogues.
26 Sampath (2010) states that in the early era of recording, the recordings would be made in India, and since the pressing and manufacture was done in Hanover, for the technician there it would be anonymous voice. Hence, the need to announce the name on the part of the artist so that the German technician could identify the voice and label the record accordingly.
27 Excerpts of the interview of the author with *Ustad* Abdul Rashid Khan.
28 The word Rasa can barely be translated into English and vaguely refers to the emotion.

29 Excerpts of the interview of the author with *Pandit* Jasraj.
30 Interview excerpts of author with Smt Girija Devi.
31 Interview excerpts of author with Smt Girija Devi.
32 Interview excerpts of author with Dr. Suresh Chandvankar.
33 Interview excerpts of author with Mr. V.A.K. Ranga Rao.
34 Interview excerpts of author with Dr. Suresh Chandvankar.
35 Interview of author with Dr. Suresh Chandvankar.

4 THE PROTAGONISTS*

Although scholars have written about the early years and the monpolistic establishment of The Gramphone Company in India, little is known or discussed about the artists who gave the Company the strong foundation on which it built its Indian fortunes. In the previous chapter, it was mentioned that during the first three recording expeditions of The Gramophone Company – in 1902, 1904–05, and 1906–07 – women's recordings of Indian classical music accounted for 80.95%, 83.51%, and 85.36% respectively of the total recorded catalogue of Indian classical music. A majority of these women belonged to the background of *tawaifs* and *devadasis*, across India. They disregarded the social taboos and inhibitions that were prevalent among the hereditary male musicians regarding recording and circumvented the logistical challenges that the new technology posed to adapt to it readily. Singing in high-pitched voices in the absence of microphones during the era of acoustic recording and limiting one's presentation to a mere three-minute capsule were creative challenges that could unsettle any artist. However, with their grit and ingenuity, these women, led by the pioneer Gauhar Jaan, devised a wondrous formula to present a holistic portrait of the raga and the genre in the limited time available and also managed to entertain the customer enough to buy the record. So who were some of these women and what were their lives like?

Gauhar Jaan of Calcutta (1873–1930)

The first commercially recorded artist in India, Gauhar Jaan of Calcutta (1873–1930), was born to a Hindu courtesan grandmother, a British grandfather, and a Christian father, Robert William Yeoward. She was born on 26 June 1873 in the town of Azamgarh in the United Provinces of northern India and was baptised as Eileen Angelina Yeoward. When the little girl was all of six, the parents had a bitter divorce and Robert disowned his wife and daughter. Her mother, Victoria Hemmings, then moved to the North Indian town of Banaras with a Muslim paramour, Khursheed, and converted to Islam to take to her mother's profession, becoming a courtesan named Badi Malka Jaan. The daughter was renamed as Gauhar Jaan. The mother and

DOI: 10.4324/9780367822026-4

daughter took to music and dance as a profession and became well-known *tawaifs* of the temple town of Banaras. It was here that the girl came of age and the ceremony of *nath-uthrai* was conducted. But in a tragic turn of events, she was raped by an old landlord and went through the subsequent pain of an abortion that left a deep scar on her psyche.

Mother and daughter migrated to the then capital of British India, Calcutta (now Kolkata), seeking better professional prospects. They were invited regularly to perform at soirees of wealthy landlords, royal families, and British parties. Both Banaras and Calcutta offered the young Gauhar a wide range of opportunities at honing her innate skills in music, dance, and poetry. Unlike the male singers who were strictly bound to a *gharana*, or hereditary style of music, the *tawaifs* had an eclectic range of musical training from several *gharanas* and in varied genres. After subduing the uprising of 1857, the British had deposed the Nawab of Awadh Wajid, Ali Shah, to Calcutta. The courtly patronage to the arts and the bustle of his hitherto capital of Lucknow, in Awadh, now shifted to Calcutta. It was hence natural for the artists of Northern India to migrate to the new locus of patronage that Calcutta was becoming in search of a better life. Both Badi Malka Jaan and Gauhar Jaan established themselves as court musicians in the deposed Nawab's estate. From the days of penury in Azamgarh and Banaras, they managed to buy several properties in Calcutta, including a house that became famously known as the "Gauhar Building" in the city's Chitpur area that was known for its *tawaifs*. By the time Gaisberg came to the city in 1902 looking for "native voices" Gauhar Jaan had established herself as the leading artist of the town and, in fact, the country with performances in several royal courts. Recording transformed her life and made her a national and international superstar in her own right. She was called upon to perform, along with another contemporary *tawaif* Janki Bai of Allahabad, at the Imperial Darbar in 1911 before Emperor George V when the capital of India was shifted from Calcutta to Delhi. She charged exorbitantly for her live concerts, including what would have been considered an astronomical sum those days of Rs. 1000 for her performance at the Prayag Sangeet Samiti.

The musical sensation that Gauhar was in her heyday is illustrated in the memoirs of eminent musicologist D.P. Mukherjee who had stealthily heard her sing by sneaking into her house:

> In our days there was a singer, Gauhar Jan, and she was unapproachable. Yet, where there is a will, there is a way. I managed to sneak into her house one night in the company of somebody belonging to the underworld of music. She was entertaining a Nabab. She sang Adana, Bahar, Suha and Sughrai, but the Nabab's preference was for thumri, which she sang in one of her sensuous veins with lots of bhava-batana for which she was famous...I vividly remember the occasion when she sang a dhruvapad in Adana, a sadra in the same raga, and yet a third

khayal in Adana. Since then, I have found it difficult to concentrate on Adana even when it is sung by the best in the country... Later on, I had more public opportunities of hearing her. It is a pity that today's world does not know what a great khayal singer was lost in the voluptuous folds of thumri. To please her audience, Gauhar Jan would sing Pushtu songs, anything bizarre and clever... She had a magnificent and scintillating personality. There have been many excellent khayal singers among women after her, but I would feign call them masters. They are exceedingly competent, but always fall below the standard that Gauhar Jan occasionally set in khayal.

(Sampath 2010: 118)

Noteworthy is his assertion too that "a great khayal singer was lost in the voluptuous folds of thumri" meaning to suggest that the thumri was a lesser art form than the weighty khayal that demanded more classicism and musical virtuosity.

But despite the celebrity status that she attained, Gauhar was cheated by several male lovers – including a young secretary whom she married and who embezzled all her funds, leaving her in utter penury. She died a lonely death in Mysore on 17 January 1930, in Southern India, far away from her hometown Calcutta and lies buried there in an unmarked grave. Kinnear's (1994) catalogues show that her records with The Gramophone Company are labelled "First Dancing Girl, Calcutta," confirming her pioneering role in the recording industry in India (Figure 4.1).

But what set Gauhar Jaan apart were her flamboyant lifestyle and a sense of nonchalance for the men in positions of power. As senior musician Girija Devi recounts:

For someone like me who grew up in Banaras, Gauhar Jaan was always a figure we looked up to with awe. Our elders would tell us that she was so fair and beautiful, almost like an English *memsahib* (regal European woman). There were so many stories about her I have heard in my childhood. When the King of Datia, a small province in Central India, invited her to perform at his court, she thought it below her dignity to sing at such small soirees. Hence she demanded an entire train to be booked for her! And the King actually conceded her request and she went to Datia with almost hundred people accompanying her, including a retinue of servants, doctors, cooks, students, friends and even her horses! (*laughs*). She paid a fine of Rs. 1000 to the Viceroy of India when he obstructed her from going around the city on her joyrides in her horse-driven buggies that she loved to ride. Even Mahatma Gandhi was not spared. When he requested her to sing for the Congress Party and raise funds for the Independence movement, she agreed but with a pre-condition that he should be personally present at the concert! Imagine any of the musicians of today imposing such conditions on the tallest political

Figure 4.1 Photograph of a young Gauhar Jaan.

Source: Picture courtesy *My name is Gauhar Jaan!*

leaders of our time? She flouted British Government rules, and even paid fines to ride through the streets of Calcutta in her horse buggy. I do not know how many of these stories are indeed true, but we grew up listening to them in complete awe and admiration of this lady.[1]

Binodini Dasi of Calcutta (1863–1941)

Kinnear (1994) mentions another early recorded artist of The Gramophone Company, a superstar actress of her times, Binodini Dasi of Calcutta (1863–1941). She recorded several songs in Bengali and semi-classical compositions in the first recording expedition of The Gramophone Company in 1902. Binodini was the first actress of the country to write her autobiography in 1912: *Amar Katha* (My Story). She repeatedly calls it a "narrative of pain." Being aware of the stigmatisation that women such as herself faced in the early decades of the twentieth century, Bhattacharya (1998) quotes Binodini:

Let them not read it who will despise or ridicule this insignifcant piece of writing. Let them refrain from sprinkling salt to further irritate the deepest wound in a woman's life...Because I have no relations, I am despised. I am a prostitute, a social outcast. There is no one to listen or to read what I feel within. That is why I have let you know my story in pen and paper...The talented, the wise, and the learned write in order to educate people, to do good to others. I have written for my own consolation, perhaps for some unfortunate woman who taken in by deception has stumbled on to the path to hell. (104–107)

Bhattacharya (1998) documents that Binodini began working in the public theatre in Calcutta in 1873 when she was eleven years old to help her family escape abject poverty. About her maiden stage appearance she writes poignantly:

> When I saw before me the rows of shining lights, and the excited gaze of a thousand eyes, my entire body became bathed in sweat, my heart began to beat dreadfully, my legs were actually trembling and it seemed to me that the dazzling scene was clouding over before my eyes. Backstage, my teachers tried to reassure me. Alongwith fear, anxiety and excitement, a certain eagerness too appeared to overwhelm me. How shall I describe this feeling? For one, I was a little girl and then too, the daughter of poor people. I had never had occasion to perform or even appear before such a gathering. In my childhood I had often heard my mother say, "Call on Hari [God] when you are frightened." I remembered him and followed the instructions I had received during the rehearsals, uttered the few words I had been trained to deliver with the appropriate gestures, and then came back to the wings. As I did so, the audience clapped loudly to show their appreciation. I was still shaking all over, whether with fear or excitement, I do not know. My teachers embraced me as soon as I went backstage. But I did not know then what the clapping signified. Later, the others explained to me that people clapped in pleasure if the performance was a successful one.
>
> (Bhattacharya 1998: 67)

Binodini retired from the stage when she was only in her mid-twenties. In this short time span, she played over 80 major roles; worked with several leading playwrights and directors of the time, and was instrumental in setting up the renowned Star Theatre of Calcutta. People thronged to see her on stage, and directors lauded her as a rare combination of talent, professionalism, beauty, and intelligence.

In my interview with music afficianado and record enthusiast of Kolkata, Shankar Lal Mehta, he mentions:

> *Noti* (actress) Binodini, as she was popular, is a cult figure in Bengal's cultural history. The spiritual teacher of the late nineteenth-century Ramakrishna Paramahamsa not only visited the theatre to see her performance but also blessed her after this. In *Amar Katha*, she writes

movingly that this was a blessing and purification that would haunt her for the rest of her life. She wrote this autobiography at the request of another stalwart of the times: Girish Chandra Ghosh, who was hailed as the father of modern Bengali theatre and was her mentor. It is believed that he inspired her to write this autobiography, so that in the process it would help bring her unruly heart under some semblance of control and also contain her pain.[2]

I compare the theme and motivation behind *Amar Katha* to the Urdu poetry of Binodini's contemporary and Gauhar Jaan's mother, Badi Malka Jaan. In 1886, Badi Malka Jaan published a *Diwan* (or collection) of more than 500 of her poems, titled *Makhzan-e-Ulfat-e-Malka* (or The Treasure Trove of Malka's Love). The opening verses of her collection are poignant:

Every sin of even a habitual offender such as me will be forgiven; such is the infinite grace of the Protector of this Universe. I am steeped in sin, that I have committed all my life, and of which I am terribly ashamed. But my condition does not baffle me because I know that the ocean of Mercy that my Almighty is, my sins too will be washed away. On the Day of Judgement, the odds would be placed heavily against me due to my sins; but my sincere repentance born out of disgust for my own actions will see me through; my faith in His mercy will not be belied. The entire cosmos, which is a garden of His creation, sings His praise. And when the all-merciful creator sees that despite my sins, I have burnt in the fire of repentance and always had praise on my lips for Him, I will surely be pardoned. Malka has always chanted His name; she is not the one who will be tortured in her grave when her acts in this world are judged.
(Sampath 2010: i)[3]

Bhattacharya (1998) notes that Binodini, however, is less confident about the mercy of God, whom Malka repeatedly beseeches to pardon her supposed sins:

You say that if you heard the entire story of my life you would be able to explain to me how I have been created for the Lord's work. I too will unfold these incidents to you from beginning to end. If you listen, you would understand how unbelief has only deepened and how impossible it would be to uproot it. (60)

There is however a uniformity in the emotions of despair, betrayal, and a sense of hopelessness in the writings of the courtesans. Malka rues in her poems:

No wish of mine ever gets fulfilled; there is nothing to look forward to. My mind is barren and forced to accept the inevitable.
(Sampath 2010: 290)

Was it not enough to have troubled me all my life? Is it necessary to ruin my peace even in my grave by kicking my tombstone?

(Sampath 2010: 291)

There is none who would understand the plight of my heart. Even the memories of the past are foes who tear my heart asunder. Whom do I confide to about my plight?

(Sampath 2010: 298)

My foolish footsteps lead me involuntarily to your streets. This, despite your treacherous nature and the advice of well-wishers to avoid you.

(Sampath 2010: 299)

I can bear his betrayal of commitments to promises. But it breaks my heart to see him in the salon of another.

(in Sampath 2010: 298)

Binodini laments similarly:

I wondered afterwards, was all their love and affection only a show of words in order to get some work out of me?

(Bhattacharya 1998: 89–90)

Gauhar Jaan, a poet in her own right, has written verses, which she recorded for The Gramophone Company, and which became hugely popular. Ironically, musicians perform these songs even today, being unaware of the authorship of the lyrics. One of her popular *thumris*, *Kaisi Yeh Dhoom Machayi*, which she recorded in raga *Kafi*, has the same element of hurt at being betrayed in love, but is presented in a flippant, playful manner:

What preposterous behaviour is this Krishna? Such tumult you cause in my life.

You splash colors on me, and twist my arms, and in return chide me as well?

What do you take me for? For heaven's sake, let me go, leave me alone.

You wait and watch, you will not succeed in laying your hands on me despite your hideous plans.

You make tall claims of love for your beloved Gauhar, and yet at the very first opportunity, dally with other women?

What commitment to love is this?

(Sampath 2010: 48)

A question that arises from these works of prose and poetry by courtesans, in an autobiographical mode, is the implication of life stories of the ones who are debarred from life. It creates dissonances that jeopardises the very genre of autobiography. The unease, the guilt, and self-critical observations are a reflection of societal attitudes to these women and their presence in society. In dissonance with the Gramscian theory of the need for histories to create an inventory of the self, the narratives of the women are inventories of what did not, or could not happen, in their lives and the resulting deep sense of despair and hopelessness about this. The despair even turns ontological, as in Binodini's case, where she pleads: "My restless heart asks time and again, 'What is my work in this world?...in which part of the Lord's scheme have I ever been of any use?'" (Bhattacharya 1998: 56).

Analysing the literary works of these courtesans, I speculate that it was possibly this sense of despair; of wanting their stories, their pain, and their voice itself to be heard by a society that sexually accepted them on the one hand, and publically shunned them on the other, motivated the courtesan to seek the agency of the gramophone. Every media and new technology, be it print or the gramophone, had to be seized to amplify their stories to people who possibly did not care enough to listen; treated them as bodies for pleasure, and seldom as human beings with emotions. While literate and gifted women such as Binodini, Badi Malka, and Gauhar had their works published, the gramophone gave the lesser read courtesan an immediate opportunity to imprint her legacy for posterity. The monetary motivations apart, the urge to leave behind this bequest for the future, I speculate, is what led these women to adapt to recording technology so easily.

In the first decade of recording, all the musicians announced their name at the end of the recording. The reason for this was logistical. Although the recordings were made in India, the manufacture was in Hanover. For the technician there, this was an anonymous voice which would be recognised by this announcement, multiple copies then stamped with the label of the artist. This loud announcement of one's name at the end of the recording, further consolidated the authorial sense of ownership and achievement of having created a work of art in history.

There was criticism of this announcement of the artist's name, such as expressed by a music critic H.P. Krishna Rao in his review of Gauhar Jaan's concert in Bangalore in 1912 mentioned by Sampath (2010):

> Miss Gauhar is known through the gramophone records even to the villager. Her records are enjoyable but there is a disparity between the copy and the original leading to disappointment. She has made a name and fortune far above the reach of even masters of the art, of whom there are plenty in India and if the key to such success is to be sought for, it will be found to lie in the invisible and self-advertisement through the gramophone: MY NAME IS GAUHAR JAAN. (46)

The scorn and contempt for a woman musician such as Gauhar Jaan having achieved success and popularity much more than "masters of the art," and the manner in which the critic attributes it all to "self-advertisement" rather than the announcement of an artistic identity is indicative of the popular societal attitude to women performers.

About Binodini's recording for The Gramophone Company, Bhattacharya (1998) elaborates:

> There appears to be three Binodinis whose voices have been recorded: a Miss Binodini, a Binodini Dassi and a Gayika Binodini. There is also some confusion regarding a turn-of-the-century actress, who went by the familiar name of 'Hadi' but whose stage name was Binodini. The matter of recordings is as yet quite controversial. By the first decade of the twentieth century, Binodini Dasi had long left the theatre world. Her inaccessibility to the public coupled with the incident of being blessed by Ramakrishna [Paramahamsa], transformed her into something like a 'living legend.' It seems reasonable to suppose that her recordings – songs and dialogue from plays such as Girishchandra's *Bilwamangal* or *Jona* would find a good market. (164)

This confusion with female artists bearing similar names is a common roadblock when one looks for them in The Company's catalogues. The fact that there were several women with the same name (more so, if one of them achieved cult status) that was spelt varyingly by The Company makes matters complicated when it comes to ascertaining to whose recordings we are actually referring. For instance, along with Gauhar Jaan of Calcutta, there was Gauhar Jaan of Patiala, Gauhar Jaan of Jaipur, Miss Gohar (of the Parsi Theatrical Company in Bombay), Gohar Mamajiwala (singer and actress who was also the mistress of film producer Chandulal Shah of Ranjit Studios in Bombay), and Miss Gohar Bai Karnataki of Bijapur (who was associated with Marathi thespian Bal Gandharva and was his longtime mistress). Along with Gauhar's mother Badi Malka Jaan, there were three other famous artists with the name 'Malka' during the time – Malka Jaan of Agra, Malka Jaan of Mulk Puhkraj and Malka Jaan of Chulbuli. So an incomplete description of the artist in the catalogue, without the place she came from, would lead to a complete dead end for the researcher.

Zohra Bai of Agra (1868–1913)

Another popular recorded woman musician of the early twentieth century was Zohra Bai of Agra (1868–1913). Very little is known about her life, and references about her musical virtuosity appear to be more anecdotal than factual. Speaking about her, Tembe (1988) mentions in his Marathi book:

> Along with Gauhar Jaan of Calcutta and Bablibai of Bhavnagar, name of Agrewali Zohra Bai has to be mentioned. She had sung for me when

she came to Mumbai for recording her gramophone records. She had a wonderful combination of both male and female singers. She was a renowned female singer of India. (163)

What Tembe possibly means when he refers to Zohra being a combination of both male and female singers, is her virtuosity in the puritanical and classical genres, such as *khayal* and *dhrupad*, that were seen as being strictly the male preserve. The semi-classical and romantic *thumris* and *dadras* were the preserve of women singers. Zohra broke this stereotype. Also, Bhole (1964a) mentions that her original voice was quite masculine and with a lot of training "she infused sweetnesss to it and sweetness clings to the musical notes she takes, as can be heard from her records" (67).

Sampath (2010) states that Zohra was possibly born in Agra in 1868, received her training from her father Ahmed Khan, who was both a vocalist and a *sarangi* player. There are references claiming that she learnt under eminent ustads such as Mehboob Khan and Kale Khan of the Agra *gharana*. She is also credited to be a dancer of great repute (57).

For the 1908–09 recording expedition, The Gramophone Company secured Zohra Bai. The EMI Music Archive records that Zohra Bai of Agra, Mumtaz Jaan of Delhi, Bedana Dassi of Calcutta, Miss Acchan of Bombay, Nawab Jaan of Meerut, Zeban Jaan of Delhi and Miss Vanajatchi of Madras were placed under an "exclusive contract." The agreement was signed between The Gramophone Company and "Zohra Bai (formerly living in Agra and currently in Patna City, at Mohalla Machharhatta, Thana Khowaja Katan)" on 5 February 1908.[4] The agreement describes her as the daughter of Hussaini Jaan of Agra. She was contracted for a period of three years, with an annual salary of Rs. 2500 and was required to sing the best of her songs for The Gramophone Company "in good and sweet tune" of 25 records or songs every year. She was promised to be paid within six months of the completion of the recording. Being an "exclusive" contract, she was forbidden from recording for any rival company. The Gramophone Company pledged to provide a recording expert, the machines needed to make the recordings, and also for her travel and lodging, with "foodings" for herself and her companions for recording sessions held outside Patna.

Kinnear's catalogues (1994) show that during late April 1908 Gaisberg recorded 25 songs of Zohra Bai in Calcutta, along with those of Kali Jaan of Delhi and Gauhar Jaan. The catalogues also demonstrate that on 21 and 22 November 1909, 26 recordings of Zohra were undertaken by recording expert George Walter Dillnutt in Lucknow. The same expert recorded 12 songs of hers in Delhi on 21 November 1910 and 15 songs on 22 November 1910 (Figure 4.2).

The Gramophone Company catalogues at EMI Music Archive have the above photograph of Zohra Bai, holding a child in her lap. I speculate that it almost seems necessary for her to demonstrate her maternal side, possibly to deflect attention from her courtesan status.

Figure 4.2 A photograph attributed as Zohra Bai, credited to have been taken by
        Arthur Clarke.

Source: Photo courtesy EMI Music Archive, London.

Bhole (1996) writes effusively about her musical virtuosity and tunefulness:

Aalaapchaari (rendition of *aalaap*) of Zohra Bai was undoubtedly beautiful. This can be judged through her gramophone records. Even today,
her music gives an immense pleasure to her listeners. Records do testify
that she did have a natural melodious voice...she has cut many gramophone records and the *vilambit* (slow renditions) was her specialty.
I used to listen to her records again and again and each time could
feel something unusual. Whenever Ramakrishna Bua Vaze visited me,
we would listen to her '*Kajaraare*' record in raga *Gaud Sarang*, and he
would ecstatically remark: 'What a *Shuddha Madhyam*, Keshav Rao.
I am trying very hard, but can't sing as she has, and hence I listen to
this record again and again...one day he [Vaze] told me an interesting
incident, which occurred during his stay at her house-'During my stay,
Ghulam Abbas Khan and Nathan Khan came to her house. Everyday,
we used to listen to her. She also sang many ragas again and again.
One day her father requested them to sing. Since they were very senior
and renowned singers, he thought that his daughter would also learn
from them. But they just smiled and kept quiet but did not sing. I was

surprised, as I had thought that they would definitely sing for this little girl Zohra. Her father repeatedly requested and finally asked whether his daughter does not deserve to listen to them. They said: She is so melodious and tuneful that we are afraid that we would be quite out of tune if we sing! Her father thought that they are making fun and he requested again and again. Finally they took the oath of Allah and all of us were stunned!'...her style of singing for records has been imitated by many including Khansahab Abdul Karim Khan and is being followed till today. In other words, like sages of the past, she has created her own tradition and school of music. Her rendition style of *Sthayi*, *Antara*, stretching and twisting of musical notes was followed also by Bhaskar Bua Bakhle in his singing. In 1918, while listening to Abdulla Khan, elder brother of Vilayat Hussein Khan and to Bhaskar Bua, I could immediately spot the influence of Zohra Bai's *laykari* style of singing on these two great singers. (104–105)[5]

Bhole (1996) credits Zohra as being the pioneer of the formula to condense a weighty khayal into a three-minute capsule on a gramophone record. He claims that several renowned male musicians simply heard these records and copied her format of condensation:

Zohra Bai of Agra chose best *bandishes* of various ragas, recorded prolifically and proved the popularity of these among the music loving and record buying public. Her *gayaki* as could be heard in these records is undoubtedly great and graceful. Her records in ragas Basant, Marwa, Puriya Dhanshree, Jogiya, Gaud Sarang, Todi, Multani, Kedar, Khamaj, Bhupali, Jaunpuri and many others prove this amply. She was equally great in her records of thumri, dadra and ghazal. After singing *Sthayi* and *Antara* gracefully, she weaves the words of the *cheez* in *Aalaap*, *Murki*, and *Khatka*, improvising on the raga. She then slowly begins to sing layakari taans and in fast tempo presents faster and faster taans and suddenly concludes her name- 'Zohrabai Agrewali' in English and in the same tempo. This formula became so popular that it was religiously followed by several gramophone singers almost till the end of 78 RPM era. This is just a small condensed version of three-hour proper concert of Hindustani classical music where an elaborate and improvised singing of a raga is presented. Several instrumentalists followed this formula too and no one dared to change it or divert from it. Those who tried to evolve some other formula have failed miserably and their records did not become popular and bestsellers. Her formula is based on firm footing that has taken into account factors like taste of the audience, their psychology and attitudes towards this medium of 'canned music.' In this respect, she is considered to be a trendsetter. This could be seen in the 78's of Bade Ghulam Ali Khan and Moghubai Kurdikar. In about 1927, Narayanrao Vyas recorded two sides- *Yeri*

Mohe Jaane na de and *Avinashi ha Atma Jagati*. He had studied Zohra Bai's formula by listening to her records carefully and this is the reason of the nationwide popularity of his records. (104–105)

Although Zohra died around 1913, she has left behind a huge corpus of her records that speak volumes of her talent and virtuosity.

Janki Bai of Allahabad (1880–1934)

Janki Bai of Allahabad (1880–1934) was another popular gramophone recorded artist. Sampath (2010: 57) mentions that she had a curious nickname, *Chappan Churi*, meaning 56 slashes. It was said that a jealous suitor, who was madly in love with her, permanently scarred her face with 56 slashes of his knife, when she rebuffed him (Figure 4.3).

Kinnear's catalogues (1994) postulate that Janki Bai first recorded for The Gramophone Company in March 1907 in Delhi. The sessions were conducted by recording experts William Conrad Gaisberg, assisted by George Walter Dillnutt.

The catalogues of the EMI Music Archive demonstrate that she recorded proflifically for The Gramophone Company in subsequent expeditions (see Table 4.1).

Figure 4.3 Photograph of Janki Bai and her accompanists in a recording studio. Photograph is supposed to have been taken by Frederick William Gaisberg.

Source: Photo courtesy *My name is Gauhar Jaan!*

Table 4.1 Recording sessions of Janki Bai of Allahabad

Year of recording	Place of recording	Recording expert
Late November 1908	Calcutta	George Walter Dillnutt
November 1909	Delhi	George Walter Dillnutt
December 1910	Delhi	George Walter Dillnutt
November 1916	Allahabad	George Walter Dillnutt
Early 1923	Lucknow	Robert Edward Beckett
1928 (electrical recording technique)	Lucknow	Robert Edward Beckett
Late 1928 (electric recording)	Delhi	Arthur James Twine

Source: Kinnear (1994).

Janki was an expensive artist for The Gramophone Company. As Gaisberg (1942) notes:

> Janki Bai was one of the best classical singers and her fee was 3,000 rupees for a recording session. To attend a wedding celebration her fee varied with the standing of the parties; from a wealthy family she would get 5,000 rupees, and the festival on such an occasion would last several days. (57)

The Record News (January 1994: 5–8) reports that she was paid Rs. 250 for 20 titles in the 1907 recording session and Rs. 900 for 24 titles in the 1908 recording session. It also notes that she recorded for other recording companies as well, and by late 1910 The Gramophone Company began recognising her celebrity status and sought an "exclusive contract" with her. By 1913 the Company started releasing violet-coloured Gramophone Concert Records of Janki Bai, which was a measure of an artist's celebrity status that The Gramophone Company bestowed to only select artists. By the 1920s, she was at the peak of her performing career and was offered Rs. 2000 for her live performances. She proved thereafter to be a tough negotiator with The Gramophone Company, demanding higher fees. This is possibly why after 1916, we see her being recorded again only in 1923.

Gautam (1987) traces Janki Bai's lineage to Banaras, where she born in 1880. Janki had a troubled childhood. Her stepmother Laxmi, and father Shivbalak Ram betrayed Janki and her mother Manki, forcing the mother and daughter to become *tawaifs* in Allahabad to earn a living. In my interview with senior musician Girija Devi, she mentions:

> I was told that Janki Bai was very talented in music and learnt the art under *Ustad* Hassu Khan of Lucknow and had very accomplished accompanists too. She learnt English, Sanskrit and Persian and wrote a *Divan* of Urdu poetry too called *Divan-i-Janki*. She used to be embarrassed by her bad looks and scarred face and sang from behind a curtain

or veil. It is said that once while performing for the King of Rewa, he was so captivated by her melodious voice that he ordered her never to cover her face because a true artist's worth was her talent and not her looks.[6]

Sampath (2010) documents that Janki Bai, along with her contemporary and rival Gauhar Jaan, had the rare privilege of being selected to sing for Emperor George V during the famous Delhi Durbar of 1911 in the presence of all the royal families of India. Among other songs, they sang *"Yeh Jalsa Taajposhi ka Mumbaarak ho, Mubaarak ho"* (Congratulations to His Majesty on this grand coronation ceremony) (142). She was also an accomplished poet and published an anthology of her Urdu poetry titled *"Deewan-e-Janki."*

Gautam (1987) documents that at the peak of her career Janki fell in love with a handsome lawyer in Allahabad, Sheikh Abdul Haq, and married him. But the marriage ended after a few years. She thereafter lost interest in materialistic pursuits, established a charitable trust (which still exists as "The Janki Bai Trust") and willed away all her property to the trust, which provided financial help to poor and needy students, distributed blankets to the poor, charity to temples and mosques, and ran free kitchens for the needy. She died on 18 May 1934 in Allahabad and was cremated there.

Malka Jaan of Agra

Another illustrious courtesan whom The Gramophone Company recorded was Malka Jaan of Agra (her dates of birth and death are unknown). Sharma (2012) documents that she trained under several teachers of the Agra *gharana*, such as Ghulam Abbas Khan (1825–1934) and later Faiyyaz Khan with whom she had a torrid love affair (138). The other gramophone celebrity, Maujuddin Khan, who was a master of rendition of soulful *thumris*, was captivated by Malka Jaan and professed his love for her. But her rebuff, Sharma (2012) claims, led him to the path of destruction and addiction to alcohol (139). Sampath (2010) documents that Malka Jaan became popular for developing a full-throated *thumri* style of singing and some of her *thumris Beete jaat barkha ritu sajan nahin aaye* in raga Desh and *Papihara piu piu kare* in raga Sawan, recorded by The Gramophone Company, were widely popular all over India (57).

Bai Sundarabai Jadhav of Pune (1885–1955)

The year was 1929. The royal Darbar of the Nizam of Hyderabad Mir Osman Ali Khan Siddiqi Asaf Jah VII glittered with the best musicians from across the country. In deference to the Nizam, many of the singers performed standing in front of him. But there was one singer who made the Nizam sit up and take note of the wonderful voice he was listening to and

Figure 4.4 Bai Sundarabai of Pune.

Source: Pic courtesy: SIRC, Mumbai.

forced him to accord the due respect of allowing the performer to sit down and finish the song. That talented singer was Bai Sundarabai Jadhav (1885–1955) from Pune, who, although forgotten now, was one of India's most celebrated recording artists of her time and whose repertoire spanned several decades and became popular through different forms of media. So pleased was the Nizam with Bai Sundarabai's Urdu diction and rendition of ghazals that he also permitted her to sing his compositions (Figure 4.4).

Born in 1885 in Pune, Sundarabai's father Marotrao was a contractor, who had noticed the innate musical talents in his daughter quite early. She was among the few recorded women artists who did not belong to a *tawaif* background. The father took Sundarabai, who did not attain any formal education, to Satara where she trained initially in light classical music. It was here that Sundarabai added a vast corpus of Marathi folk songs (known as *Laavni*) to her musical talent from her guru Dabhade Gondhali. In Pune, she learnt Hindustani classical music under Shankarrao Ghorpadkar. She also found an unusual teacher in a mystical Thakurdasoba, who enriched her repertoire with several devotional songs or bhajans. Such was the dedication of Sundarabai and her father that when Thakurdasoba suddenly decided to migrate to Bombay, Marotrao who was not quite well off, decided to rent a small room in Chirabazar near Girgaon in Bombay – close to a temple where Thakurdasoba had decided to spend his life. In the holy precincts of this Gora Ram temple of Thakurdwar in Girgaon, Sundarabai's voice blossomed to greater heights with several soulful bhajans that she later popularised all her life. Polishing her Hindi and Urdu diction, she also learnt ghazals and Hindustani music, as well as the folk songs of the Banaras region under a wide range of gurus like Dhamman Khan, Gulam Rasool Khan, and Keshav Bhaiyya.

With this kind of eclectic training, it was just a matter of time before Sundarabai took to live performances. She received wide acclaim from connoisseurs within and outside Maharashtra. Her guru, Dhamman Khan, was a tabla maestro and often accompanied her to her classical concerts. During her many concert tours, Sundarabai came in contact with the musical divas of her time – Vidyadhari Bai, Siddheshwari Devi, and Rasoolan Bai (all from Banaras), and incorporated the *purabi* style of singing from them into her own. From Lucknow to Banaras to Hyderabad, Sundarabai was a rage across India.

Quite expectedly, her music soon caught the attention of the veteran Marathi theatre thespian Bal Gandharva. He was conceptualising a new play *"Ekaach Pyala"* in 1920 and asked her to compose the music for it. She readily agreed and the outcome was a series of hit Marathi natyasangeet songs and ghazals that were used in the play.

In October 1921, The Gramophone Company and its recording agent George Walter Dillnutt solicited Sundarabai for recording sessions. Ever the innovator, she agreed to this offer as well. In Bombay, she cut about 12 records under the Zonophone label for them in this session. There was no looking back after this for Sundarabai. With the entry of electric recording in 1925, artists could sing without the limitations that they faced during the acoustic era, including having to scream at high pitch. She recorded for numerous labels such as Odeon, Regal, Young India, The Twin and Columbia. In a recording career that spanned later for 30 years, Sundarabai cut close to 100 records, recording about 180 songs on them. So popular were Sundarabai's records that The Gramophone Company (His Masters' Voice or HMV by then) awarded her with a gold medal around 1927–1928, for highest sales. Unfortunately, very few of these best sellers survive today, nor have there been any serious attempts to protect those available for posterity.

In the same recording session with Odeon in August 1934, she recorded her famous Hindi bhajan *"Mathura hi Sahi"* – possibly learnt under Thakurdasoba. But quite interestingly, in a subtle manner, midway in the bhajan, a line is inserted: *"Deen Bharat ka dukh door karo Prabhu!"* (Oh Lord! Ameliorate the sufferings of my oppressed country). This was quite in keeping with the political climate of freedom struggles and how the gramophone was an effective tool in conveying patriotic sentiments. The finesse with which Sundarabai rendered the sensuous lavni is remarkable, giving them a new sense of respectability and stripping off the normal lewd and bawdy associations with it.

In her long and momentous career, Sundarabai witnessed so many changes in the world of music and entertainment – the gramophone recordings, the rise and fall of Marathi musical plays or natyasangeet, the radio and the wonder of the twentieth century – the talkies or cinema. Ever ready to adapt to any medium, Sundarabai experimented and succeeded in each one of these. She worked with the Bombay Radio station since its inception. It is said that it was under her persuasion that Bal Gandharva, who considered her as his sister, gave performances on radio. She remained employed with the radio in her last days as well. In fact, she is believed to have played the role of an active campaigner with several musicians, especially women and *tawaifs*, imploring them to eschew their inhibitions and adapt to modern technology – first with the gramophone and then the radio.

Sundarabai acted and also sang in two Marathi films produced by the doyenne of Indian cinema V. Shantaram, through his Prabhat Film Company – *Manoos* (which later got remade in Hindi as *Aadmi*) in 1939 and *Sangam* in 1940–41. The immensely talented Master Krishnarao provided the music in the films and HMV-issued records of the songs as well.

Sundarabai had obviously earned a lot of wealth to be able to reserve the entire third floor of Bombay's Empire Hotel as accommodation. She also owned two expensive cars of which she was very enamoured. Generous to a fault and ever fond of children, Sundarabai's velvet bag was always full of chocolates, expensive perfumes, and gifts that she happily distributed to anyone she met. Her little notebook with jottings of songs and notations too was freely shared with anyone who asked for it. Obviously, with such generosity, she was bound to face numerous tricksters, many of whom duped her of her wealth. Some of them coaxed her into starting a gramophone recording business and establish a company called "Navbharat Record Company." Sadly for her, the company went broke and she lost all her fortunes. Selling away her cars and giving up her regal life, she returned to a life of more modest means, but she struggled to earn enough while working in the radio.

The pressure of it all eventually got to her and Sundarabai breathed her last breath in 1955 in Bombay – unsung, uncelebrated, and completely forgotten. But her rich legacy across so many different media platforms still speaks to us, as eloquently as ever and with as much finesse and love.

Salem Godavari

Documentation about the *devadasis* of the South who recorded for The Gramophone Company are very scant in comparison to the Hindustani musicians discussed in this chapter thus far. Possibly the erasure of their life stories was deemed more necessary, given that the intensity of their social boycott (discussed in the next chapter) was felt more in South India. Historical fragments of archival material and anecdotal information are all that are available of these women.

Among the earliest superstar singers to be recorded by The Gramophone Company in South India was Salem Godavari. No details are available of her birthdate or background. The first account about Godavari is in recording expert Noble's (1913: 48–49) memoirs, when he came to record her voice. He braved the tropical heat of Madras (now Chennai), where Godavari lived in the Thambuchetty Street in George Town, which was the city's *devadasi*

stronghold. He writes about being led into a house whose interior was constructed of marble and a "faint glimmer of a blue-shaded light cast an interesting and warm sensation over the interior that was at once fascinating and
seductive" (48). The house was donated by her patron and cost Rs. 18,000
Noble was informed. Noble's Pathé Company secured her for 16 titles for
the sum of Rs. 300. Thereafter she negotiated for a higher fee, and at the end
of two days was paid Rs. 900.

The same memoirs have a photograph of Godavari, which is grainy and
unclear, but shows her, as Noble describes, with her accompanists on the
violin and the *ghatam* and she playing the drone instrument, the *tanpura*
(Figure 4.5).

The Hindu newspaper dated 14 August 2014 records how the nationalist
leader C. Rajagopalachari is supposed to have attended a party in Salem
hosted by a famous advocate of the city, Vijayaraghavachariar, and was
captivated by Godavari's performance (n.pag.). Sampath (2010) writes that
in 1910, she hosted Gauhar Jaan of Calcutta, who was a close friend, at her
residence when the former came to Madras for a performance (144). The
archives of *The Hindu* report Godavari's demise on 20 October 1911.[7] Akin
to the philanthropic work undertaken by courtesans such as Janki Bai, the

Figure 4.5 Photograph of Salem Godavari in the recording studio.

Source: Photo courtesy *The Talking Machine World* 1913.

1 November 1911 issue of *The Hindu* newspaper reports several bequests made in her will to institutions such as the Pachaiyappa College, Society for Protection of Children, Annanda Samajam, Salem College, Vedic School attached to Salem Theosophical Society, and for temple cars and a rest house for pilgrims at a Shiva Temple in her hometown Salem.

Dhanakoti Ammal of Kanchipuram

Dhanakoti Ammal of Kanchipuram was another of the *devadasi* artists recorded in the Second recording expedition of The Gramophone Company in 1904–05. From Kinnear's (1994) catalogues it is evident that she did not record very prolifically. She had close ties to the prima donna of Carnatic music, Dhanammal. Sankaran (1962) traces the lineage of the women and states that both Dhanakoti and Dhanammal belonged to the *shishya* tradition or lineage of one of the Trinity of Carnatic music – Shyama Shastri – but belonged to two different branches. Sankaran states that Dhanakoti was a direct disciple of Kacchi Shastri, great-grandson of Shyama Shastri. He documents that a renowned *devadasi* of Kanchipuram, Mettu Kamakshi Ammal, had two daughters: Thayammal and Chinnakanniammal. The former was a violinist and the mother of four children: Dhanakoti, Kamakshi, Velu Mudaliar and Palani Ammal. Dhanakoti and Kamakshi performed together as the "Dhanakoti Sisters," and Kinnear (1994) reveals that they have even recorded duets for The Gramophone Company (Figure 4.6).

Figure 4.6 Photograph of Dhanakoti Ammal of Kanchipuram.

Source: Picture courtesy Isai Medaikkal.

Musicologist and scholar Dr. Ritha Rajan mentions:

> Dhanakoti Ammal possessed a powerful and resonant voice and it seems that she met with success wherever she performed. She was supposedly very popular in Andhra Pradesh, in Kakinada, Eluru, Rajamahendrapuram and so on. She had a wide repertoire of Tamil songs too and knew several Ramayana *kritis* of Arunachala Kavirayar. There is a very popular anecdote about Dhanakoti that we often hear. During one of her concerts at the soiree of a rich *zamindar*, a young man of the family supposedly addressed her disparagingly by first name and ordered her in a rough tone 'Sing a song from the Ramayana, eh Dhanakoti!'. Everyone was angered by this discourteous way of asking for a song to be sung and Dhanakoti herself was stung for a moment. But quickly regaining her composure, she turned towards him, focusing on him with the slight squint that she had in her eyes and in a loud voice started '*Yaru Daa nee Korange?*' (Who are you, Oh Monkey?). While the repartee seemed apt for his discourtesy, this was actually one of the songs from the Ramayana, where Ravana says this to Hanuman when the latter goes to Lanka with the ring of Lord Rama! The audience and the intemperate young man were stunned into silence by this timely musical retort.[8]

Sankaran (1962) notes that many of the rare songs Dhanakoti sang are no longer available even on palm leaf manuscripts. He lists some of these rare compositions that were part of Dhanakoti's repertoire: Palani Andavar's *Chandra Jataadhara Jagadeeshwara* in raga *Nadanamakriya* (which was a very popular one that she sang on concert stages and won the appreciation of audiences), *Appane Pazhani Appane* in raga *Kapi*, Doraiswamy Iyer's composition *Inthaparamukhameno* in raga *Begada*, and Muthuthandavar's famous *padam: Theruvil Varaano* (140).

Dr. Ritha Rajan mentions:

> It is said that Dhanakoti also knew several rare *padams* of Subbarama Iyer. One of them, *Naanange varuveno* was very popular and later even transformed into a Tamil film song! In her live concerts, it is said that Dhanakoti would go to the extent of singing some of the *charanams* 10–15 times too, savouring the meaning each time as she gave as much importance to the lyrics as to the tune. Sometimes her niece Kuppammal would also accompany her and the sister in concerts. It is said that in a live concert she started with *Saroja Dalanetri*, the famous composition of Shyama Sastri in raga *Shankarabharanam* and would exhaust all the possibilities of improvisation offered on the lyric *korivacchina varike-llanu*, by singing it so many times and in so many different ways. It is said she would make the gestures of playing on the *veena* while singing and so one can assume that she was perhaps trained in that instrument

too. Her understanding of what the audiences wanted in a live performance too was good. I have heard this story that in one instance while
singing the line *Ennai tirumbi paaraano* (literally meaning, will he turn
back to look at me) which she sang many times, each time she would
turn to different sections of the audience making them all feel she was
singing this for them and them alone! Sadly the gramophone records
do little justice to her virtuosity as they sound pretty bad and today we
wonder if these stories are indeed true or apocryphal! Dhanakoti had
gifted a *tanpura* to my family and was close to my great grand father.
Dhanakoti's style of rendition of Shyama Shastri's compositions is
markedly different from what has now become the trend. However, I
feel, that unlike Dhanammal, the two sisters Dhanakoti and Kamakshi
lacked a sense of musical sophistication. This conclusion I am drawing
only from hearing some of the recordings and I do not know if this was
the limitation of the technology that caused it and if they were different
in live performances.[9]

Sankaran (1962) mentions that Dhanakoti's sister, Kamakshi, had a son
on 25 July 1889 – Subramania Pillai, famous later as Kanchipuram "Naina"
Pillai. It is said that the name "Naina," an endearing and affectionate nickname, was given by Dhanakoti and it stuck with him for all his life as his
first name. As a child it was Dhanakoti who gave him the initial musical
training. Dhanakoti's date of demise is unknown.

Salem Papa

The other artist to be recorded by The Gramophone Company in the first
decade of the twentieth century was Salem Papa. Sundaram (2003: 73) col-
lates scanty biographical details about her. She was the daughter of a famous
devadasi singer of Salem, Meenakshi Ammal, who shifted to Madras (now
called Chennai) in search of better opportunities and settled down there in
the nineteenth century. Papa and her sister Radha showed musical promise;
and, hence, the mother made arrangements to invite the renowned composer
and musician Patnam Subramanya Iyer to come to Madras to teach them.
The girls were also trained in dance initially under Chennai Jagannnatha
Nattuvanar, and later from his son, Kumarar Nelliappa Nattuvanar. The
daughters of Papa and Radha carried on their legacy in music and dance
until the anti-*devadasi* campaign ensured that they lost all opportunities of
performance.

Bangalore Nagarathnamma (1878–1952)

One of the more popular recorded women musicians of the South is
Bangalore Nagarathnamma (1878–1952). Sriram (2007) documents that she
was born in Mysore on 3 November 1878 to an unwed mother and *devadasi*,

Puttulakshmi. The father deserted a year-old child, and Puttulakshmi was left to take care of herself and her daughter. They took shelter under a Sanskrit scholar, Giribhatta Thimmayya Shastri, who worked in the royal court of the King of Mysore. Under his tutelage the young girl nurtured her interests in Sanskrit and music. But Shastri soon turned hostile and threw the mother and daughter away with an invective that the young Nagarathnamma was destined to collect cow dung in the streets of Mysore (3). Deeply insulted by this, Puttulakshmi made it her life's mission to make her daughter a great musician and vowed never to enter Mysore until that dream was fulfilled. The mother-daughter shifted to Bangalore where young Nagarathnamma's vigorous musical training progressed. By the time, she was 15, she was ready for performing in public and soon the King of Mysore, Chamarajendra Wodeyar X, invited her to sing at the Palace. This was Puttulakshmi's ultimate revenge for all the insults heaped on her and her daughter.

Senior record collector V.A.K. Ranga Rao mentions:

> Nagarathnamma started receiving concert invitations from all over South India, the royal courts of Mysore, Travancore, the *zamindaries* of Bobbili, Vizianagaram and then ultimately the urban centre for excellence in Carnatic music, Madras. As a scion of the *zamindari* of Chikkavaram, I remember interacting with her. People had started attributing all kinds of special powers to her, that with her blessings women would lead a long and happy married life or become pregnant! After all, a *devadasi* is considered sacred in our traditions. My mother Saraswathi Devi was childless for long and had invited Nagarathnamma for a performance and sought her blessings. Nagarathnamma gave her a blessed lime fruit and asked her to worship it regularly. It is said that, that is how I was born! She had come and even sung at my naming ceremony.[10]

Nagarthnamma faced a major public controversy when she published the translation of an erotic poetry collection called the *Radhika Santhvanamu* (discussed in detail in Chapter 5). She then decided to lead a quiet and spiritual life. She willed all the wealth she had earned to a trust that undertook philanthropic work and used her resources in getting a memorial constructed for one of Trinity of Carnatic music, Thyagaraja, in Thiruvaiyaru (Tamil Nadu). Sriram (2007) documents that this came at a heavy cost of fighting long drawn patriarchal battles and attempts at appropriation of the memorial shrine by men, which she single-handedly battled and eventually triumphed. To this date her idol at Thiruvaiyaru stands opposite the Thyagaraja shrine, as a testimony to her single- minded courage and determination. Nagarathnamma passed away on 19 May 1952 (Figure 4.7).

Vasudevacharya (1999) writes about her music:

> Raga *aalaapana*, *swara kalpana*, *neraval* everything was there as in a traditional concert...her style of singing was religiously classical. She

Figure 4.7 Photograph of Bangalore Nagarathnamma with her initials "B.N.R."

Source: Courtesy *A Dictionary of South Indian Music and Musicians.*

had accurate *laya gnana* (sense of rhythm). Her voice combined the melodic sweetness of a female voice with the dignity of a male voice. She had a sound knowledge of *Bharatanatya* and her singing had an emotional appeal. *Yadhukulakambodhi* (raga) was her favourite. She was never afraid of any challenge from a musician…a queen among dancers and singers, she was an apostle of modesty, pride of the Kannada land, selfless soul and had the beauty and wealth in equal proportions… her respectful conduct in the presence of senior *vidwans* attracted my attention. She stood in front of them as though to offer worship…never looked up at them and spoke little in their presence. (69–72)

Coimbatore Thayi (1872–1917)

Another important celebrity singer of the gramophone era was Coimbatore Thayi (1872–1917). Kinnear's (1994) catalogues and the EMI Music Archive reveal that from 29 August 1910 to 2 September 1910, The Gramophone Company held special sessions called "Coimbatore Thayi Recording

Sessions." As mentioned in the case of Janki Bai, records were colour coded based on the artist's popularity. Thayi was coded violet, which indicated she was one of the most popular and celebrated artists. The Gramophone Company made nearly 60 recordings in this session.

Sundaram (2003: 49–51) documents that Coimbatore Thayi was not only a renowned singer but also a talented dancer. She hailed from Avinasi near the town of Coimbatore. He traces her lineage to her grandmother, a *devadasi* named Visalakshi, and her mother Vengammal. Vengammal moved from Avinasi and settled down in the town of Coimbatore, which is where Thayi was born in 1872. Her name was Pazhanikunjaram, and she was affection-ately called Thayi. Soon everyone began calling her by the latter name and she became known as Coimbatore Thayi. Vengammal ensured the best train-ing in dance for Thayi under stalwarts such as Sivananda Nattuvanar and Subbaraya. At the age of eleven, in 1883, Thayi gave her maiden dance per-formance. Thayi was also gifted with a melodious voice and showed a keen interest in training in Carnatic music. Vengammal put her under the tutelage of Kadur Bhagavathar of Tirunelevlli and later under Ramachandra Iyer, a direct disciple of the renowned maestro Mahavaidyanatha Iyer of Tanjore. Thayi also had the opportunity of learning several Kannada javalis from Mysore Kempegowda. With the raging sentiment against the dance of the *devadasis*, Thayi restricted herself to musical performances only by the time she was nineteen years old. Sundaram writes that the mother and daughter soon travelled to the city of Madras in search of better opportunities and took up a residence in the Nattu Pillaiyar Koil Street in George Town where all the renowned *devadasis* of the city lived. Dhanammal was a neighbour who introduced her to several composers and musicians of the city.

In Madras, Thayi continued her musical training under Tiruvottriur Thyagayya and learnt the erotic *javalis* from Dharmapuri Subbarayar, who was an authority in that art. By the time she was 31 years old, she completely eschewed dance and dedicated herself to musical performances alone.

It was in 1910 that she was solicited by The Gramophone Company to record. Sundaram (2003) states that for the recording sessions, she used either Coimbatore Periyasami Pillai, his brother Kaliya Pillai, Thatchur Singaracharlu, or Thenmadam Varadachari as her regular violin accom-panists, and Mysore Muthuswamy Thevar was the permanent mridangam accompanist. The records made her more popular and awards and invita-tions for performances started coming in from the royal courts of Mysore and Travancore, and rich *zamindaries* of South India. Sundaram (2003) doc-uments that in a public gathering, she was felicitated for her musical talents by the people of Coimbatore. Prominent citizens of the city presented her a thick golden bracelet embedded with diamonds and emeralds during this event. Thayi died at her house in Madras on 17 August 1917.

Pasler (2000: 103) mentions an incident related to Coimbatore Thayi, and an unlikely collaboration that she was part of, because of her record-ings for The Gramophone Company. Maurice Delage was heir to a shoe

Figure 4.8 A portrait of Coimbatore Thayi.

Source: Picture courtesy *The Hindu* 4 March 2013.

polish manufacturing fortune in France. Born with a severe eye problem, he developed his hearing to an amazing degree. He studied composition with Maurice Ravel for about ten years, and became a pianist and composer. Pasler (2007) states that it was in Paris in 1911 that he became fascinated with Coimbatore Thayi after hearing a record of hers, and that he wrote they "sent chills up and down my spine" (272). His keen ear "detected the subtle microtonal effects she produced while singing."[11] Pasler (2000) mentions that Delage came to India and heard Coimbatore Thayi in a performance in one of the temples of Mahabalipuram. He described her as "a master of open and closed mouth singing"[12] (276). Delage composed *Ragamalika*,[13] which seems to have been a direct inspiration of Thayi's renditions of *Arulpa* songs recorded on the gramophone discs (Figure 4.8).[14]

Speaking of the *Ragamalika*, Pasler (2007) writes:

In every way *Ragamalika* reflects its model; in its changing modes (*ragamalika* means "a garland of ragas"), its recurring refrain, it's multipartite form, and its tempo relationships. The piano takes the place of the *tabla* and the droning accompanimental [sic] instrument. Its ostinati octaves serve principally to support the vocal line, except in one very important instance. To articulate the system tonic, B-flat, and to bring attention to the change of mode in the middle of the piece, Delage asks that one note on the inside of the piano be muted. This creates an unusual otherworldly effect for the drone. It is perhaps the first example of 'prepared piano' in European music. The publisher Durand was so 'enchanted' by this music that on 20 June 1914 he paid Delage 500 francs to orchestrate it. With the help of these recordings, Delage succeeded better than his contemporaries in reproducing the spirit and the style of the music of North and South India. With its emphasis on self-criticism, sound for its own sake, and respect for traditions in their own terms, the modernist aesthetic prepared Delage to hear Indian music in its own terms. (277)

Pasler (2007) mentions that Delage listened widely to Indian gramophone recordings and undertook field trips across India and experimented with "unusual timbres produced by altered tunings and vocal techniques, special kinds of ornaments that modify the Western sense of internal and pitch, improvisatory rhythms, new forms and novel performance techniques" (272). Along with the composition of *Ragamalika*, this osmosis resulted in Delage's major work *Quatre Poèmes Hindous* for soprano and small chamber orchestra, written during his India travels between 1912 and 1913. These compositions are richly influenced by Hindustani and Carnatic music recordings, as well as folk music that Delage might have heard in the course of his travel. These musical interactions between Western and Indian music, and between Coimbatore Thayi and Delage and the subsequent outcome were unintended consequences of the gramophone recordings. For the first time, it brought Indian music from its local confines to not only a wider Indian audience, but also to Western listeners and musicians.

Impact of Recording on the Women Musicians

Recording made brands of many of the singers who adapted to the technology and performed well. In many cases they were now being globally recognised too, as had happened in the case of Coimbatore Thayi. Similarly, Sampath (2010) notes that a *tawaif*, such as Gauhar Jaan became a national celebrity with her photographs appearing on matchboxes with a "Made in Austria" sign on it and on picture postcards (116–117). In some of those pictures, she looks quite imposing in traditional Bengali attire. The postcards sold as briskly as her records (Figures 4.9 and 4.10).

Although the recognition and wealth that came their way with recording technology for many successful *tawaifs* and *devadasis* might have liberated them from their exploitative patrons, it might have further accentuated the hatred against them and provided momentum to the morality campaign that was being led against them (details in Chapter 5). The increased income that came their way made many of the *devadasis* and *tawaifs*, such as Gauhar Jaan, feisty and hedonistic in their lifestyle. Sampath (2010) writes that Gauhar owned a huge mansion in Calcutta called "Gauhar Building," had costly cars, phaetons with exquisite silk curtains, imposing Victoria carriages and,

Figure 4.9 Gauhar Jaan on Matchbox with a "Made in Austria" sticker.

Figure 4.10 Gauhar Jaan on picture postcards dressed in royal finery.

Source: Picture courtesy *My Name is Gauhar Jaan!*

according to eye-witnesses, drove along thoroughfares of Calcutta every evening in a majestic phaeton driven by six white Arabian stallions (117). Apocryphal stories abound in the musical world of how she spent recklessly.

Senior musician Girija Devi recounts:

> Gauhar Jaan was a flamboyant lady. I used to hear stories about her from my parents, teachers, and music lovers. As much as she was celebrated for her music and her recordings, they would tell us that the money she earned through her concerts and recordings made her a reckless spender both in Banaras and Calcutta, who spent on lavish parties for events as insignificant as the wedding of her pet cat and another when the cat had a litter![15]

It is possible that this profligacy in the lifestyles of these courtesans came about after their taking to recording and charging huge fees to the recording companies. This hedonistic lifestyle possibly induced both a sense of awe and admiration and also intense envy in the minds of their male musician counterparts and the social reformers. A social revolution was brewing against them, ironically contemporaneous to the times when they were scripting histories on shellac. This disdain for the performing women was to manifest as the "Anti-Nautch" campaign and was to banish them from their art forever.

Notes

* Significant content for this chapter has been drawn from a series of articles written by the author himself for a news portal ThePrint. More information and links to these articles can be found in the Bibliography.

1 Excerpts of interview of author with Smt. Girija Devi.

2 Excerpts of interview of author with Shankar Lal Mehta.

3 Translated by Urdu scholar Dr. Iqbal Ahmed and included in *My name is Gauhar Jaan*. The only copy of this *Divan* is extant in the British Library, London.

4 Source: EMI Music Archive, London. Agreements and correspondences of the 1908–09 Indian Expedition.

5 Ramkrishna Bua Vaze (1871–1945) was a stalwart exponent of the Gwalior *gharana* of Hindustani music. Bhaskar Bua Bakhle (1869–1922) was another stalwart who received training under multiple *gharanas*. The Gramophone Company tried very hard to convince him to record, in 1911, but Bhaskar Bua refused and, hence, there is no recorded legacy of this artist.

6 Excerpts of interview of author with Smt Girija Devi.

7 *The Hindu* Archives, 1900–1930.

8 Interview excerpts of author with musicologist Dr. Ritha Rajan in Chennai.

9 Interview excerpts of author with Dr. Ritha Rajan in Chennai.

10 Interview excerpts of author with Mr. V.A.K Ranga Rao in Chennai.

11 He possibly refers here to her *gamaka* and fast paced or *bhriga* laden phrases.

12 This is possibly referring to what she did while rendering *taanam*.

13 *Ragamalika* of Maurice Delage was written sometime between 1912–22, according to Pasler and was published by Durand Et Fills, Paris.

14 The *arulpa* was a devotional composition of Ramalinga Swamigal, a nineteenth-century mystic who grew up in Madras. The *devadasis* sung these routinely to please the Gods of the temples to which they were attached.

15 Excerpts of interview of author with senior musician Smt. Girija Devi.

5 THE ABOLITION AND THEREAFTER

Miss Tennant was a British Anglicist, who, like several other Christian missionaries of her times, deemed it a divinely ordained responsibility to check the moral decadence of Indians. She had come all the way from England to India with a specific purpose in mind. In a circular dated 19 June 1893 that appeared on behalf of the "Punjab Purity Association" in all newspapers, she made a passionate appeal to the educated elite of the Punjab, seeking their opinions on a matter, in her view, of great importance. The letter read as follows:

> The custom of celebrating festive occasions by nautches prevails in our country. The nautch girls are as a rule, public prostitutes. To encourage them in any way is considered immoral by some people. They hold that the nautches only give opportunities to the fallen women to beguile and tempt young men. There are some, again, who consider dancing girls to be the depositaries of our music and see nothing objectionable in attending nautches. This is a question of vital importance for the moral welfare of young men.
>
> (in Sampath 2010: 183)

Among the many respondents who wrote back, Lala Harkishan Lall, Bar-at-Law, replied:

> According to our ancient beliefs and ideas, music and dancing are heavenly, while prostitution is hellish. With you the question ought to be how to divorce blessing from curse and separate one from the other, in this way you may increase purity of life in India and lessen the chances that the devil has to ensnare the youths of the country.
>
> (in Sampath 2010: 188)

A certain gentleman named H.C. Mukerji wrote:

> Let us teach our wives and daughters to practice music at home, so that they may entertain their husbands and brothers. Musical clubs

DOI: 10.4324/9780367822026-5

should be organized at all important places, not simply for the private entertainment of the members among themselves but for giving performances on festive occasions.

(in Sampath 2010: 190)

Sampath (2010) argues that the social movement against performing women, popularly known as the "anti-nautch" movement, had its roots in the social developments in Britain where evangelical movements such as the "Second Great Awakening" (1790–1840s) and "Third Great Awakening" (1880–1900) sought to purge the sins of society and restore its moral fabric through religious means. From the middle of the nineteenth century, Social Purity movements began to gain ground in Britain. Towards the end of the century, Max Nordau's concepts of "degeneration" in the arts and the means to stem this "mental illness" and the Lamarckian theory of evolution furthered these ideals. It was believed that a preoccupation with gambling, alcohol, sex, and other vices would spiral into further indulgence and thus degeneration. The effect of this physical and moral decadence would be passed on to future generations as well. Of all the vices, sexual indulgence was considered the most harmful to the health of society. The State needed to come down on licentious behaviour with a heavy hand, it was argued. The spread of sexually transmitted diseases like syphilis both in England and India in the 1850s seemed to vindicate the reformers' claims and made the authorities sit up and take notice. Several "social purity organisations" sprang up in Britain like the National Vigilance Association, the White Cross Army, The Salvation Army, and The Church of England Purity Society of the White Cross League (CEPS). Given the deep entrenchment of the Missionaries in the social and political life of Britain's most famous colony, India, since the time of the East India Company's hegemony, many of these supposed ideals percolated down through society in India as well. Social Purity organisations like the ones seen in Britain in the mid-eighteenth century were established in Northern India to rid society of the pernicious influence of the *tawaif.* The "Punjab Purity Association" (Lahore), the "Social Service League" (Bombay), and a host of others took it upon themselves to work for this hallowed goal. All these developments were to irrevocably impact the position of the courtesan in Indian society in times to come.

But other factors also contributed to the courtesan coming under strict scrutiny and surveillance. Immediately after the British ruthlessly crushed the First War of Indian Independence in 1857, it became known that many *kothas* (or salons) in North India were used by the revolutionaries of the movement as hideouts and that the revolutionaries had been actively helped by the *tawaifs.* Jafa (1998) postulates that since the *kotha* of the *tawaif* was an active social meeting point for the elite and for people from various backgrounds as they gathered for an evening of musical entertainment (*mujra*), the *kotha* also became a place of sedition where revolutionaries took shelter.

The latter were protected by the *tawaifs* who seemed to have a patriotic streak that propelled them to support the soldiers fighting a nationalist cause. Jafa contends that the British Government was baffled by this discovery and decided to take strict action against *kothas*, which began coming under increasing surveillance (157–160).

Oldenburg (1990) mentions that The British government also seemed affected by reports of liaisons that several young British soldiers had with the *tawaifs* and in 1864 passed the *Contagious Disease Act*. She details the manner in which the royal city of the Nawabs, Lucknow, was transformed into a British colonial cantonment with strict laws passed particularly against the performing women (46–50). Oldenburg refers to one such letter that was published in the newspaper *Oudh Akhbar* where all *tawaifs* are instructed to be

> registered and classified...each woman should be given a wooden ticket with her name, age, address and fixed rates...this ticket should be fixed on her front door...each prostitute should carry a certificate stating whether or not she is free from venereal disease...those who refuse registration...should be branded on the chin, cheek or forehead of their beautiful faces...it is essential that women are branded to save the respectability of innocent men. (46–50)

It was a blanket definition of all women in the performing space as prostitutes, although the community had several hierarchical categories ranging from the high-browed performer to the prostitute, as was discussed in Chapter 1.

There was also a class of neo-literate Indians that was armed with a modern, English education in schools set up by Christian missionaries and which freely embraced Western ideals. These Indians began to look down upon various aspects of their own culture and traditions, especially the performing arts, which were now seen to be synonymous with a debased and debauched feudal setup dominated by courtesans, prostitutes, nawabs, and zamindars. Coincidentally, from this very same class of neo-literate Indians emerged the various social reform movements and, to an extent, the early branches of the Indian freedom movement. They too held the *tawaif* in utter contempt. Sampath (2010) quotes the eminent reformer Keshab Chandra Sen:

> Hell is in her eyes. In her breast is a vast ocean of poison. Round her comely waist dwells the furies of hell. Her hands are brandishing unseen daggers ever ready to strike unwary or willful victims that fall in her way. Her blandishments are India's ruin. Alas! Her smile is India's death. (186)

In Southern India the degeneration of the process of dedication of women to temples as *devadasis* by patrons who sexually exploited them was a matter of concern for several social reformers. One of the first concrete efforts at tackling the custom of dedication to temples was taken in 1881 when social reformer Viresalingam started a movement that received support from both missionary and Hindu organisations from the Madras State. *The Hindu* newspaper struck the first blow in 1893, opining that nautch performances appealed to the baser instincts and condemned the practice of such programmes held for visiting dignitaries to the Madras Presidency. In April 1894, it published an article condemning the nautch party held at the eminent gentleman Dewan Bahadur Venkataswamy Rao's residence in Mylapore in Madras and the Thanjavur Bar Association for organising such a party for the Governor.[1]

The same year, Viresalingam mobilised public opinion for the Hindu Social Reform Movement to hand over a memorandum to the Governor of Madras, Beilby Lawley, third Baron Wenlock, appealing to the Viceroy and Governor not to attend nautch performances and thereby give them a modicum of credibility. The archives of *The Hindu* newspaper reveal that this memorandum, signed by 2000 signatories, urged the British authorities not to give credence to a practice that "necessarily lowers the moral tone of society" and "also tends to destroy that family life on which national soundness depends, and tends to bring upon individuals ruin in property and character alike." To dispel any connections with Hinduism, which perhaps the petitioners thought was the reason why the Government was reluctant to intervene, the petitioners pointed out that the nautch practice, which they considered to be equivalent to prostitution, had no sanction in religion or antiquity. Considering the "strong feeling springing up among the educated classes of this country against the prevalence of this practice, as is evinced among the other things by the proceedings at a public meeting in Madras, on the 5th of May 1893," the memorandum ended with a plea "to discourage this pernicious practice by declining to attend any entertainment at which nautch girls are invited to perform, and thus to strengthen the hands of those who are trying to purify the social life of their community."[2]

The colonial authorities initially seemed guarded in their reaction, viewing the matter as a purely native problem and preferring to stay out of temples and local politics. In response to the memorandum, Viceroy Landsdowne stated[3] that he had himself been present in several such entertainments and did not find anything improper in them. Governor Wenlock too stated that he had "been present on several occasions on which nautches have been performed at none of which has he ever seen anything, in the remotest degree, be considered improper; and that it has never occurred to him to take into consideration the moral character of the performers at these entertainments, any more than when he has been present at performances which have been carried out by professional dancers or athletes either in Europe or India."[4]

But the debate against the performing women started gathering momentum in different parts of India, starting from the South. Sampath (2008) mentions that by 1909, the Mysore government became the first to formally ban the dedication of girls to temples for music and dance (671). Temples in the state were forbidden from utilising the services of *devadasis*. Dance performances in public places, known as *taffe*, were banned across the State. The news was received with great jubilation across the country and gave a further boost to the reformers' zeal. Mysore was hailed as a pioneer of social reform.

A declaration of the King of Mysore, Nalwadi Krishnaraja Wodeyar, dated 28 January 1910 mentions:

> Whatever may be the euphemism by which the true nature of the ceremony is concealed, *Gejje Puje*[5] has an intimate connection with dedication to the profession of a prostitute singing-dancing girl. They are not allowed the performance of such a ceremony in a *muzrai* temple[6] and are satisfied from the depositions and the opinion of the *Muzrai Agamik*[7] on record that no hardship will be caused by the prohibition of the performance of *Gejje Puje* or any similar ceremony within the precincts of any temple under the control of government in the Muzrai department.[8]

Gautam (1991) mentions that "Social Purity movements" began in the Nizam's dominion of Hyderabad in Southern India too, in the form of a *Jagan Mitra Mandali* (Global Friendship Society) established in 1906. Madari Bhagya Reddy Varma (1888–1939) founded the Mandali at Hyderabad. He traces the evolution of this movement that eventually culminated in the Adi Andhra movement in 1917. This movement passed a resolution at its All India Adi Hindu Social Conference in 1922, held at Hyderabad. Gautam (1991) states that the resolution declared "dedication of girls to deities as *devadasis*—known as *Joginis*, *Murlis* and other names in different parts of India should be declared immoral and the custom be abolished" (11).

In the Madras Presidency, Vijaisri (2004) describes that, along with Viresalingam, the active leadership of Venkataratnam Naidu (1862–1939) gave the anti-nautch movement a new impetus (158–162).

Naidu postulated that:

> legislation may punish immodest soliciting of attention in public; but it needs a strong public opinion to note indecent song and suggestions out of court; while chastity that would rather pluck out the offending right eye than tarnish its native purity, is bred only in the soul that delights in the law of righteousness...Legislation compels the unaided helplessness of man; public opinion works upon his 'gregariousness'; personal responsibility draws out his manliness.[9]

He took the discourse from the beseeching of government, colonial powers, and legal courts right to the court of the people and believed creating a strong public opinion against the courtesan was the only way forward. Vijaisri (2004) mentions that The Social Purity Association of Machalipatnam that Naidu formed made all its male members take pledges of purity, of not attending nautch performances, singing indecent songs, or using lewd gestures, postures, words, or thoughts and being pure in body, mind, and soul (158–162).

The Case of Bangalore Nagarathnamma

Around this time, Bangalore Nagarathnamma, the celebrated *devadasi* of Madras who was discussed in the previous chapter and who was also among the earliest musicians in South India to record her songs on a gramophone created a stir in the orthodox society of Madras. Nagarathnamma had come across the work titled *Radhika Santhvanamu* or the Appeasement of Radha,[10] by Muddupalani, an eighteenth-century courtesan of Thanjavur King Pratapasimha. It had a unique storyline: The Hindu God Lord Krishna's soulmate Radha is in love with him though he is much younger than her. The two of them indulge in sexual gratification even though he is a minor. But eventually Radha lets her lover marry her niece Iladevi. In her translation of *Radhika Santhvanamu*, Sandhya Mulchandani writes that the very thought of the two making love fills Radha with jealousy and she demands that her sexual needs be met as well (Muddupalani, 2011). She abuses Krishna and even kicks him hard when he bends down to touch her feet. Eventually, a situation arises where Krishna appeases her and makes love to her as well, even as he keeps his young wife happy. The bold theme of the story underlined that a woman's sexual needs were equivalent to that of a man and that she too had the right to seek gratification (xxix).

In her translation, Mulchandani mentions that in 1855 Telugu scholar Charles Philip Brown discovered a ready-for-print manuscript of *Radhika Santhvanamu* in the Oriental Manuscripts Library (Muddupalani, 2011). In 1887 this was published under the supervision of Paidipati Venkatanarasu, an associate of Brown and reprinted in 1907 (ix–xxi). Uncomfortable with some of the highly erotic contents of this text, Venkatanarasu dropped them from the text as also the long prologue of Muddupalani detailing her ancestry and *devadasi* lineage. Bangalore Nagarathnamma found this sanitised version distasteful. She searched for the original palm leaf manuscript and was fascinated.

Bangalore Nagarathnamma (1910) stated:

> I was introduced to *Radhika Santhvanamu* in a *prabandham* called *Panigruhita* by Tirupati Venkata Kavulu. As I read it with great curiosity, I came across many printing mistakes…on knowing my interest for the work I got an annotated manuscript from a friend, and I came across many inconsistencies as I compared the printed work and the manuscript. The earlier work lacked a prologue and certain verses had disappeared. (80)

Bangalore Nagarathnamma decided to get it published herself in its entirety. She loved its lyrical poetry and mentions in her prologue that she was tempted to read the masterpiece over and over again.

Bangalore Nagarthnamma (1910) writes:

Poetry so suffused with *rasa* could only have been written by a *gan-ika*[11] and I undertook this task as the work was not only composed by a woman but a woman born into our community, I publish it with the intention of bringing out a better version by overcoming the mistakes in the earlier published volume. (80)

Nagarathnamma also decided to correct the attempt to make the author of the original text, Muddupalani, anonymous and therefore described her lineage in detail, as a courtesan and mistress of the king of Tanjore, Pratapasimha, as someone who had written this work in four chapters, and as the daughter of another courtesan Muthyalu.

The consequences of this brave act of Nagarathnamma set the Madras literary and cultural scene ablaze. It was considered blasphemous to be publishing something as erotic as this, and a campaign against the book and Bangalore Nagarathnamma was led by noted literary critic Kandukuri Veeresalingam. Sriram (2007) mentions that he became her harshest critic, condemning her work in the following manner:

having been written by a woman whose hereditary profession was prostitution. It is bereft of the innate female virtue of modesty that one expects of woman and she has filled the book with graphic details of lovemaking in a very crude manner and is a shame in the name of romanticism. Parts of the work are such that they should not be heard or read by women. (40)

He chided Bangalore Nagarathnamma as a "prostitute and adulteress who loved to put out in public such detailed and graphic descriptions of sexual intercourse" (41).

In a strongly worded rejoinder published in the women's magazine *Grihalakshmi*, in its January 1910 edition, Bangalore Nagarathnamma punctured holes of factual errors in Veeresalingam's critique. She mocked his self-righteous moral indignation and asserted that "marrying a man and eloping with another could be termed as adultery, but a prostitute is not an adulteress…shame or modesty was natural only to women and not to men?" She decried his hypocrisy and attempts to set different standards for men and women when it came to sexual gratification. She wrote:

Is he implying that it is acceptable for Muddupalani to write about con-jugal pleasures in minute detail and without reservation because she was a courtesan? Are the 'obscenities' in *Radhika Santhvanamu* any worse than those in *Vaijayantivilasam*, a book he had personally reviewed and approved for publication? (19)

Despite the harsh reactions of her critics such as Veeresalingam, Bangalore Nagarathnamma sent the edited manuscript with her prologue to Vavilla Ramaswami Sastrulu and Sons; a renowned publishing house for Telugu books in Madras. The book was formally released on 30 March 1910. The controversy around the book seemed to die down for a year, and many scholars commended the publication.

But a year later a Telugu magazine *Sasilekha* wrote a stinging editorial against the book stating that "it was to be regretted that wretched books full of rude, depraving and obscene descriptions are now brought out in good and attractive editions in Telugu literature...a prostitute composed a book under the name *Radhika Santhvanamu* and another prostitute corrected errors therein and edited it!" Sriram (2007) states that the editorial also wondered how "the firm of Vavilla Ramaswami Sastrulu and Sons have printed such a book on good paper without any fear of law and openly distributed it for sale" (42). Since the theme of the book was the erotic relationship that Lord Krishna had with both Radha and her niece Ila, causing considerable jealousy in Radha's mind as she secretly watches her niece make love with her lover, the editorial states that "no well-behaved literate gentleman can realize God by reading descriptions depicting God that He without heeding the prohibited degrees of relationships enjoyed sexual embrace in forty different ways with an adulterous woman." (42) The editorial wondered if, following the success of the book, Nagarthnamma would now plan an illustrated edition with pictures as well to depict these graphical descriptions and concluded that it was not "possible to gauge the evil effects of this book, seeing that it is written in fine composition within the grasp of even ordinary minds"(42). [12]

A letter with copies of the review in *Sasilekha* was sent to the Chief Secretary of the Government of Madras who deemed it fit to forward the same to the Criminal Investigation Department, which assured the petitioners of an investigation and prosecution. On 22 May 1911 Deputy Commissioner of Police Cunningham raided the offices and depots of the publisher of the book and 388 copies of *Radhika Santhvanamu* were seized. A government translator Goleti Kanakaraju Panthulu certified that the content was indeed grossly obscene and needed to be banned. The book was declared illegal and was alleged to be an unhealthy influence on the morality of its readers and under Section 293 of the Indian Penal Code its publication was declared a criminal offence.[13]

Publisher Vavilla Venkateswara Sastrulu was summoned to submit an apology and undertake a promise not to indulge in such indecent literature in the future. Sastrulu however maintained in his letter to the Commissioner of Police F. Armitage dated 5 September 1911 that while publishing the books he did not feel even momentarily that he "was doing anything wrong, particularly because they were widely current and well-known works, freely published by others" in the publishing trade. He pleaded innocence, claiming that the very possibility of looking upon these publications as objectionable came to his knowledge only when the police seized the printed copies of the books in his possession.[14]

The entire Telugu literary establishment headed by Veeresalingam lobbied against Nagarathnamma's work with the Government. Eventually, on 27 September 1911, the British government formally issued a memorandum to the Commissioner of Police stating that it had been decided, "that all copies of the book *Radhika Santhvanamu* should be destroyed as objectionable passages are found on nearly every page of that work."[15]

Sriram (2007) mentions that the publisher, however, continued to distribute copies without waiting for the government response until 1927, when a complete ban was imposed through 1947 (52).

This episode underscores the popular public discourse and sentiment that raged across South India around the same time that the gramophone made its entry into the cultural scene. Hence, despite these social inhibitions, the fact that The Gramophone Company sought the participation of courtesans, such as Nagarathnamma who were looked down upon in society, was in itself noteworthy.

Sriram (2007) describes how after this episode, from a *devadasi* Nagarathnamma refashioned herself completely into a saintly figure, contributing to the construction of the *Samadhi* or resting place of saint composer Thyagaraja. As mentioned earlier, her statue in a reverential pose stands to this day at the *Samadhi* in Thiruvaiyaru in present-day Tamil Nadu.

The entire backlash from the social censoring and cleansing movements and Bangalore Nagarathnamma's own reinvention of her *devadasi* identity perhaps also seemed to impact the kind of recordings she made thereafter for The Gramophone Company. She eschewed the erotic compositions such as *padams* and *javalis* and stuck to devotional music only. She did not record prolifically, but her discs sold for many decades after she stopped recording, and it was largely the devotional recordings that were the source of brisk business. This was in line with the prevalent social situation in South India at that time. In the process, the few *padams* and *javalis* that were recorded in the early gramophone recording expeditions disappeared gradually from her repertoire, as they did from the repertoire of other *devadasi* singers of the time.

Hounding the courtesan

Innumerable cases, such as that of Nagarathnamma, of legal hounding of *tawaifs* and *devadasis* are reported from the 1910s through the 1940s. Jafa (1998) mentions that in 1939 the *deredar tawaifs* of Delhi who were under their *chaudhrayan* or matron, Mumtaz Jaan, were asked to move out from their *kothas* that were located in the Chawri Bazar area of the city because the municipality had planned a locality for "respectable families" in Chawri Bazar. The new area demarcated for them was on Garstin Bastion Road (63).

Speaking about this episode in my interview with him, the senior musician *Ustad* Sabri Khan, who knew Mumtaz Jaan personally, mentions:

> Mumtaz who was the *chaudhrayan* of the *tawaif* community in Delhi was a brave lady. She and the other *tawaifs* were not the ones to give up easily. Mumtaz took the local municipality to court with a lawyer Jamna Das fighting their case. But in the end the *tawaifs* lost the case and were forcibly evicted from a locality in which they had lived in for centuries.[16]

Notably, Mumtaz Jaan of Delhi also recorded prolifically for The Gramophone Company in the early expeditions.

Although the British government had decided to invite the renowned Gauhar Jaan to the Imperial Durbar to sing in the presence of Emperor George V in 1911, by which time her gramophone records had already made her a nationwide celebrity, there were several instances where even a celebrity such as her struggled for social recognition and sanction from the moral police. Sampath (2010) mentions one such when the Government of the United Provinces had planned a unique exhibition, the first of its kind, at Allahabad in 1910–11. Several leading citizens of the city were also involved in its preparation. The three-month long exhibition, which would showcase arts and crafts, agricultural produce, industrial equipment, entertainment shows, and amusement parks, was intended to create a veritable paradise on earth and to be the show of the century. An obvious choice for the entertainment section of the event was Gauhar Jaan of Calcutta. She was to be felicitated with a gold medal at this concert.

As news of her inclusion trickled out, widespread protests in the form of letters to the editors of various newspapers were made for weeks on end. The objection was against the government's decision to invite a *tawaif* to perform at a public function; thereby in a way legitimising their status in society. It was argued that the inclusion of a *tawaif* would be a bad influence on society and would corrupt the youth. The conservative section of the city that included both Hindus and Muslims wrote bitter letters condemning this decision.

A look at some of the newspapers of the times shows the intensity of this disapproval. The *Saddharma Pracharak* of 28 December 1910 from Bijnor remarked that, "the sanctity of the exhibition would be defiled by the intemperate use of wine within its walls and the music and dance of the nautch girl of Calcutta."[17] The editor deplored the fact that "the convenors of the Exhibition had included the performance of the "dancing girl" Gauhar Jaan merely as a crowd-pulling stunt and to make up for the loss they had incurred due to their mismanagement."[18] He expressed surprise that while "the students of the Muir Central college and Hindu Boarding House were encouraged to witness her performance at a reduced fee, they had to apply to the principal of the college for permission to attend Arya Samaj meetings."[19] The editor thundered that this only reflected the skewed priorities of the government and urged eminent people such as Pt Madan Mohan Malviya (Congress leader, educationist and social reformer) to help save the situation.

The *Fitna* of Gorakhpur dated 8 January 1911 protested the inclusion of a *tawaif's* performance in a public event of this magnitude and remarked that if "entertainment and money-making was the only aim of the Exhibition, the Committee should have allowed twenty prostitutes instead of one to perform at the venue."[20]

The renowned newspaper of Allahabad, the *Leader* dated 21 January 1911 contains a lengthy letter from one Satish Chandra Banerji in which he expresses his disapproval of the Exhibition Committee's decision to present Gauhar Jaan with a gold medal.[21] Barely a week later, on 27 January 1911, the *Musafir* of Agra took exception to Gauhar Jaan's presenting a concert and receiving a gold medal, and also to the inclusion of Acchanbai of Rampur, who was to sing at the same venue. It asked the people of Allahabad not to take this lightly and protest against such "immoral" acts.[22]

The *Abhyudaya* of Allahabad of 9 February 1911 published a translation of articles in the *Prabasi* (Calcutta) regarding the inclusion of Indian and European music in the United Provinces Exhibition and remarked that "although political dependence was inevitable in the prevalent circumstances of the country, still people should try and cultivate independence in the arts."[23] In the *Hindustani* of Lucknow dated 20 February 1911 a writer protested against Gauhar Jaan's singing and dancing at the event and remarked that its "effects on the social and moral progress of the people of the Provinces will be very injurious."[24] Continuing the tirade, the writer remarked that "European officers should discourage nautch parties which are given in their honour and they should try and assist the people in introducing social reforms."[25]

However, despite this concerted campaign, the concert of Gauhar Jaan was held as scheduled. The protests could do nothing to undermine her popularity. Her concert was a huge success. It drew one of the largest crowds and proved to be the most profitable investment of the whole exhibition. The already highly priced tickets were sold for three or four times the original price and were fully sold out in no time, leaving thousands disappointed. On the day of the concert there was a stampede at the venue, and the police had to be called in to control the crowds. Gauhar's popularity had not diminished despite the tirades against her in the newspapers across the state.

Of course, the exhibition was a matter of discussion until almost the end of 1911 with one disparaging comment or another about its organisation appearing in the newspapers of the times. The focus slowly shifted away from Gauhar's inclusion to the colossal waste of money at the exhibition by the government.

But what is noteworthy was that even an artist such as Gauhar Jaan, who had already made her triumphant "entry" into "respectable families" through the agency of the gramophone records that were the country's best-sellers, was not to be tolerated to be "seen" performing in public. Just the voice – without the female body – was acceptable; not her live performance that would show her to her audience and thereby "morally corrupt" them.

The Reform Movements

Soneji (2012) postulates that the issue of courtesan reform was embedded in the larger public debates centered on women and sexuality in colonial India. The reform project sought to "detach modern India from the archaic and patriarchal symbol of temple dedication by creating a new paradigm of citizenship" (114) for these women. In South India many women with links to the *devadasi* community, such as Dr. Muthulakshmi Reddy, Yamini Purnatilakam, and Muvalur Ramamritammal, spearheaded some of these reform movements. The promise that was held out to the women was one of respectability in an emergent nation. However, this respectability never materialised because the movement itself was hijacked by men (115). Soneji (2012) rightly describes the movement as "men's reform of women cloaked as reform for women that enabled the unusually high prominence of men... in the official mechanisms of the state" (115).

Soneji (2012) mentions that Muthulakshmi Reddy continued the foundational work, on *devadasi* reform, of Viresalingam and Venkataratnam in the Madras Presidency. Notably, she came from a *devadasi* background herself. Despite this background, she became the first female medical graduate in the country and obtained her degree from Madras Medical College in 1912. Two years later, she married Dr T. Sundara Reddy whose family was associated with the Justice Party, a political party in Madras Presidency. She also became the first female Indian legislator before Indian Independence and an important member of the All India Women's Conference. She took up several issues related to gender justice, women's sexuality, their rights and also the abolition of the *devadasi* practice. She undertook a long and arduous intervention in the Madras Legislative Assembly to abolish the *devadasi* system: something that took almost three decades to materialise (120–122).

On 4 November 1927, Muthulakshmi recommended "the Government to undertake legislation to put a stop to the practice of dedication of young girls and young women to Hindu temples for immoral purposes."[26] The British Government, which had been reticent so far saw the growing social mood against the performing women and accepted her suggestion. The *devadasis* immediately took to organising protests against Reddy. Many of them, such as Nagarathnamma, being educated women, also used the press to present their viewpoint through articles and open letters.

In 1930 Reddy's resolution was drafted as a bill entitled "A Bill to Prevent the Dedication of Women to Hindu Temples," which was placed before the

Legislative Council in 1930. However, it took seventeen years for the bill to become an act, passed by independent India and was called The Madras *Devadasi* (Prevention of Dedication) Act of 1947. As Soneji (2012) states that in both her interventions, Reddy actively championed "the enfranchisement of *devadasi* lands (known as *inaams* and *maaniyams*) in the names of women" (112) as rightful property holders and to liberate them from the obligations of dancing, singing, and other tasks to lay claim over this land. This was, however, something that was completely sidelined and ignored as the movement progressed.[27]

The newspapers of the times are replete with letters to the editor and opinion columns of people taking favourable and dissonant stands on the issue of the abolition of the *devadasi* tradition.

Muthulakshmi Reddy made regular interventions in the press to create public opinion in favour of a ban on performing women. In the newspaper *The Hindu*, dated 3 July 1928,[28] she wrote that it was impossible to even imagine the plight of young girls who are trained from their infancy with "the full knowledge and consent of our society that on attaining their womanhood they may administer to the vile and baser passions of the other sex. Could anyone picture to himself or herself a worse perversion of the human mind or an act more inhuman and unjust?" She stated with horror the anecdote of two girls, aged 10 and 9, who were already dedicated to a temple and "who were too young and innocent to understand the real significance of '*Pottu*' tying and the horrors of a prostitute's life." She mentioned that quite regrettably the women in several *zamindar* (landed gentry) families bought children from poor families by paying a heavy price for them just for their recreation and once they grew up they would dedicate them to temples and make these girls available for the pleasure of their male relatives. Muthulakshmi recommended that following the example of the League of Nations, the Madras Presidency too must appoint a committee of experts to investigate the social evils of trafficking women and children and create a vigorous propaganda to educate both the *devadasis* and the ignorant public against this practice; stop using the shield of religion and tradition to perpetuate the practice, and empower the police to take stricter action against defaulters.

Interestingly, several men of the upper castes opposed the anti-*devadasi* stance of reformers such as Muthulakshmi with the argument that it would eventually lead to a death of the arts if women from respectable families were not brought into the field soon.

One such instance is that of the artist and critic E. Krishna Aiyar writing to the same newspaper *The Hindu*, in his letter to the Editor dated 7 December 1932, on what he termed as practical aspects of art and social reform.[29] Aiyar maintained that while he agreed with Muthulakshmi Reddy's proposition to curb the social menace of dedication of young and innocent girls as *devadasis* and their subsequent exploitation by the elite and upper caste men, he warned that in "a conscious or unconscious over-emphasis merely on the social reform aspect of the matter, the arts themselves are made to be mistaken for the medium by which they are represented." He calls the 50-year struggle that Muthulakshmi said she had put into abolishing nautch parties as a "tragedy in success" because in that time span, three generations of women musicians and dancers belonging to the so-called respectable backgrounds could have been produced, but there is no such evidence of respectable women artists. He also mentions that people, such as himself, made several efforts to have musical education introduced at school and college levels. But, terming that programme a failure due to the lukewarm response from women and girls of respectable families, Aiyar rhetorically asks "whether Mrs. Muthulakshmi Reddi and her Women's Association have moved their little finger to prevent that tragedy?" He bemoans a complete absence of women in the field of arts, be it dance, music, or the nascent film industry, which could have benefited with these *devadasi* girls trained in the arts. In his letter, Aiyar raised several pertinent questions to the reform zeal of Muthlakshmi:

> Should the art be penalized for a defect of society? Cannot social reform take the shape of making girls become regular wives and family women by giving up prostitution and at the same time cultivate the art? Is it really the arts that lead them to concubinage? If that is so, how is the learned Doctor going to solve the general problem of the relation of art and morality, even when respectable classes take to it, according to her wish.[30]

The arts, Aiyar opined, needed to thrive somewhere and cannot do so in a vacuum, in the wake of the proposed abolition of a whole generation of performing women, before it could be ascertained whether this abolition would be replaced with a new set of women artists from respectable families. The absence of such a mechanism could lead to the death of the arts due to lack of practitioners, according to Aiyar. In conclusion, Aiyar summarises his arguments:

> It is easy to destroy a culture, that is a legacy of ages; but not so to build it up. If India lives today and can hold up her head proudly even in these degenerate days, it is more on account of her culture and art than by her kings, ministers, or legislators. The legacy of the art, hallowed by the names of Gods and Royal ladies, is too precious a treasure to be destroyed or dimmed by the confusion of purpose and method of over-enthusiastic reformers with no proper perspective of Indian life and its amenities.[31]

In her spirited reply to Aiyar's letter, in *The Hindu* dated 10 December 1932,[32] Dr. Reddy wrote back saying Aiyar had confusedly mixed health and social purity activities with those of social reform and that saving young girls from a life of infamy was not social reform but "a universally recognized elementary code of morality that all creeds and all nations have accepted," which is why the League of Nations too was deeply concerned about illegal and immoral trafficking in women and children. She argued that no art, however great and lofty, could be cultivated or encouraged at the expense of these fundamental universal principles of justice to all human beings. She reminded Aiyar that the voices for change were coming from within the community of the *devadasis* themselves and these were not external reforms that were planted by outsiders. Pointing to a dangerous trend, she said girls who learnt music or dance, even from the *devadasi* community, were not able to get married because society saw the learning and practice of the art as being inseparable from a life of prostitution. This scenario could change only when art lovers and enlightened individuals, such as Aiyar "firmly set their faces against disreputable women-performers, so that women of culture may take their place, learn and cultivate the art and restore it to its high status." She strongly dismissed his fears of the arts dying out and maintained that music was becoming a very popular subject in schools, and the sole credit for that fact should go to the work of women's associations and women's conferences. Muthulakshmi concluded her defence saying:

> The duty of all lovers of art is to help the work of social purity by encouraging the cultivation and the practice of the art by the establishment of a school of music and dance by attracting women of culture and character to the noble profession with special scholarships, in the same way as women have been attracted to the profession of medicine, teaching and nursing, and as the Indian School of Medicine has been established to keep alive, the Ayurvedic and the Unani systems of medicine.[33]

While all these social debates and legal actions framed the context in which music was being produced and consumed, on their part, many of the *devadasis* were baffled by the arguments posed on either side without ever taking them into confidence about the matter and grouped themselves under several "*Devadasi* Associations." Soneji (2012) mentions that 25 of them met in Cheyyur, outside Madras, to unanimously pass a resolution to "severely oppose" Reddy's resolution and held that "the ancient honorable religious practice of tying *pottu* in the temples is not related whatsoever to the mean practice of prostitution. Hence this meeting requests our benevolent Government not to appeal any bill that will put an end to our ancient traditional rights." Other meetings were held at places such as Kanchipuram, Madhurantakam, Tiruchendur, and Tirunelveli (125).

The Secretary of the Madras *Devadasi* Association, T. Duraikkannu mentions in a pamphlet of 1927:

> It is certain that the bill to abolish the practice of tying the *pottu* will put an end to the social practices and hereditary rights of our community,

and this has created unending worries for us…it is unbelievable that prostitution can be eliminated by putting an end to the practice of tying the *pottu*. The supporters of this bill can give a lame excuse that a majority of *isai velalars* support this agitation to destroy this practice of tying the *pottu*. *Isai velalars* are none other than the male members of this community, and it is strange that they support this agitation. Let's think about the intention behind this carefully, which is nothing but selfishness. It should be noted that women of this community alone are entitled to inherit entire property and perform funeral rites as well. It is well known that every human being works in his or her selfish interests alone. The men of this community, who are like axes felling their own community, are responsible for this bill. It is clear that they are doing so with the selfish intention of inheriting property.[34]

Several of the women also signed a petition entitled "The Humble Memorial of *Devadasis* of the Madras Presidency" (1928), addressed to Sir C P Ramaswami Iyer, law member in the Government of Madras. Eight members of the Association called *Chennai Uruttirakkanikai Sangham*, which included several prominent *devadasis*, including Bangalore Nagarathnamma, urged the Government not to take such a radical step. They demanded reforms through education, as Soneji (2012) mentions: "Give us education, religious, literary and artistic. Education will dispel ignorance and we will occupy once again the same rank which we held in the national life of the past," (125) they urged. They referenced the ancient Tamil cultural past and the role played by *devadasis* in it, to buttress their claims of being a race that has traditionally been in this profession.[35] Smaller groups such as the Tirukkalukunram *Devadasi* Association and others made similar pleas.[36]

Sharma (2012) mentions similar associations also formed by the *tawaifs*, to counter the anti-nautch campaign. In Banaras, courtesans came together to form a *Tawaif Sabha* or Association and unanimously elected one of the most reputed *tawaifs* of the town, Husna Jaan, as their President (153–155). Music aficionado and record collector of Banaras, Krishna Kumar Rastogi, mentions:

Husna Jaan is supposed to have given an electrifying speech at this congregation. She urged her fellow *tawaifs* to draw inspiration from Joan of Arc and fight for their rights. She reminded them that if they really wanted freedom they must be prepared to wear iron shackles instead of ornaments of gold. She made all of them pledge support to the Independence movement of Mahatma Gandhi, boycott foreign goods, and commence all their performances with patriotic songs. Another famous *tawaif* of Banaras, Vidhyadhari Bai, was called upon to set some of these patriotic songs to tune. In fact, it is said that Vidhyadhari used to include these songs of protest in all her recitals thereafter even in concerts at royal courts, much to the chagrin of the Kings who were subservient to the British! Her performances would be held under police surveillance. Thus, not only were the courtesans concerned about their own freedom, but through the medium of music, they played a very important role in galvanizing public sentiment in favour of the nationalists who were fighting for India's freedom from British rule. It was sad that these nationalists never recognized this effort of these women and instead worked for their abolition.[37]

Rastogi then played a gramophone recording for me of the opening lines of a patriotic song that was one of Vidhyadhari's favourites in her performances, *Chun Chun Ke Phool Le Lo*. He summarised the purport of the song to me thus:

India shall not remain a land of slaves. It will be free, the time has finally come. Who cares if one lives or dies. Getting executed has become child's play for the brave people of India. For our motherland, we, the children, would happily get our heads cut off, but will no longer allow the despotic rulers (the British) to loot this garden.[38]

Soneji (2012) mentions that the 1920s saw the birth of the *isai velalar* class in South India. They were hitherto the teachers of *devadasis*: the *melak-kaarars*, and *nattuvaanars*, *(chinnamelam)* and ritual musicians in temples *(periyamelam)* (112–115). Srinivasan (1985) illustrates how the men who lived or worked as part of the *devadasi* community perpetually felt a deep need to develop a closed patriarchal tradition for themselves within the *chinnamelam*, independent of their illustrious womenfolk (112).

Reddy's 1927 bill, "The Madras Hindu Religious Endowments Act" sought to give hereditary *inaam* lands or gifted lands, the largely tax-free *maanniyam* lands that *devdasis* received from patrons and temples and also inherited from their mothers to be handed to them legitimately without the need for them to perform to be able to continue to maintain a stake upon them. Soneji (2012) describes that many men of the community strongly opposed such a move. They began mobilizing themselves as a major political force that sought to wrest these properties. Successive interventions in the legislative process and their own redefined role in the new politics of the Madras Presidency ensured that they eventually had their way. This class continues to be a dominant force in contemporary politics of the Indian state of Tamil Nadu (115).

The Arts Revival Project

Bakhle (2005), Subramanian (2006), Sampath (2010), and Soneji (2012) argue along similar lines that the arts were perceived to be the best way of creating a shared history and culture, a sense of identity, and self-respect for an emerging free nation. The first four decades of the twentieth century also being the time of the freedom struggle in India against British imperial rule, created this sense that nationalism and identity were important. India's ancient civilisational heritage and culture had to be utilised to pave the way for a present and future where tradition and modernity co-existed peacefully and were not in conflict with one another. In this objective, Sampath (2010) argues, the narrative of the courtesan did not fit the objectives of the neo-literate Indians and the reformers who saw the institution of the courtesan as a blemish on their shared cultural past. The ancient and sacred arts of music and dance were seen as being degenerative in the hands of these supposedly immoral women who were willing to even sell these arts to recording companies to make money. Liberating the arts from these women, sanitising them, and making them accessible to respectable families was an important concern that Krishna Aiyar too referenced in the letter discussed in the preceding section.

As Bakhle (2005) sums up some of the major developments in Indian music in the first few decades of the twentieth century:

> Music went from being an unmarked practice in the eighteenth-century to being marked as classical music in the twentieth. From performing for small audiences in princely courts, musicians moved into the larger cultural public sphere to give ticketed-entry performances in modern auditoriums. Music's content, which ranged from raucous and ribald to devotional, was rewritten into respectable fare. Music was viewed as one type of entertainment among many others in princely courts, but by the twentieth-century, it had become a high art form that occupied pride of place in the national imagination. While its upper-level pedagogy remained dominated by hereditary musicians, it became possible even for respectable middle-class Hindu housewives to imagine themselves as performers. Last but not least, a modern history was authored for music. The authors of this history aimed to restore to music its ancient origins and address colonial denigrations of it as native caterwauling. (4)

Sampath (2010) writes that between 1920 and 1940 many dancers, such as the legendary ballerina Anna Pavlova from Russia and Ruth St Dennis and Ted Shawn from America, contributed to creating a new and modern structure for Indian dance based on sanitised themes. They actively worked with Indian pioneers in the field such as Rabindranath Tagore, Uday Shankar, Madame Menaka, Krishna Aiyar, and Rukmini Devi Arundale. The nautch dance of the *tawaif* and the *sadir* dance of the *devadasi* were recast and recreated into the modern Indian classical dances of *Kathak* and *Bharatanatyam*, respectively. While they retained elements of the ancient traditions, they were suitably adapted to create a new and modern idiom suited to the current times and prevalent socio-political conditions. Ironically, the art of the *tawaif* and *devadasi* was rescued and reinvented, but the *tawaif* and *devadasi* themselves were destroyed (188–189).

The Hindustani Music Renaissance

Bakhle (2005) mentions that Hindustani musical reform was spearheaded by two of the most influential modern musicologists of India—*Pandit* Vishnu Narayan Bhatkhande (1860–1936) and *Pandit* Vishnu Digambar Paluskar (1872–1931). Both were concerned that the traditional music of the country had fallen into the hands of illiterate Muslim *Ustads* or maestros of various *gharanas* (musical families literally differentiated by no major demarcation) and the immoral *tawaifs*. The *gharanas* were disorderly and, more importantly, inaccessible to the public as they offered limited entry to students other than the men in the *Ustad*'s family. Neither was there any public area for informed discussions and debates on musicology. *Gharana* musicians had to adapt to this new drive for music's modernisation, and this created a conflict between them and the nationalists. Bakhle (2005) writes that while secular musicologists such as Bhatkhande envisioned Indian classical music as a "new, modern, national and academic art that would stay away from religion," Paluskar spoke more of "sacralized *bhakti*/devotionalism" (7). Bhatkhande tried, according to Bakhle (2005), to "classify, categorize and classicize music, whereas Paluskar worked to cleanse and sacralize it. Both men tried to bypass the authorial role played by the *Ustads* and together they both posed a serious challenge to *gharana* musicians"(8). Both these schools of thought, however, converged in their assessment that "music itself was on the verge of extinction, either because it had lapsed into degeneracy or because it had failed to become adequately modern" (8).

The approach to a recovery of music from this perceived morass for both men was, as Bakhle (2005) postulates, the creation of a connected and shared musical history, a systematised and orderly pedagogy and bestowing respectability to the art. For the creation of this music history that connected the ancient textual prescriptions and theories to contemporary practice there was the necessity for the creation of musical literature and performance norms, which being in the hands of the *gharanas*, was kept secretive and inaccessible. It was more anecdotal and family memory than a textual archive.

Bhatkhande was of the firm belief that the original and pristine music of India was Hindu by character. Bhatkhande (1917) wrote:

The rise of the Muslim power in North India marked the date of the decline of all arts and sciences purely Hindu. The conquerors, we can easily understand, were no lovers or patrons of learning. During those unsettled times the progress of the study of the science or theory of music was bound to decline and, as a matter of fact, did decline. The practice, however, continued with more or less success until the time of

Mahomed Shah, one of the successors of Aurangzeb... The Mahomedan rulers naturally patronized at their courts their own co-religionists as musicians, who knew their tastes much better, and who by pandering to the tastes of their masters commenced to take all sorts of liberties with the orthodox Sanskrit melodies. We are told that many of the first class Hindu *Pandits* of those times were scared away or ceased in course of time to take the same interest in their science of music as they did formerly. I do not think anybody will be able to deny that the majority of the musicians at the court of even such a very tolerant monarch like Akbar were *Mussalmans*. (17–18)

Bhatkhande presented his above hypothesis on 20 March 1916 at the First All-India Music Conference, which was held under the patronage of the King of Baroda, Sayajirao Gaekwad III, in the Hall of Baroda College. The Conference was attended by some of the greatest names in the world of Indian classical music, court musicians, and music scholars. Bakhle describes that by then Bhatkhande had travelled across India extensively to study various forms of Indian classical music and musicology, interviewed several contemporary musicians and musicologists, recorded their views on phonographs, and had come out with his four-volume magnum opus *Hindustani Sangeet Paddhati*. This was a distillation of the musicological knowledge of several centuries available to him at that time in the form of theoretical treatises: Pundarika Vitthala's *Sadragachandrodaya* (c.1560–70), Somanatha's *Ragavibodha* (1609), Ahobala's *Sangitaparijata* (c.1665), Lochana Kavi's *Ragatarangini* (c.1665), and Muhammad Reza Khan's *Usul-al-Naghmat-i-Asafi*.

Bhatkhande dedicated his life to systematising the prevailing forms of Hindustani music and building on that system a coordinated theory and practice of music. Hindustani ragas were classified into ten musical scales called *thaats* by Bhatkhande. He also created a time cycle for music where particular ragas were presented only at certain time of the day and named as morning ragas, afternoon ragas, evening ragas, night ragas, and so on.

As Bakhle (2005) notes:

> For Bhatkhande, classicization meant at least two things: system, order, discipline, and theory, on the one hand, and antiquity of national origin, on the other...the first set of elements he could not find in contemporary practice, and he had toured the country in search of them. He found confusion, not order, and an emphasis on spontaneity rather than disciplined performance. So he set out to impose order on contemporary music. (124)

Bakhle (2005) notes that by 1928, at the age of 68, Bhatkhande had authored 18 works on Indian music, which included compilations, textbooks, treatises, and booklets. Six volumes titled *Hindustani Sangeet Kramik Pustak Maalika* were compiled by Bhatkhande to serve as textbooks on musical theory, notation, and compositions. This made music an academic subject that children of "respectable" households could learn without the taboo of the presence of a *tawaif* or the reluctance of a *gharana ustad* to teach an outsider. These volumes had nearly 1800 compositions, which Bhatkhande collected from hereditary musicians during his travels (117).

Bhatkhande was also an institution builder and established several music schools and colleges where Hindustani music could be taught systematically. He started All India Music Conferences to create a platform for Hindustani and Carnatic musicians to meet and discuss musical theories. He also spent considerable time rewriting several compositions and expunging them of their original erotic content. Music had to be freed from the influence and memory of the *tawaif* for it to be widely accepted.

The musical instrument that bore the brunt of this socio-cultural transition in Indian music was the *sarangi*, a stringed instrument that is played with a bow like a violin. Sampath (2010) writes that *sarangi* players came from the lowest rung of the socio-economic pyramid of Hindustani musical society in terms of both prestige and pedigree and were looked down upon as pimps. They lived off *tawaifs* and sometimes stayed at the *kotha* (salon) and even fathered the illegitimate children of the *tawaifs* (161).

Senior musician and *sarangi* player *Ustad* Sabri Khan mentioned:

> The *sarangi* ustads were repositories of great musical knowledge and imparted training to several *tawaifs*, corrected them when they performed or even prompted them when they forgot the lyrics of a song. Many *tawaifs* had two *sarangi* players on either side of them. The unwritten law was that the one on the right was the more senior and respected one while the other was the junior. Even during gramophone recording sessions, it would be the *sarangi* and *tabla* players who would keep time and inform the singer to wind up before the recording ends.[39]

Neuman (1980) underscores this transition for the *sarangi* and its player when he quotes *Ustad* V.H. Khan:

> There is one thing about the musical sittings, which I still remember. *Sarangi* players were not allowed to take *tanpura* and sing…in one such *mehfil* (concert) a *sarangi* player who sang very well started singing in the *mehfil*. The *sabhapati* (music event organizer or sponsor) asked him to stop playing the *sarangi* and then only would he be allowed to sing in all the *mehfils*. So he completely stopped playing *sarangi* and started singing. After that he was praised by good vocalists and became famous. By mentioning this I mean to say that in those days music was the purest and highest form of education and it was necessary to respect it. (102)

The association of the *sarangi* with the *tawaif* and the *kotha* made it "impure" and hence with the abolition of the *tawaif* all musical remnants related to her had to be excised too. These could be compositions or genres associated with her or instruments that reminded audiences of the *tawaif.* The Delhi *gharana* is usually underrated because its founder *Ustad* Mamman Khan was a *sarangi* player and traced his lineage to several other *sarangi* players. A published pamphlet and excerpts of the diary maintained by Mamman Khan's son Chand Khan was shared with me during an interview with *Ustad* Iqbal Ahmed Khan, Chand Khan's grandson who calls himself the *Khalifa* (or Head) of the Delhi *Gharana.* Reading out excerpts from the diary, Iqbal Khan told me in my interview with him:

> My grandfather (Chand Khan) was bitter about the scorn heaped on the *gharana* for its association with the *sarangi.* He has claimed here (in the diary) that it is the oldest instrument and is capable of magical music in the hands of a fine master. He has mentioned that his father Mamman Khan and his cousin Bundu Khan were such stalwart musicians gifted with great virtuosity. The women artists of Delhi who recorded on the gramophone such as Mumtaz Jaan Choudhrayan and Kali Jaan were disciples of Mamman Khan, who also accompanied Gauhar Jaan in concerts.[40]

Sampath (2010) writes that the stigmatisation of the *sarangi* led to its replacement in concerts and recordings with the stiff-reeded Western harmonium as a melodic accompaniment for Hindustani vocal music (58). Bhaiya Sahib Ganapatrao, an eminent musician who was also the son of the king of Gwalior and his courtesan, was the man who is credited with adapting this Western instrument to Hindustani music.

Ustad Sabri Khan mentions:

> Proponents of the harmonium say that its fixed tuning makes it very convenient to maintain the same key throughout a performance. But that is hardly an advantage when its tempered scale is fundamentally out of tune with Indian scales. Furthermore, its inability to handle certain slides makes it difficult to perform many ragas on it. It is obvious that when the melodic accompaniment shifts from a stringed instrument that mirrors the human voice so closely (like the *sarangi*) to a reed instrument like the harmonium that could not produce several of the glides on notes (*meend*) that characterize Indian classical music, there is a shift in aesthetics.[41]

These were side effects of the anti-nautch movement and the arts revival project.

The mission of Bhatkhande's contemporary and another significant musicologist-scholar Vishnu Digambar Paluskar (1872–1931) was threefold.

Bakhle (2005) states that the first objective of Paluskar was to raise the status of music and musicians by de-linking the association with entertainment and linking it instead to devotional music highlighting religious themes. The second mission was to establish a number of institutions for the spread of musical education around the country and also sending his students to different parts of India as evangelists to spread this new pedagogy. Lastly, and perhaps, most importantly, "Paluskar reinstated a modern version of a bhakti-based, but Brahminized, understanding of the *guru-shishya parampara*" (137–138). He established the first modern school of Hindustani music known as the Gandharva Mahavidyalaya as early as 1901 in Lahore, and the school later shifted to Bombay.

Despite the difference in their approach to music modernisation, their commonality also hinged on contempt for the "debased" *tawaif* and how she should be ejected from the musical ecosystem. That these revival projects were contemporaneous to social movements like the anti-nautch movement that sought to abolish performing women made matters worse for the courtesan, leading to her gradual fading away from the collective musical and national consciousness despite her chivalrous attempts at embracing technology in the form of gramophone recording.

The Carnatic Music Renaissance

In South India, too, the urge for modernisation in music started gathering momentum. Sampath (2012) writes that there was a growth spurt in the number of *sabhas* that were established in various parts of South India. The *sabhas* were concert halls or public salons, which were also associations where music could be enjoyed as a shared communal and cultural experience (118). Raghavan (1958) likens *sabhas* to "earlier gatherings of old Madras, called *sadas*, convened by rich patrons at fixed intervals or whenever there was a happy event" (97).

Sampath (2012) elaborates that by 1924, musicians of the South under the leadership of renowned musicologist, scholar, and court musician of Mysore and Travancore princely states, Harikesanallur Mutthaiah Bhagavathar, put forth demands to the Madras University that music should be included in the curriculum along with other subjects on offer. The clamour for relocating the teaching and learning of the ancient art form of Indian classical music in modern institutional spaces was thus increasing (118).

In December 1927, the Congress Party held its annual session in Madras, and on the sidelines a weeklong Music Conference was organised. At the end a resolution was passed, stressing the need for establishment of an Academy of Music in Madras. Sampath (2012) mentions that a constitution was drafted, an advisory panel of experts was nominated to advise on technical matters related to music, its dissemination, and education, to arbitrate on theoretical matters of music and also to set performance standards. (119).

The Journal of the Madras Music Academy (1930) quotes its first President Dr. U Rama Rau, a leading physician and music aficionado of Madras, about the aims of the Academy as being the following:

- To arrange for exposition of the art by competent artists and to encourage new and deserving talent.
- To provide facilities for widespread instruction in music on proper lines by establishing a College of music and otherwise.
- To promote the study and practice of music by instituting competitions and scholarships and awarding prizes.
- To form and maintain a music library and museum.
- To collect and preserve compositions in music.
- To organize music conferences.
- To construct a music hall. (79–80)

The Madras Music Academy set in motion a vibrant debate among all its stakeholders, artists and connoisseurs alike, of what constituted the aesthetic and pure when it came to performance. In its 1935 journal it states that the Academy was "not a mere music *sabha* but aimed at purifying Indian music, setting standards, educating the audience and training teachers who would ensure that the 'classicism' was maintained" (161). It was postulated that training women of respectable families would wean the men away from the *devadasis*.

The genres that *devadasis* popularised, such as the erotic *padams* and *javalis*, had to be exorcised from performance repertoire, and in their place devotional and spiritual songs and themes became the mainstay in classical Carnatic music. The gramophone discographies from as early as the 1910s show a gradual, yet marked, decline in the number of erotic *padams* and *javalis* recorded even by the *devadasis*.

An investigation of the Carnatic music discographies, from Kinnear (1994), of the 1904–05 recording expedition and the 1906–07 recording expedition of The Gramophone Company illustrates this point (Table 5.1).[42]

Almost 48% of the recordings were of women, split mainly between five *devadasi* artists: Dhanakoti of Kanchipuram, Salem Papa, Salem Godavari, Salem Ammakannu and Bangalore Nagarathnamma.

A split of the artists and the composers and genres they recorded are shown in Table 5.2.

Table 5.1 Number of Carnatic recordings in the 1904–1905 expedition of the Gramophone Company and the number of women who recorded

1904 expedition	7-inch	10-inch	12-inch	Total
Number of Carnatic recordings	96	167	60	**323**
Number of Women recordings	44	73	37	**154**

Table 5.2 Number of recordings per artist and their split across the Trinity (Thyagaraja, Dikshitar, and Shyama Shastri), other classical composers, devotionals, and the erotic *padams* and *javalis*

Artist vs. composer/genres	Thyagaraja	Shyama Shastri	Muthuswami Dikshitar	Other classical composers	Padams and javalis	Devotional
Dhanakoti of Kanchipuram	1	4	2	4	9	
Salem Papa	10		3	4	5	
Salem Godavari	12	2	2	7	23	4
Salem Ammakannu	2		1		18	3
Bangalore Nagarathnamma	5	1		3	7	2
	19%	4%	6%	11%	41%	5%

The recordings show a wide range of the repertoire of the *devadasi* singers. The "other classical composers" include eminent composers such as Patnam Subrahmanya Iyer, Bhadrachala Ramadas, Karur Dakshinamurthy, Subbaraya Shastri, Veena Kuppaiyer, Gopalakrishna Bharati, and Mysore Sadashiva Rao. This shows a pedagogical underpinning steeped in classicism. Most of the *devadasis* seem to follow the disciple lineage or *shishya* tradition of Thyagaraja, followed by Dikshitar and lastly of Shyama Shastri. But what is striking is that 41% of the recordings are of the erotic *padams* and *javalis* that identified the *devadasi*. This is significant considering it was almost contemporaneous with the moral brigade's proscription of Bangalore Nagarathnamma in the *Radhika Santhvanamu* episode, detailed earlier in this chapter.

During the 1905–1906 expedition, the following number of recordings was made of Carnatic music; see Table 5.3.

From 48%, there was an increase to 63% of the recorded music being of the *devadasi* singers divided among just four of them. Salem Godavari was the only one repeated from the first expedition while Vadammal, Bhavani of Tiruvadaimaradur and Sivakalundo of Madras were the new additions (Table 5.4).

Despite the majority of the recordings (63%) being that of the *devadasis*, the percentage of *padams* and *javalis* shows a fall from 41% to 25%. At the same time, there is an increase in the devotional repertoire from 5% to

Table 5.3 Number of Carnatic recordings in the 1905–1906 expedition of the Gramophone Company and the number of women who recorded

1905 expedition	10-inch	12-inch	Total
Number of Carnatic recordings	112	52	**164**
Number of Women recordings	70	33	**103**

Table 5.4 Number of recordings per artist and their split across the Trinity (Thyagaraja, Dikshitar and Shyama Shastri), other classical composers, devotionals and the erotic *padams* and *javalis*

Artist vs composer/ genres	Thyagaraja	Shyama Shastri	Muthuswami Dikshitar	Other classical composers	Padams and javalis	Devotional	Other forms
Vadammal	2			2			
Salem Godavari	11	7	3	3	10	5	3
Bhavani of Tiruvadaimaradur	10		1		4	4	2
Sivakalundo of Madras		1		1	6	3	2
	29%	10%	5%	8%	25%	15%	9%

15% and the compositions of Thyagaraja from 19% to 29% between the two recording expeditions. Interestingly, a lot of recordings (not accounted here) are of classical raga *aalaapanas* and less of compositions of other classical composers. Several new forms too were recorded in this expedition, such as *Varnams* and *Thillanas* and also a Hindustani music genre of the *Ghazal*.

By the time of the next expedition, we see an almost complete disappearance of *padams* and *javalis*, which account for just about 4% of the total recorded repertoire. This trend clearly shows a shift in musical choices that the market was demanding and to which the artist and The Gramophone Company had to cater to.

The entire nationalistic project of defining what "pure classical" meant was also related to how not to sound like the *devadasi*. An aesthetic quite different from that of the *devadasi*, as heard on gramophone records, was sought to be created. In the next chapter, related to musical analysis, we will note that gramophone recordings of the 1930s are distinctly different from those of the early recordings of the *devadasis*. The structure and presentation of ragas and compositions in Carnatic music display a visible aesthetic and structural shift.

These changes in performance repertoire, style and recording discographies were influenced by the social conditions and the construction of a new and modern aesthetic that could be termed as "pure" and "classical". The gramophone records played an indirect role in this transition of musical standards. On the one hand, the early recordings, particularly of the *devadasis*, demonstrated what music should not sound like in this new paradigm; and on the other, the newly created aesthetic was disseminated and popularised through the later recordings.

All these social movements and debates eventually sounded a death-knell for the entire class of performing women. Sampath (2010) quotes a popular proverb of the times that describes their plight most aptly: "The dancing girl was formerly fed with good food in the temple; now she turns somersaults for a beggar's rice" (187). With no plans for the rehabilitation of these "fallen" women, these condemned practitioners of an ancient art were to fend for themselves or die in penury or reinvent their art and adapt it to the modern situation. Having no options for an alternate profession, some of them resorted to prostitution, while others reinvented themselves. Many *tawaifs* and devadasis slowly gave up the dance element in their performances and concentrated on music only since it was perceived as a more "pure" art. Even there, there was censorship of what was considered erotic or obscene lyrics and genres. All these changes had their impact on the musical instruments as well. As mentioned, the *sarangi* became synonymous with the decadent *tawaif* tradition. The harmonium gained respectability as a worthy accompaniment and replaced the *sarangi*. The word "Bai" acquired derogatory connotations in the North, and many *tawaifs* gave up the suffix in their names in favour of "Devi" or "Begum" which signified their "respectable" background. While music itself began to enter both a university pedagogical system as a systematised subject that could be taught to both boys and girls of "respectable" families, the custodians of the art form for centuries, the courtesans, were slowly excised from national and musical consciousness completely.

As Nevile (2009) notes poignantly:

> Honoured by royal lovers, rewarded by nawabs and nobles, patronized by the European elite, immortalized by poets and chroniclers, pursued by love-sick gallants, the Indian nautch girl, a symbol of glamour, grace and glory and a queen of performing arts, passed into the pages of history.
>
> (in Sampath 2010: 190)

Notes

1 The archives of *The Hindu* newspaper, Chennai; correspondences of 1880–1900.
2 The archives of *The Hindu* newspaper, Chennai; correspondences of 1880–1900. Full text of Memorandum, see Appendix 1.
3 Viceroy's Private Secretary to the Secretary of the Hindu Reform Association, Madras, 23 September 1893, *The Hindu* Archives
4 Ibid.
5 The *devadasi* performed ritual worship to her anklets, which was called *Gejje Puje*, which marked her entry into the performance world.
6 Muzrai temple was a temple supported, controlled and patronised by the government.
7 Government official in charge of all the state-owned and funded temples.
8 Muzrai Department, Karnataka State Archives, Bangalore documents of the Mysore Kingdom from 1881 to 1947 "Proceedings of His Highness the Maharaja of Mysore" dated 28 Jan 1910, No 1872–9; 08–6.
9 The archives of *The Hindu* newspaper, Chennai; correspondences of 1880–1900.
10 In Hindu mythology, Radha or Radhika is the most important female lover of Lord Krishna.

11 *Ganika* is another synonym for a *devadasi* or dancing and singing girl.
12 See Appendix 1 for full text.
13 Tamil Nadu Archives; notes to GO No 348: Judicial; 4 March 1912, p. 14.
14 Tamil Nadu Archives GO 348; Judicial; 4 March 1912; Enclosure to letter from F Armitage, Commissioner of Police to Chief Secretary, Government of Madras 1911; p. 6
15 Tamil Nadu Archives GO 348; Judicial; 4ᵗʰ March 1912; Official Memorandum No 4370–1: Judicial; 27 September 1911; p. 9.
16 Interview excerpts of author with *Ustad* Sabri Khan.
17 *Saddharma Pracharak* 28 December 1910, National Archives of India, New Delhi.
18 Ibid.
19 Ibid.
20 *Fitna*, 8 January 1911, National Archives of India, New Delhi.
21 *Leader*, 21 January 1911, National Archives of India, New Delhi.
22 *Musafir*, 27 January 1911, National Archives of India, New Delhi.
23 *Abhyudaya*, 9 February 1911, National Archives of India, New Delhi.
24 *Hindustani*, 20 February 1911, National Archives of India, New Delhi.
25 Ibid.
26 The archives of *The Hindu* newspaper, Chennai; correspondences of 1910–1930.
27 For more details, please see 'Legislative Assembly Debates of Madras, 1924–26', Tamil Nadu State Archives, Chennai.
28 The archives of *The Hindu* newspaper, Chennai; correspondences of 1910–1930. Original article by Muthulakshmi Reddy, in full, is found in Appendix 1.
29 The archives of *The Hindu* newspaper, Chennai; correspondences of 1930–1940. Text of complete letter of Krishna Aiyar found in Appendix 1.
30 The archives of *The Hindu* newspaper, Chennai; correspondences of 1930–1940. Text of complete letter of Krishna Aiyar found in Appendix 1.
31 The archives of *The Hindu* newspaper, Chennai; correspondences of 1930–1940. Text of complete letter of Krishna Aiyar found in Appendix 1.
32 The archives of *The Hindu* newspaper, Chennai; correspondences of 1930–1940. Full text of Muthulakshmi Reddy's letter in reply to Krishna Aiyar is in Appendix 1.
33 The archives of *The Hindu* newspaper, Chennai; correspondences of 1930–1940. Full text of Muthulakshmi Reddy's letter in reply to Krishna Aiyar is in Appendix 1.
34 T. Duraikkannu, handbill, dated 1927, the Muthulakshmi Reddi Papers, Nehru Memorial Museum and Library, New Delhi, subject file II (part II), p. 72. Also quoted by Soneji (2012) (124-126)
35 Ibid. pp. 283–287.
36 Ibid. pp. 90–91.
37 Interview excerpts of author with Krishna Kumar Rastogi in Banaras.
38 Ibid.
39 Interview excerpts of author with *Ustad* Sabri Khan.
40 Excerpts of Interview of author with *Ustad* Iqbal Ahmed Khan in Delhi.
41 Excerpts of Interview of author with *Ustad* Sabri Khan in Delhi.
42 Source for data is Kinnear (1994) and validated at the EMI Music Archive, London in its Sales catalogues.

6 ANALYSING THE RECORDINGS

Analysis of Carnatic Music Recordings

Theoretical Background and Stylistic Parameters in Carnatic Music

The Gamakas

Much like modal musics of the world, the identity of ragas in modern Carnatic music is defined by characteristic, note-centric inflexions called *Gamaka*. Every raga in addition to being described by its pitch positions (*swara sthanas*) in relation to the tonic (*Shadja*) is heavily understood within the Carnatic music tradition as a set of melodic behaviours that encompass typical inflexions on certain notes, rules to avoid certain musical gestures, or to feature certain quintessential micro-tonalities in the scale. A simple *gamaka* could be a vibrato, or a quick oscillation between a quartertone or semitone. Sometimes, the range of the oscillatory inflexion can span a whole tone, often implicated in fixed melodic gestures or manoeuvres.

Chelladurai (1991) defines the *gamaka* as a particular shake of the note, which is employed to bring out the distinctive shape of the raga. He terms the *gamaka* as an "indispensable aspect'" of Carnatic music. He quotes ancient treatises such as Bharata's *Natyashastra* (dating c. 500 B.C.E.) and Sharangadeva's *Sangita Ratnakara* (13th century C.E.) to emphasise their importance. *Dashavidha Gamakas*, or ten different types of archetypal inflexions, are prescribed in these ancient treatises: *Arohana, Avarohana, Ahata, Pratiyahata, Sphurita, Tripuscha, Dhalu, Andolita, Kampita*, and *Murchana* (200–202).

The concept of *gamaka* is an established construct in Carnatic music and thus, one of the pivotal parameters to study the impact of recording technology on this music. The presence of the kind of *gamaka*, the phrases that showcase the *gamaka*, the microtonal pitch displacements it produces, the shape of the *gamaka*, the behaviours associated with its usage are well documented in modern Carnatic literature as aesthetic values of the music.[1] Compositions in Carnatic music, curate and reinforce the staggering importance placed on the aesthetic rules of presenting this music and is thus well

DOI: 10.4324/9780367822026-6

documented for comparison before and after the arrival of the gramophone in India.

Improvisation in Carnatic Music: The Aalaapana

Deva (1973) mentions that Indian classical music (both Hindustani and Carnatic) has two broad categories of musical forms: the *anibaddha* (open or unbound) and the *nibaddha* (closed or bound). *Anibaddha* refers to music that is not set within the limitations of a composition like a song. It has no rhythmic structure or defined sectional arrangements (36–38).

Improvisation is the defining feature of Indian classical music. An important component of this improvisatory music is the *Aalaap* (in Hindustani music) or *Aalaapana* (in Carnatic music). *Aalapana* in Carnatic music is unraveled much like a modular middle-eastern *Taqsim* in a particular *Maqam;* at the level of musical motifs and patterns that are concatenated into larger cadences and musical rhetoric.

Deva (1973) defines this as the process where a raga is developed and elaborated slowly, note by note, phrase by phrase with due prominence given to all the emphatic notes, characteristic phrases and graces of the raga. The usual practice is to start with the lower pitches and gradually work up the octave. He explains that a certain set of notes is taken as the base and variations of this theme are improvised in such a way that the raga is slowly unfolded. While there are set patterns in which a raga is delineated step by step from lower to middle to higher registers, touching upon the important notes of that raga and characteristic patterns, the manner in which each artist does this bears an individualistic stamp. How an artist exposes a raga also differs from one concert to another. Thus, within the broad perimeter of the grammar and semantics of the raga, the musician is challenged to imagine newer ways to portray the raga *swaroopa* (or the portrait of the raga) (36–38).

In modern Carnatic music recitals, an *aalapana* can last from anything between five minutes to even forty-five minutes where an artist displays his/her musical virtuosity by weaving interesting patterns and creates the "mood" of a raga.

Composition Structure and Inherent Improvisation in Carnatic Music

Carnatic music has a substantial repertoire of *kritis* (or compositions) composed by several bards and mystic poet-composers (*vaggeyakaras*) of the past. Sambamoorthy (1952) states that passing these on from generation to generation with utmost fidelity to lyrics, pronunciation and an unwritten notation in an oral tradition is an integral part of Carnatic music pedagogy (122). Modern Carnatic practice is quasi notated, to acquire the skeletal compositional structure.

A composition or *kriti* usually has three parts: the opening refrain called the *Pallavi*, the second portion of the composition called *Anupallavi*, and the final bit known as the *Charanam*. Only in the compositions of one of the Trinity of Carnatic music, Mutthuswami Dikshitar (1776–1835), a concluding portion is sung in faster tempo, and is called *Madhyamakala Sahitya*. Each component of the composition allows the artist to make improvisations over phrases of the lyrics, and every component takes ones back to the refrain (*pallavi*) (Figure 6.1).

As depicted in the schema above, the improvisation built into the composition is called *neraval* (or idiomatic improvisation over particular verses of a composition) and *kalpana swarams* (or extempore solfege syllables). In contemporary Carnatic music performance, there is equal emphasis given to the improvisatory portions (*aalaapana*, *neraval* and *kalpana swarams*) and the composition (*kritis*).

Deva (1973) details the process of presentation in a contemporary Carnatic music concert where typically an artist would essay the raga in an

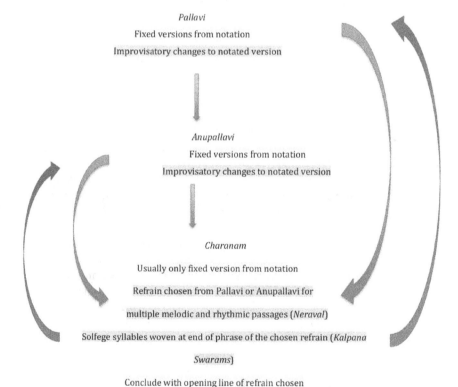

Figure 6.1 Flow of a Carnatic composition with composed and improvisatory sections.

Key: Light grey: Improvide portion. Dark grey: Composed portion.

expansive *aalaapana*, follow this up with a composition in the same raga, pick up one or two lines of the composition and weave multiple melodic and rhythmic patterns (*neraval*) and end with a volley of impromptu solfege syllables in multiple patterns (*kalpana swaram*). This entire exercise takes anything from forty-five minutes to a little over an hour and depends on the scholarship and virtuosity of the musician (42–45).

Other forms of *nibaddha* (closed or bound) music in the Carnatic idiom include *varnams, thillanas, bhajans, padams,* and *javalis*. All of these are pre-composed musical pieces. They generally do not lend themselves to as much improvisation, as a *kriti* does and have been outlined above.

Among the various genres of Carnatic music, the *padams* and *javalis* were the trademark of the *devadasis*. Deva (1973) mentions that the texts and music of *padams* and *javalis* are more lyrical than *kritis*, and they deal with romantic and erotic themes (42). The common themes dealt in *padams* and *javalis* are the pangs of separation or the joys of union of two lovers, misunderstandings that arise between them, uncertainty of anticipation, and the nostalgia of memory of union. *Padams* are allegorical and human love is usually a euphemism or reference to the yearning of the human soul for the Supreme Being. According to Deva (1973), *javalis* are more direct descriptions of human love and considered non-allegorical. As well, *padams* are rendered in a slow tempo while *javalis* are usually sung faster (43).

Observations of Archived Catalogues of Carnatic Music Recordings

As discussed earlier, an analysis of the catalogue of the early South Indian recording expedition of 1904–05 reveals that *padams* and *javalis* constituted 41% of the recorded repertoire. This number fell to 25% by the time of the next recording expedition in 1905–06 and decreased to 4% by the end of the decade. With time, we find a near complete disappearance of the entire repertoire of erotic compositions of *padams* and *javalis*, not only in the catalogues but also from Carnatic music performances.

The recorded *padams* and *javalis* are largely unknown songs and have been recorded by several of these women singers. Table 6.1 lists some of the rare songs archived by this project. Sadly, barring one or two, none of these records is available anywhere for purchase today even in scrap dealer shops or in flea markets.

The disdain for *padams* and *javalis* because of their association with the *devadasi* has been discussed earlier. This contempt is apparent in the observation of noted musicologist Sambamoorthy (1952):

> Mundane love might be the dignified type or of the voluptuous type…there are…*padams* treating of base love and commercialized love. From their very nature these are detestable to read and sing. One really wonders why some responsible composers should have descended to such a low level and prostituted their gifts in composing such compositions. (208–209)

Table 6.1 *Padams* and *javalis* recorded by the women singers in the first decade of the twentieth century

Artist	Title	Raga
Dhanakoti	*Antasthu Marechi*	*Behag*
	Balimini Bilechi	*Kedaram*
	Mohapaahtukari	*Thodi*
	Sankalp Metili	*Kharaharapriya*
	Mohappatukkaari	*Thodi*
	Yinnamundu rani karkandu	*Ragamalika*
Bangalore Nagarathnamma	*Baro Priya*	*Thodi*
	Ekanemanduni Chaliye	*Kambhoji*
	Ponnar Meniyane	*Kamas*
	Matharpirai	*Devagandhari*
Salem Ammakannu	*Yavananudhane Baare*	*Khamas*
	Ekanemandune Chaliye	*Yadukulakambhoji*
	Talaraa Baalama Raa	*Athana*
	Buludu Naa To	*Mukhari*
	Yethulane Vegintune	*Khamas*
	Yetane Vinavinthune	*Shankarabharanam*
	Kopa metikipo chali	*Behag*
	Komali Rao Balagopala	*Saveri*
	Nettru Ratthiri	*Surati*
	Baro baro doreye	*Yamuna Kalyani*
	Sakhi ninna chaturya	*Hindusthani Kapi*
	Ennadimettha	*Thodi*
	Yena Maadali	*Kamas*
Salem Papa	*Samayamide Ramaswamy*	*Behag*
	Samiki Saryeya	*Dhanyasi*
Salem Godavari	*Yerata Guntara*	*Kedaragowla*
	Tapamidene Chappu Kovalan	*Bhushavali*
	Mohamedhi Sahikka	*Khamas*
	Innamen Pichi	*Janjuti*
	Yenna Solven Di	*Nadanamakriya*
	Praana Kaanthane	*Pharazu*
	Yela Ontarigaa	*Punnagavarali*
	Ye matalaadi nee nee matale	*Yadukulakambhoji*
	Sohasulludheera	*Khamas*
	Vanjiyunmel	*Behag*
	Ariyaanai	*Yadukulakambhoji*
	Intiki Vachina va daya raada	*Janjuti*
	Entaro Vaani Manasu	*Bilahari*
	Prana Kaantane	*Pharaz*
	Sohusulladheera	*Kamas*
	Vanjiyunmel	*Behag*
	Ariyaanai	*Yadukulakambodhi*
	Yentati Kulake	*Kalyani*

Source: Catalogues of The Gramophone Company, EMI Archives, London and Kinnear (1994).

About another *padam*, *Payyeda Paijeri* in raga *Nadanamakriya*, Sambamoorthy (1952) states that in this composition "disappointment and frustration are depicted powerfully. It is inauspicious for married girls to learn this *pada(m)* and perform *abhinaya* for it" (211).

Critical Perspectives from Some Key Respondents on Specific Carnatic Music Recordings by the Women Singers

Salem Ammakannu

Two early recordings of Salem Ammakannu, dating back to the 1904–05 expedition of The Gramophone Company were heard and analysed with contemporary musician Jayanthi Kumaresh: *Baro Baro Doraiye*, a *javali* in Kannada, and *Appane Pazhani Appane*, a Tamil devotional. Jayanthi Kumaresh notes:

> I find in this recording that her pitch is pretty stable except for a few cadenzas that she takes up and down. But in view of the lyrical content of a leisurely, erotic *javali*, where the singer is cajoling her lover to come back soon and without whose presence her nights seem scary all alone, the mood is sedate and the pitch, therefore, uniform too. I also notice that the *Kaala pramaanam* (or tempo) of both the renditions is *Madhyama kaala* (or medium tempo). A noticeable feature of her singing is that there are only a few glides in the notes unlike in contemporary Carnatic music. I find *shruti shuddham* (or pitch adherence) in her rendition. A good pronunciation of the language of the *javali* – Kannada, clear voice, well-enumerated *bhrigas*, and lack of too many *sangathis* (or melodic iterations) and complicated *gamakas* seem to mark her singing. The mood she creates in the other devotional song is also appropriate and I find it markedly distinct from the emotion of eroticism that is created so successfully in the *javali*.[2]

Bangalore Nagarathnamma

Bangalore Nagarathnamma has a very limited recorded repertoire on the gramophone as is demonstrated in her discography. According to the EMI Music Archive catalogue and Kinnear (1994) during the 1904–05 expedition she recorded many songs; see Table 6.2.

While the *padams* and *javalis* disappeared from gramophone recordings, they began disappearing from the repertoire of Nagarathnamma too. Possibly, as discussed earlier, after the controversy around the *Radhika Santhvanamu* episode, she eschewed recording erotic compositions and stuck only to devotional music. The main pieces recorded after 1912–15 were Sanskrit devotionals such as *Gacchami Achyuta*, *Srimadgopavadhu*, and *Vyamohaprathamaushadham* which were all in praise of Lord Krishna.

Table 6.2 Recordings of Bangalore Nagarathnamma

Genre	Title	Raga
Kritis	Raghuvamsha	Kadanakutoohala
	Alakalella	Madhyamavati
	Garuda Gamana	Nagaswaravali
	Nee Bhajan Gana	Nayaki
	Nijamarmamulanu	Umabharanam
	Anuradhamu	Kharaharapriya
	Maa Janaki jatta battaga	Kambodhi
	Nitya Kalyani	Ragamalika
Javalis	Dharma dore kuvade	Kalyani
	Hegguve yaako	Ananda Bhairavi
	Tore to yaja netrana	Khamas
	Baaro Priya	Thodi
	Jaanatanamu Nilupane	Hindustani
	Eka nemandhu ni chaliya	Kambodhi
	Matharpirai/Ponnar Meniyane	Devagandhari/Kamas
	Maathaadabaradeno	Khamas

She did not record prolifically, but Kinnear's (1994) catalogues show that her records sold till many decades after she stopped recording, and it was largely the devotional recordings that made brisk business.

Jayanthi Kumaresh notes:

> When I hear some of her early recordings to those after 1912, I do notice the change in the voice texture and singing style, as compared to the shrill, child-like renditions of the earliest expeditions. She has clear Sanskrit diction and it is apparent that she is trained in the language as well.[3]

Dhanakoti Ammal of Kanchipuram

The EMI Music Archives catalogues and Kinnear (1994) demonstrate that Dhanakoti Ammal's recordings for The Gramophone Company are limited and after the first expedition, she does not feature in any new recordings, but only reissues. In the 1904–05 expedition she recorded many songs; refer Table 6.3.

Of the above, *Saroja Dalanetri, Himachala Thanayabrochuta, Diname Sudiname*, and *Varamulosagi* were heard, along with Jayanthi Kumaresh. She notes:

> In all the recordings, I observe that her voice displays great felicity and *shruti shuddham* (pitch adherence), as was the case with Salem Ammakannu and Bangalore Nagarathnamma. However, when I compare this to contemporary renditions of the same compositions, I find a significant absence of raga *bhaavas* (or emotional content) and finesse

Table 6.3 Recordings of Dhanakoti of Kanchipuram

Genre	Title	Raga
Padams/Javali	Antastu Marechi	Behag
	Balimini Bilechi	Kedaram
	Sankalp Metili	Kharaharapriya
	Mohappahtukari	Todi
	Yinnamundurani pagukarkandu	Ragamalika
Kritis	Himachala Thanayabrochuta	Anandabhairavi
	Diname Sudiname	Latangi
	Brova Samayamidhe	Gaurimanohari
	Saroja Dalanetri	Shankarabharanam
	Ninnu vina gati gaana	Kalyani
	Varamulosagi brochuta	Keeravani
	Sri Subrahmanya Namasthe	Kambhoji

in many of her renderings. The *vallinam* and *thallinam* (vocal dynamics and modulation), which provide the flavor to the renditions are almost singularly lacking in all her recordings. Whether this is an impact of the gramophone recording or her natural style is difficult to tell. The emotional content is on the lower side in most of the recordings and she seems to be rendering them in a very matter-of-fact and non-creative manner. In the rendition of *Varamulosagi*, I find it quite alarming to see the complete lack of the *Kakali Nishadham* (or augmented seventh note of the scale) in the rendition, an otherwise essential ingredient of the raga. This perhaps means ragas had a different grammar a hundred years ago or that these digressions of using other notes or deleting a note that is so essential to a raga was acceptable. According to me, it references to a period when rules of the dos and don'ts in a raga where still not set and that was to come much later.[4]

Salem Godavari

In terms of virtuosity, two of the most versatile singers of the gramophone era were undoubtedly Salem Godavari and Coimbatore Thayi. The sheer range of their recordings as evidenced from the EMI Music Archives catalogues and Kinnear (1994) and the musical value of some of these make them stand apart. This substantiates also what Noble (1913) had said about Godavari in particular, of being a practiced musician who knew the demands of the medium and suited her renditions to the same. From the EMI Archives catalogue and Kinnear (1994), we observe that in the very first expedition (1904–05) itself Salem Godavari recorded a wide array of songs; see Table 6.4.

From *padams* and *javalis* to classical compositions or *kritis*, not only was she a prolific artist, but also extremely versatile with a wide repertoire. One finds a tilt towards Thyagaraja *kritis* in her repertoire, which might

Table 6.4 Recordings of Salem Godavari

Genre	Title	Raga
Padams/Javali	Yerata Guntara	Kedaragaula
	Intiki vachina vaa	Janjuti
	Tapamidene chappy kovalan	Bhusavali
	Mohamedhu sahikka	Khamas
Kritis	Paridana Michite	Bilahari
	Chetashri Balakrishnam	Dvijavanthi
	Nee Bhajana gana	Nayaki
	Neevada ne gana	Saranga
	Kshirasagara Shayana	Devagandhari
	Devi Minakshi mudam dehi	Purvi kalyani
	Thyagarajaya Namasthe	Begada
	Mayateetaswaroopini	Mayamalavagowla

indicate she must have learnt under someone of the lineage of Thyagaraja. Her records continued to be reissued and remained in circulation until the end of the 1920s, even after her death.

In my interview with contemporary musician Neela Ramgopal, we heard *Kshirasagara Shayana, Intiki vacchina vaa, Paridana Michite,* and 1906–07 recordings of her *aalaapanas* in s *Shankarabharanam* and *Kalyani*. We also heard a 1918–20 recording of Dhanammal presenting the *kriti, Mahima Theriyama Tharama* in raga *Shankarabharanam* to observe stylistic differences. Neela Ramgopal notes:

If I were to describe the rendition style of Godavari by listening to her recordings, I would term it as being analogous to bees hovering around a particular note, creating patterns. The emphasis is on the main staying note. This is a marked departure from contemporary Carnatic music where the approach to a note is usually taken as a "journey between the notes" rather than staying on it for too long. I observe a very marked difference in the handling of raga *Shankarabharanam*, for instance, in the early recordings of some of these women and that of Dhanammal. In the latter case the *valli gamakas* (or gliding notes) are very similar to contemporary practice, but that is not the way Godavari or Nagarathnamma seems to have treated the raga. Perhaps the fact that the violin and its influence on Carnatic music, in comparison to the harmonium that was sometimes used as accompanying instrument earlier and as heard in some of these recordings, further defined the construction of this tradition of excessive gliding of notes within contemporary Carnatic music. In Godavari's recording of the raga *Kalyani aalaapana* as well as the *aalaapanas* by the other singers, I do not hear the profusion of scatting syllables: *Tha Dha Ri Na Na* that are used for enunciation in contemporary Carnatic music. Instead, there is more *akaaram* or *aa* syllables used and open-mouthed pronunciation. In the second part of this record, I notice several rounds of *neraval* (or idiomatic improvisation) on a particular line of a composition. We find this to be much in consonance with the *neraval* that one observes today in concerts. Godavari displays her virtuosity here with a lot of improvisation on each line of the *neraval* rendition. What I find noteworthy again is that the ornamentation is minimal and it is centred around the note and the note placement is where it should be. The rendition is marked by a lack of any deep and scooping *gamakas* and instead by a profusion of plain, straight notes. The *gamakas* are all restricted to around the note and do not tread beyond their loci.[5]

Coimbatore Thayi

Another of the early singers with an extraordinarily vast repertoire recorded was Coimbatore Thayi. The EMI Music Archives catalogue and Kinnear (1994) provide details of the special *Coimbatore Thayi Sessions* of 1908 made in Madras by George Walter Dillnut. The catalogue demonstrates the breadth of her musical knowledge, the ragas employed, and the wide range of composers whose compositions she recorded. Her main interests, however, seem to have been more in Tamil songs and devotionals.

Among the classical pieces, it is predominantly Thyagaraja's compositions that have been recorded. Just one of Dikshitar and two of Shyama Shastri were recorded. This illustrates the arguments of Subramanian (2006) and Weidmann (2006) on the increasing clout and canonisation of the lineage of Thyagaraja in the Carnatic pantheon and the popularisation of his compositions through gramophone records and print medium. Very few of Thayi's records have been available, especially in genres such as *padams* and *javalis*.

As observed from the EMI Music Archives catalogues and Kinnear (1994), Coimbatore Thayi made several recordings; refer Table 6.5.

In my interview with Neela Ramgopal, she notes:

> Despite the range of her repertoire, when one compares the recordings of Thayi to those of Godavari or Dhanakoti, I find that Thayi has a very soft voice, which does not seem well suited to the acoustic recording era. In the 1910 recording of the Thyagaraja *kriti Maa Janaki* in raga *Kambodhi*, I notice the acceleration of *kaalapramaana* (or tempo). However, this does not affect the emotional content of the rendition. The voice modulations and twists are characteristic of Thayi's recordings, which her soft and supple voice seems to manage well. I, however notice, that unlike the other female singers there are occasional slippages of *shruti* (or pitch) at times. There is an element of *shringara* (or romance) in her voice and modulations that she successfully brings forth in the *javalis* recorded in 1910, *Enthadi Kuluke* and *Yemi maayamu*. I feel that the softness of her voice brings that element of longing

Table 6.5 Recordings of Coimbatore Thayi

Genre/composer	Title	Raga
Thyagaraja *Kritis*: (17)	*Kaddanu Variki*	*Thodi*
	Triloka Matha	*Pharazu*
	Chakkani Raja margamu	*Kharaharapriya*
	Ksheera sagara Shayana	*Devagandhari*
	Entha nerchina	*Shuddha Dhanyasi)*
	Bhajana parula kela	*Surati*
	Evarani	*Nadachintamani*
	Nee Bhajana Gana	*Nayaki*
	Rama Bana	*Saveri*
	Ninnu vina namadhendhu	*Navarasa Kanada*
	Maa Janaki jetti battaga	*Ragamalika*
	Jaya jaya Gokula bala	*Kambhoji*
	Thalli Thandrulu	*Balahamsa*
	Sugunamule	*Chakravakam*
	Nagumomu galaneni	*Abheri*
	Kali narulaku	*Kunthalavarali*
	Nanu Palimpa	*Mohana*
Dikshitar *kritis*: (1)	*Sri Subrahmanyaya Namasthe*	*Kambhoji*
Shyama Shastri's *kritis*	*Meena Lochana*	*Dhanyasi*
	Birana Brovamma Thamasamyala	*Manji*
Miscellaneous *Kritis*: (4)	*Samdehamu*	*Gamanashrama*
	Neeva paripalinchutaku	*Kambhoji*
	Varugalaamo	*Maanji*
	BrovaSamayamidhe	*Gourimanohari*
***Javalis*: (6)**	*Voori varemi*	*Kedaragoulam*
	Meragadu lechi rara	*Athana*
	Sarasa Priya	*Desika Thodi*
	Maathaada baradeno	*Khamas*
	Enthadi Kulake	*Kalyani*
	YEmi mayamu	*Kalyani*
***Padams*: (2)**	*Manchi dhinamu*	*Ananda Bhairavi*
	Paiyyada Paimeethajee	*Nadanamakriya*
Tamil devotional: (24)	*Panakkai*	*Yadukula Kambhoji*
	Aruljyothi	*Panthuvarali – Arulpa*
	Pinukuillatha	*Thodi*
	Kaga mantha kodi	*Ragamalika*
	Pavana mai	*Devagandhari*
	Ponnum mai porulum	*Kambhoji*
	Vin padaitha	*Ragamalika*
	Valvavathu mayam	*Senjurutti*
	Nan Padum padoo	*Kambhoji*
	Yennaria paravithanin	*Saveri & Madhyamavati*
	Pooveru konum	*Natakuranji*
	Cararum	*Thayimanavar*
	Sankhanidhi	*Harikambhoji*
	Vaazhai yadi vaazhai	*Nadanamakriya*
	Matriyaadha	*Surati*

(Continued)

Table 6.5 Recordings of Coimbatore Thayi *(Continued)*

Genre/composer	Title	Raga
	Appa nee amma nee	*Harikambodhi*
	Etthanai vidhangalaal	*Nadanamakriya*
	Pathi yundu nidhi yundu	*Thodi*
	Maasil veenaiyum	*Poorvikalyani*
	Santhathamu vedha	*Bhairavi*
	Andha mudi Thannilo	*Thodi*
	Pathi mathi	*Thiruppugazh*
	Padamudiyaathu	*Ananda Bhairavi*
	Mathradellam Pocche	*Saveri*
Hindustani songs: (4)	*Rasoolulla*	*Kapi*
	Abahum lalana	*Behag*
	Guyyari Mero	*Dhoon*
	Savaro	*Vasantha*
Others: (6)	*Aalaapana*	*Gouri Manohari*
	Aalaapana	*Byag*
	Aalaapana	*Thodi*
	Aalaapana	*Kalyani*
	Virbhoni	*Bhairavi*
	Sanskrit hymn – *Kasturi Thilakam*	*Shankarabharanam*

and yearning in some of the phrases, much more effectively than several contemporaries that I have just heard. A good use of rhythmic patterns gives the *Yemi Maayamu* a peppiness that is characteristic of *javalis*. Her recordings are full of elaborate passages of closed- and open-mouthed singing, microtonal ornaments, and long stretches in which she changes the timbre but not the pitch of important notes.[6]

All the interviews documenting critical perspectives of respondents on the Carnatic music gramophone recording reveals a common inference with respect to the altered aesthetic aspects of Carnatic music. When one listens to the gramophone recordings from 1904 to 1925, it is noticed that the singers employ only a few glides and oscillations. The deep and scooping *gamakas* that define Carnatic music today and, in a way, characterise it, as mentioned by Chelladurai (1991: 200–202), are conspicuous by their absence in several of these renditions. Instead they are marked by a profusion of unornamented pitches. The *gamakas* are sparingly used and are restricted to around the note, rarely treading beyond the notes. Singers sang with no vibrato, much like the Baroque voice. As mentioned earlier, the quartertone bends, the vocal gestures and distinct melodic motifs that encompass these *gamakas* are somewhat missing, which leads us to ask when these elements became a quintessential feature of "classicism" in Carnatic music as evidenced in contemporary performances.

Empirical Musical Analysis of Carnatic Recordings

In this section I analyse digitised versions of the gramophone recordings, made between 1904 and 1925, for their melodic content, grammar, structure, raga presentation, and compositional structure. In some cases, these were the recordings of raga expositions or *aalaapanas* and in others the recordings were of compositions or *kritis*. These are compared with later recordings of the 1930s and also the 1960s and 1990s to benchmark the musical changes that had come about. I also analyse the recordings for changes in raga grammar, phraseology, the connection between memorised compositions, and the improvisations recorded during the gramophone era. Unlike Western Classical Music and the monumental work of scholars such as Nicholas Cook, there are no known templates, or models or parameters for empirical musical analysis in Indian Classical Music. The parameters analysed here are just a starting point for further refinement and improvisation by scholars in the field and not necessarily the only (or the last) word in the discipline.

Treatment of Improvisational Formats: Rendering of Aalaapanas

In early gramophone recordings the artists faced a major limitation of time, of only three minutes. Artists had to compress something as expansive and improvisatory as Indian classical music (both Hindustani and Carnatic) into a shorter time capsule. Hence the most essential and defining phrases and notes of a raga had to be utilised succinctly to both fit the time limit as also do justice to the artistry of the exercise.

With this time limitation of artists recording on the gramophone in mind, I analyse the *aalaapana* recordings of three Carnatic musicians to record on the gramophone—Bangalore Nagarathnamma, Mysore T. Chandra, and T.N. Manickam. The recording of Bangalore Nagarathnamma belongs to the first decade of the twentieth century. Unfortunately, nothing is known about the other two singers, Manickam and Chandra. The EMI Music Archive catalogues reveal that Mysore T. Chandra's recording belongs to the 1915–20 era and T.N. Manickam's recording belongs to the 1920–27 era.

I have picked the same raga for all the three artists – *Thodi*, which is considered a major classical raga in Carnatic music with a lot of scope for improvisation and numerous compositions set in this raga.

The recordings were analysed for:

1 Changes to Raga-specific behaviour
2 Changes in *aalaapana* structure and improvisatory syntax
3 Connection between improvisation and compositions of that era
4 Presentation of compositions

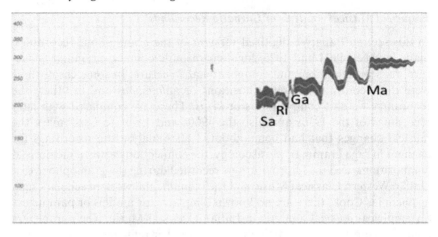

Figure 6.2 Spectrogram of the raga *Thodi* signature phrase *SaRiGa—Ma* as sung in current Carnatic practice. The third note of the scale is inflected across an interval of a whole tone (200–300 Hz).

CHANGES TO RAGA-SPECIFIC BEHAVIOUR

Figures 6.2–6.5 show spectrograms of two-signature raga *Thodi* phrases *SaRiGa—Ma* and *Ga—GaRiRi* encapsulating *valli gamakas* as sung in the gramophone era versus current practice.

In current practice, in the ascending phrase "*SaRi-Ga-Ma*", the oscillation on *Ga*, is rather large, oscillating between 200–300 Hz in frequency. As a consequence, the *Ga* has no fixed pitch value itself and is understood within the community of practitioners as that oscillatory note as such.

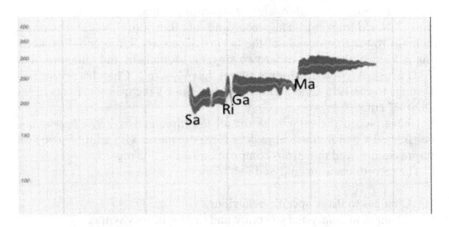

Figure 6.3 Spectrogram of the same raga *Thodi* signature phrase as sung in the Gramophone era recordings. The third note of the scale is not very inflected.

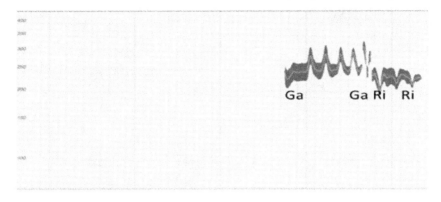

Figure 6.4 Spectrogram of the raga *Thodi* signature phrase *Ga–GaRiRi* as sung in current Carnatic practice. The third note of the scale is inflected across an interval of a whole tone (225–300 Hz).

In the descending phrase, *Ga–GaRiRi*, another signifier phrase for raga *Thodi*, the range of the oscillation decreases approximately to the interval of an equal tempered half-step 225–300 Hz. The renditions of singers from the gramophone era are distinctly devoid of this signifier phrase upon analysis and comparison.

The appearance of *valli gamakas* in the *aalaapanas* of three singers of the gramophone era – Bangalore Nagarathnamma, T.N. Manickam and Mysore T. Chandra are quantified in Figure 6.6.

In addition, comparison of the appearance of *valli gamakas* in the *aalaapanas* of the three singers (Nagarathnamma, Manickam and Chandra) from the gramophone era (1904–25), two singers who have been singing from the 1930s to 1990s (M.S. Subbulakshmi and M.L. Vasanthakumari) and one contemporary singer (Bombay Jayashri) was undertaken. The gramophone recordings of Nagarathnamma, Manickam, and Chandra are about three

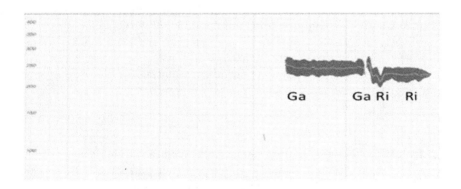

Figure 6.5 Spectrogram of the same raga *Thodi* signature phrase as sung in the Gramophone era recordings. The third note of the scale is not inflected.

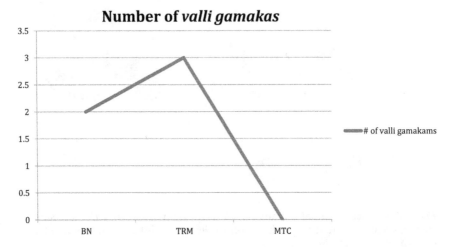

Figure 6.6 The appearance of *valli gamakas* (oscillatory inflexions on the third note in raga *Thodi* spanning a whole tone) in the improvisations (*aalaapana*) of three singers of the gramphone era was quantified. The renditions are distinctly lacking in these typical *gamakas*, which are used as classic signifiers of *Thodi* today.

Key: BN: Bangalore Nagarathnamma, TRM: T.N. Manickam, and MTC: Mysore T. Chandra (all three of the gramophone era from 1904 to 1925).

minutes, six minutes, and three minutes, respectively. M.S. Subbulakshmi's recording is about 14 minutes in duration, while that of M.L. Vasanthakumari is twenty-six minutes, and that of Bombay Jayashri about twenty-two minutes in duration. All are recordings and not live concerts.

As per the graphs shown in Figure 6.7, the renditions of contemporary singers (1930–present) are rich in *valli gamakas*, demonstrating a marked change in understanding of the raga – its melodic content and pitching. As can be seen in the figure, the *gamakas* are much wider in contemporary recordings. In my interviews with both Neela Ramgopal and Jayanthi Kumaresh, they are unanimous in their opinion that the demands of recording displaced several parameters of performance and traditional prerogatives.[7] Specifically, these early recordings demonstrate a noticeable change in understanding of the raga – its melodic content, usage of *gamakas*, and pitching, when compared to contemporary practice.

CHANGES TO *AALAAPANA* STRUCTURE

In Bangalore Nagarathnamma's *aalapana*, as with most other singers of the time, the improvisational syntax is different. While current singers, concatenate *aalaapana* with the *valli gamakas* on the *Ga* as a quintessential milestone in delineating *Thodi*, the singers of the gramophone era, improvised with more scalar/linear phrases, using long cadences and a different phrase

Number of *valli gamakas*

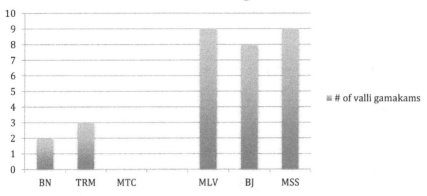

Appearance of phrase motif *Ga-Ri-Ri*

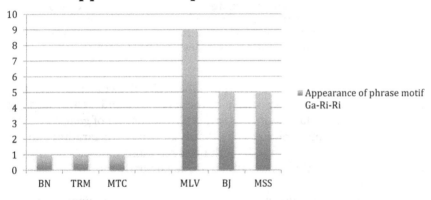

Figure 6.7 Comparison of the appearance of *valli gamakas* and signifier phrase *Ga-GaRiRi* in the improvisations (*aalaapana*) of three singers from the gramophone era and three contemporary singers. The renditions of contemporary singers (1925–present) are rich in *valli gamakas*, demonstrating a marked change in understanding of the raga – its melodic content and pitching.

Key: BN: Bangalore Nagarathnamma, TRM: T.N. Manickam, and MTC: Mysore T. Chandra (all three of gramophone era from 1904 to 1925); MLV: M.L. Vasanthakumari and MSS: M.S. Subbulakshmi (both from 1930s to 1980s); and BJ: Bombay Jayashri (from 1990s to present).

syntax. Nagarathnamma, does oscillate around the pivotal note of *Ga* making several patterns around it, such as *PaMaGaRi, RiGaMaPaMaGaRi* and *MaGaPaMaGaRi*, none of her phrases encapsulate a *valli gamaka* – i.e. it is never a scooping oscillation of a note but more straight and scalar phrases which revolve around the important note, *Ga*. She employs vocal pyrotechnic-oriented, fast-paced cadences often with disjointed octave jumps in phrasing.

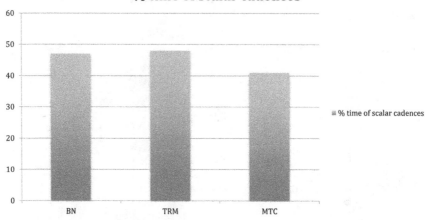

Figure 6.8 Improvisations were analysed for the total time spent singing scalar/ cadence phrases. This was expressed as a ratio of the total time of the recording to obtain percentage values. Interestingly, even though, the singers of the gramophone era displayed unique phrases in their improvisations, the melodic content of their *aalaapana* was more tightly linked to each other and scalar patterns they had memorised.

When one compares Nagarathnamma's *Thodi* with that of T.N. Manickam, another woman singer of the late 1920s and 1930s, the same observations hold. Manickam uses scalar phrases devoid of *gamakas*, longwinded cadences and a phraseology that is similar to Nagarathnamma to populate her *aalaapana*. Thus, in both these recordings we see a totally different raga portrait than is usually in vogue currently for a *Thodi aalaapana* (Figure 6.8).

Another striking feature in *aalaapana* recordings of the gramophone era is the appearance of artist specific signature phrases. The improvisations of the three singers were notated, and the combination of notes and musical phrases employed were compared within the same group and with the group of contemporary singers. The number of novel phrases in each rendition was quantified. The improvisations of BN, TNM and MTC displayed a higher average quotient of artist specific unique phrases other than the ones acquired strictly as raga grammar. In contrast, contemporary singers displayed a stricter adherence to raga grammar in the improvisations (Figure 6.9).

Specifically, to reinforce the inferences drawn above, and to map the profusion of *gamakas* in the rendition of raga *aalaapana* with the passage of time, I chose a wider range of recordings that included male and female musicians. The following set of recordings was used for this analysis:

- **1904–1930**: Recordings of Bangalore Nagarthnamma (BNR), Mysore T. Chandra (MTC), and T.N. Manickam (TNM)

of unique/artist specific signature phrases sung in *aalaapana*

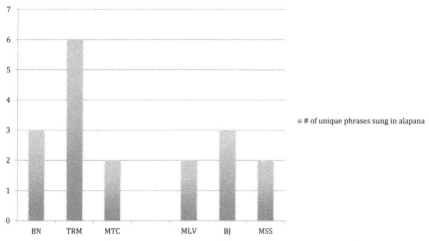

Figure 6.9 Number of artist specific phrases in *aalaapanas*.

- **1930–1950**: Recordings of male singers Ariyakudi Ramanuja Iyengar (ARI) and G.N. Balasubramaniam (GNB)
- **1950–1990**: Recordings of M.L. Vasanthakumari (MLV) and M.S. Subbulakshmi (MSS)
- **1990 onwards**: Recording of contemporary musician Bombay Jayashri (BJ)

Snapshots of the spectrograms of these recordings are depicted in the following sections.

1904–30 Recordings In the spectrograms shown in Figure 6.10, it is observed that the singer renders long, scalar phrases (marked by circle on top). The oscillations/*gamakas* are sparse and are around the pivotal note *Ga* to which the singer returns repeatedly (the return is marked in the circle at bottom). The *gamakas* too are noticed to be fast oscillating cadences and not deep and scooping.

The contrast is apparent when compared with three-minute 78-RPM recordings, (i.e. before the advent of Long Playing records in early 1950s) of the immediate subsequent era 1930–50, of male musicians: **G.N. Balasubramaniam** (1910–65) and **Ariyakudi Ramanuja Iyengar** (1890–1967). The comparison with the recordings of the 1930s here is all the more powerful in that for that era the same time constraints apply as in the earliest era, i.e. still recording (albeit electrically) onto a 78-RPM format with the three-minute limit. Hence, differences in style between recordings of the 1905 era and the 1930 era cannot be merely due to constraints of duration, but a tangible change in presentation style and aesthetics.

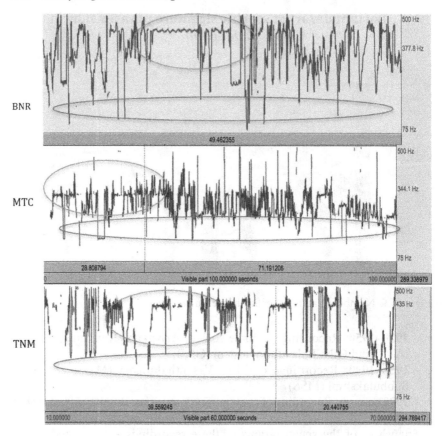

Figure 6.10 Spectrograms of *Thodi aalaapanas* recorded between 1904 and 1930.

1930–50 Recordings   The profusion of *gamaka* usage is marked in the spectrogram by circles and there is hardly any scalar phrase, which is devoid of *gamakas* (Figure 6.11). Also the return to the pivotal note *Ga* is not as marked as it was in the 1904–30 era recordings. The *aalaapana* follows a progression of highly ornamented cadences, which are more composed of phrases with scooping *gamakas*, rather than resting notes. Sampath (2012) mentions that in the 1930s a new format for a modern-day Carnatic music performance and its repertoire evolved. It was a formulaic construction of what all needs to be presented and in what manner. This concert structure (or *kacheri paddhati*) got a formal ratification by the experts of the Madras Music Academy after much debate and discussion by the late 1930s and early 1940s (122–123). Sampath (2012) quotes an essay of Sambamoorthy of 1944 where he states:

> The *vidwan* who formerly delighted in expounding a raga for hours together and earned encomiums from even his rivals, has to remodel

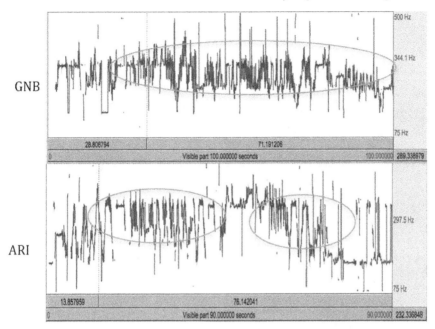

Figure 6.11 Spectrograms of *Thodi aalaapanas* recorded between 1930 and 1950.

his programme to suit the new type of audience...the performer must make sure that the concert includes a good variety of languages, ragas, and talas so as to keep the interest of the audience...the main performer should not let any of his weaknesses show, take any unnecessary risks, or draw any attention to the lapses of his accompanists. (122–123)

The codification and standardisation of what constitutes a classical Carnatic performance thus seemed complete.

1950–90 Recordings Spectrograms of snapshots of *aalaapana* recordings of prominent women singers: **M.L. Vasanthakumari** (1928–90) and **M.S. Subbulakshmi** (1916–2004) are depicted in Figure 6.12, dating to 1950–80, and from Long Playing records.

A similar trend, to that of the recordings of 1930–50, of phrases composed of deep, scooping *gamakas* executed in fast cadences is observed in these recordings as well. These portions of the spectrogram are marked by the circles.

The trend of profuse usage of *gamaka* laden, deeply scooping and ornamented phrases and an phrase-by-phrase (rather than note-by-note) exposition of a raga, seems consolidated in the spectrogram below of the recording of popular contemporary musician Bombay Jayashri in a late 1990s rendition of the *aalaapana* of *Thodi* (Figure 6.13).

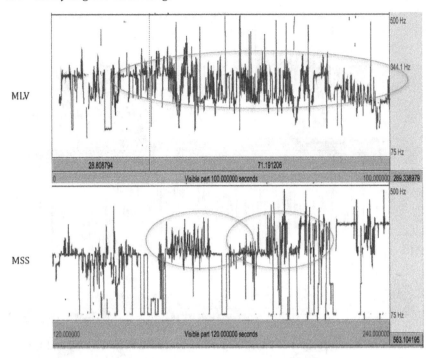

Figure 6.12 Spectrograms of *Thodi aalaapanas* recorded between 1950 and 1980.

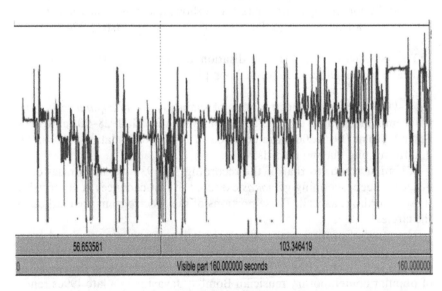

Figure 6.13 Spectrogram of *Thodi aalaapanas* recorded by Bombay Jayashri.

The spectrogram analysis clearly dates the transition period in Carnatic music when a "classical" paradigm and an accepted method of rendition were established. This points to the late 1930s/early 1940s. This period also coincides with the formal abolition of the *devadasi* practice and the establishment of the Madras Music Academy as the arbiter of classicism in Carnatic music.

CONNECT BETWEEN IMPROVISATION AND COMPOSITION

In this analysis, improvisations were notated and the phrases that were directly connected or related to the phraseology of the composition in structure, shape, and melodic idea were quantified. The total time spent singing such phrases was expressed as a ratio of the total time of the recording to obtain percentage values. Even though, the singers of the gramophone era displayed unique phrases in their improvisations, the melodic content of their *aalaapana* was more tightly linked to the compositions they had memorised. The percentage-connect between improvisation and composition was lower in contemporary singers. It was observed that although the percentage-connect of M.T. Chandra of the gramophone era is less than that of M.S. Subbulakshmi's later recordings and might seem like a contradiction, the average percentage-connect of the gramophone era singers comes up to about 35%, while that of the later singers is about 20%.

In these earlier recordings, I find the vocal delivery to be very different than later recordings. As mentioned by Jayanthi Kumaresh in my interview with her:

> Instead of a profusion of scatting syllables, there is usage of open vowels with fluid vocal resonances, open-mouthed pronunciation. Profusion of open-mouthed voicing is found, which is seldom used in modern Carnatic recitals. This is possibly influenced by the non-reliance on microphone, as this was the acoustic era of recording. This perhaps contributes to this open-throated rendition style.[8]

PRESENTATION OF COMPOSITIONS

I have considered for detailed analysis a very popular eighteenth-century composition of one of the Trinity of Carnatic music, Mutthuswami Dikshitar (1776–1835), *Sri Subrahmanyaya Namasthe* set to raga *Kambodhi*. It is in praise of the Hindu God Subrahmanya and is composed in Sanskrit. Rao (1997: 237) provides the lyrics of the composition:

(I) Pallavi

Sri Subrahmanyaaya Namasthe
Manasija Koti Koti Laavanyaaya Deena Sharanyaaya

Translation: Countless salutations to you, Oh! Lord Subrahmanya, the one who was born out of the destruction of the God of Love, but is more lustrous than crores of such gods of love, one who is compassionate, a protector of the weak and a redeemer of the downtrodden!

(II) Anupallavi

Bhoosuraadhi Samastha jana poojithaabja Charanaaya
Vaasuki thakshakaadhi Sarpa Swaroopa Dharanaaya
Vaasavaadi Sakala deva vandhithaaya varenyaaya
Daasa Janaabheeshta pradha daksha tharaagraanyaaya

Translation: He who has the lotus feet that are worshipped by devout Brahmins and others, the One who has taken the form of serpents such as *Vasuki* and *Thakshaka*, the One who is worshipped by Indra, the King of the Gods and all other celestial beings, and the One who readily fulfills every wish of His devotees – to such a Lord, I offer my countless salutations!

(III) Charanam

Taaraka Simha mukha soora Padmaasura Samhaarthre
Taapatraya harana nipuna Thatvopadesha karthre
Veeranutha Guruguhaaya ajnaana dwanda savithre
Vijaya Valli Bharthre Shakthyaayudha dharthre

Translation: The One who destroyed evil beings and demons such as Taraka, Simhamukha, and Surapadma, the One who destroys all the miseries and sufferings of His devotees and leads them to a spiritual path, the brave Commander-in-Chief of the army of the Gods, the obliterator of darkness through the sun of wisdom, the spouse of Goddess Valli, and the wise One who wields the spear of the Divine Mother or Shakti- to this Lord, I offer my countless salutations!

(IV) Madhyamakala Sahitya

Dheeraaya nata vidhaatre Devaraja jamaathre
Bhooradhi bhuvana bhokthre bhoga moksha pradhaatre.

Translation: The wise one worshipped by the Creator Brahma, the son-in-law of Indra, the King of Gods, the sovereign Lord of the Universe and the kind benefactor who bestows upon His devotees both materialistic pleasures and liberation from the cycle of birth and death- to this Lord, I offer my countless salutations![9]

It is common practice today in Carnatic music to learn a composition from a solfege-to-lyric score (A snapshot of one line of the notated refrain or *pallavi* is presented below). The time cycles are marked up; the corresponding solfas to the melodic material sung with prosody is indicated above the syllables, much as in a Western notation. The score lacks overt time signatures, as time signatures cannot vary within a composition and the role of the notation is rather descriptive, not prescriptive.

The Solfege-to-Lyric score of the Pallavi of Sri Subrahmanyaya Namaste (notated by author) is as below:

Pallavi[10]

d, , s, , r, || p, p m g, g, m r r g r, s, s, || (Solfege)

Sri....Su....bra...|| hma... ... nya... ... ...ya.na...|| (Lyric)

S̲,̲ ̲p d, s, p̲d̲ || d s, , d d s n n d p || (Solfege)

Ma... ... .sthe...na|| ma... ....sthe... ... ...|| (Lyric)

In the gramophone era, musicians were forced to innovate and rethink how to collage improvisatory demands with presenting traditional compositions, within the constraints of the three-minute imposition. One can observe a great variety in performance routines indicative of artist-specific choices; Bangalore Nagarathnamma in her recording chooses to sing more devotional songs and not indulge in too much prosodical manipulation. Dhanakoti Ammal too sings only the composition and does not render improvisatory elements of the music in her recordings. Salem Godavari, however, chooses to balance her recorded repertoire across all sub-genres and styles of Carnatic music including improvisatory solfege singing.

Changes to Raga Grammar, Gamaka Usage and Raga Signifiers

I now analyse Salem Godavari's 1906–07 recording the same composition of Mutthuswamy Dikshitar, in raga *Kambodhi, Sri Subrahmanyaya Namasthe.* Several interesting observations come to light here. In my interview with her, Jayanthi Kumaresh notes:

> The concept of the antiquity of the raga rendition or its classicism seems mythical because the version of raga *Kambodhi* of Godavari (and some of her contemporaries) is totally different from the *Kambodhi* of today. Glides of the raga are markedly different.[11]

Neela Ramgopal agrees with this postulation when she mentions:

> Today it is generally believed that most of Dikshitar's *kritis* are to be sung in a slow, stately fashion with just the two lines of the composition having their pace doubled (*Durita Kaalam*). On the other hand, compositions of another composer of the eighteenth-century who forms part of the Trinity of Carnatic music, Thyagraja, are sung a faster pace. In the renditions of these compositions by women of the gramophone era, however, we see no such rule being followed.[12]

Jayanthi Kumaresh mentions:

> In her alternation between tempos Godavari does hint that perhaps that was the normal pace of rendition of a Dikshitar *kriti* in live concerts. For example, of the two lines in the opening stanza, the second one *Manasija koTi koTi lAvanyAya dIna sharaNyAya* is sung in varied speeds, even as the first line is sung in a staid and majestic *vilamba kaalam* or slow tempo. In the *anupallavi*, the rendition at the lines of *TakshakAdhi sarpa svaroopa* is staccato and almost devoid of *gamakas*. This becomes more marked in the next line *Vasavaadhi Sakala Deva Vandithaya VareNyAya* where the glides are almost sung with Western intonation. The glide from Sa to Pa in this line is almost like a wave, devoid of any ripples of *gamakas* en-route.[13]

This is done with repeated improvisations for close to 40–50 seconds, portraying an extremely different and refreshing picture of *Kambodhi* raga. The *Charanam* is finished off in great speed in view of the diminishing time available on the record.

Neela Ramgopal, however, points out that the quality of Sanskrit pronunciations is extremely poor and this is repeatedly the case with several of the *devadasi* singers, barring of course Bangalore Nagarathnamma who had exemplary Sanskrit diction. Godavari almost gobbles up several words in the song and unless one knows the lyrics, it is not possible to understand word-to-word what is being sung.[14]

When one compares Salem Godavari's rendition with a 1930s recording of a prominent male musician **Chembai Vaidyanatha Bhagavathar** (1896–1974), we see clearly the difference in the style of rendition. As demonstrated in the analysis below, the notes in each word of the lyric are oscillated so much with deep and scooping *gamakas* in Chembai's version of the same composition.

I analyse these differences in detail in the section below.

Changes to Scheme of Performance

An important difference in Salem Godavari and Chembai's rendition of *Sri Subrahmanyaya Namasthe* is that of the schema involved in performance, compositional routines followed, and attitudes to interpretation/improvisation on compositional material.

In this double-sided record of six minutes and fifty seconds, the Pallavi portion of the composition takes up one minute and forty-one seconds. I have taken only the *pallavi* portions because both artists undertake the improvisation only in this section and not in the *anupallavi* or *charanam*. Salem Godavari unravels the performance with cyclic routines that start from the refrain (*pallavi*) (Routine 1), adds more material (Routine 2), stops to return to refrain with a short improvisational passage (Routine 3), moving to more complicated patterns of the refrain known as *sangatis* in composition (Routines 5 and 6), followed by rhythmic and prosodical manipulation (Routines 7, 8, and 9) – these elements of compositional restating, interpretation, small improvisational forays and distinct prosodical or rhythmic modulations are collaged into one powerful mix of performance.

This process is shown in the list below of Salem Godavari's recording: Routines, Improvisations on theme, Schema of unraveling composition and improvisations:

Routine 1: *sri subrahmanyaya namaste*
Routine 2: *sri subrahmanyaya namaste jaya*
Routine 3: *sri subrahmanyaya namaste* **namaste**
Routine 4: *sri subrahmanyaya namaste namaste*
Routine 5: *sri subrahmanyaya namaste* **namaste**
Routine 6: *sri subrahmanyaya namaste* **namaste**
manasija koti koti lavanyaya deena sharanyaya
Routine 7: *sri subrahmanyaya namaste* **namaste**
manasija koti koti lavanyaya deena sharanyaya (doubled up speed)
Routine 8: *sri subrahmanyaya namaste* **namaste**
manasija koti koti lavanyaya deena sharanyaya (doubled up speed)
Routine 9: *sri subrahmanyaya namaste namaste* (doubled speed in underlined)
manasija koti koti lavanyaya deena sharanyaya (doubled up speed)

KEY OF DIFFERENT FONT STLYLES COMBINATION IN TEXT ABOVE:

Jaya = improvisational filler
namaste = compositional motif
namaste = reinterpreted motif
manasija.= prosodical and rhythmic manipulation
subrahmanyaya = **rhythmic manipulation**

The routines employed by Godavari to improvise the *Pallavi* are displayed in the spectrograms shown in Figure 6.14. As can be noted, in each successive routine, she adds small incremental motifs or improvisatory patterns, seen in spectrograms of Routines 3, 4, towards the end on the word *Namaste*, and the portions of the lyrics where she doubles the tempo, displayed by wavy curves in spectrograms of Routines 7, 8, and 9.

In contrast, Chembai Vaidyanatha Bhagavathar delineates the Pallavi for about four minutes and sixty-two seconds out of the total recording time of about ten minutes for the composition. In contrast to Godavari's nine routines (*sangatis*), Chembai sings twelve. But Chembai's routines are more linear; the composition is presented with its many *sangatis* (or patterns), but without flashes of improvisation or any form of modulation. This is similar to the performance routines followed today in Carnatic music where the composition presentation is separated out from the improvisatory sections in time, space and protocols.

Figure 6.15 represents the twelve routines on spectrograms in the order of their appearance in the composition.

In addition to changes in performance routines and musicological aspects discussed in the section above, another important observation is that the structure of compositions has changed. As seen above, the *sangatis* or patterns on lyric phrases has increased in number, but not necessarily in complexity, shape and range within the scale of raga *Kambodhi*. A more formulaic presentation of a composition with gradual, linear build up of improvisational motifs is observed in the recordings of compositions after the 1930s.

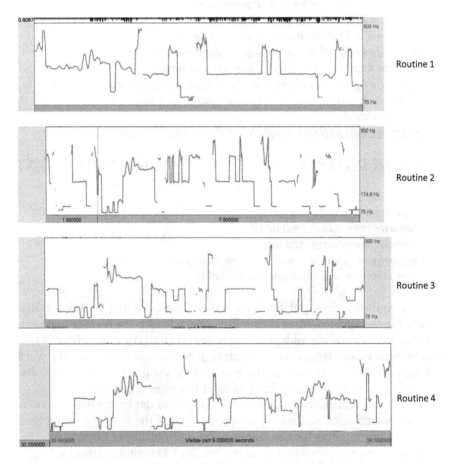

Figure 6.14 Spectrogram of Salem Godavari's nine improvisatory routines of the *Pallavi* of *Sri Subrahmanyaya Namaste. (Continued)*

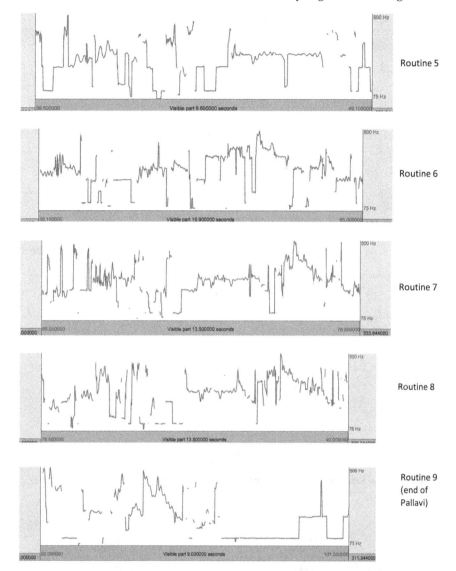

Figure 6.14 (Continued)

Another striking feature that emerges, when the compositions are compared is the distinct usage of oscillatory (*kampita*) *gamakas*, Chembai's rendition of refrain uses a staggering eighteen *gamakas* while Godavari uses only six. Chembai's stylistics involve oscillation of almost every syllable in the rendition, as opposed to a more free flowing version of Godavari, bereft of too much oscillatory notes.

Routine 1: *Sri Subrahmanyaya Namaste* (18 seconds)

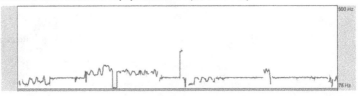

Routine 2: *Sri Subrahmanyaya Namaste* (18 seconds): No change

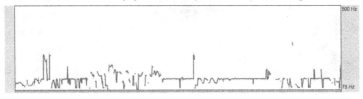

Routine 3: *Sri Subrahmanyaya Namaste* (18 seconds): No change, except in *Namaste*

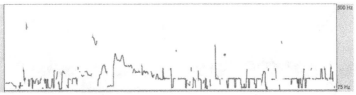

Routine 4: *Sri Subrahmanyaya Namaste* (17 seconds): No change, except minor in *Namaste*

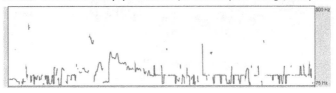

Routine 5: *Sri Subrahmanyaya Namaste* (18 seconds): No change, except minor in *Namaste*

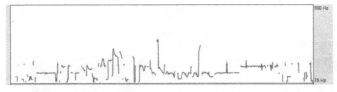

Routine 6: *Sri Subrahmanyaya Namaste Manasija*...(rest of pallavi sung) (37 seconds)

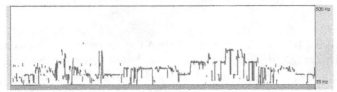

Figure 6.15 Spectrograms of the twelve routines of the Pallavi of *Sri Subrahmanyaya Namaste* by Chembai Vaidyanatha Bhagavathar. *(Continued)*

Routine 7: *Sri Subrahmanyaya Namaste Manasija*…(rest of pallavi sung) (38 seconds, no change)

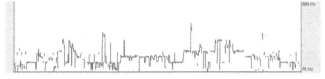

Routine 8: Tempo increase in *Koti koti lavanyaya deena sharanyaya*, rest no change (27 seconds)

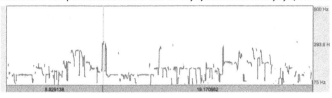

Routine 9: Tempo change in *manyaya* of '*Subrahmanyaya*' & *koti koti* as in Routine 7. Rest same. (27 seconds)

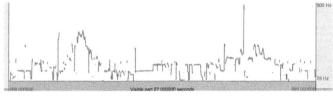

Routine 10: Tempo change in *manyaya* of '*Subrahmanyaya*' & more tempo change in *koti koti* as in Routine 7. Rest same. (23 seconds)

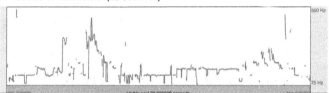

Routine 11: Different tempo change in *manyaya* of '*Subrahmanyaya*' & in *koti koti*. Rest same. (22 seconds)

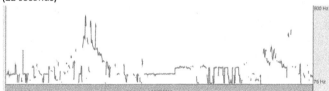

Routine 12: End Pallavi with just *Sri Subrahmanyaya Namaste*

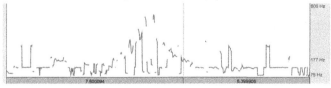

Figure 6.15 (Continued)

Table 6.6 Patterns of Salem Godavari recording vs Chembai

Salem Godavari	Chembai
1 = *Da,Sa,Ri,*	1 = *Da,Sa,Ri,*
2 = *Gapa-magari,*	*Pa,,DaSa,,Da* – *Sa,,RiGa,,Ri*
3 = *Sanipada,sa,*	2 = *Pa, PaMaGa,* - *Ga,MaRi -RiGaRi,*
3 = *Padasanidapa*	*Pa, Da Sa Da Pa* – *PaPaMaGa GaRiGaRi Sa,*
4 = *Ga Ri Ga Ma Ga*	*SaRiGaMa- PaDaSa,* - *SaSaNiDa DaPaMaGa- GaRiSa,*
	SaRiGaMa-PaDaSaRi-GaMaGaRi-SaNiDa-RiSaNiDa-DaPa-
	MaGaGaRi
	3 = Sanipada, sa,

Note: Notation symbol of underlining the notes indicates a doubling of speed of rendition.

Salem Godavari and Chembai sing the refrain *Shri Subrahmanyaaya Namaste* nine and twelve times, respectively, in the recordings. But there is no development of melodic phrases in consequent *sangatis* (Table 6.6, node 1, 2). While Godavari uses small improvisations, rhythmic and prosodical manipulations during the nine rounds of refrain, Chembai's versions are linear and show the methodical development of phrase and pattern complexity across the same nodes. This is demonstrated in Table 6.6.

Pallavi: *shri subrah[1]- manyaya[2] namaste[3] namaste[4]*
manasija koti koti lavanyaya[3] deena sharanyaya

Such changes in composition presentation could be ascribed to the sociocultural changes that occurred in the late 1920s with the creation of the Madras Music Academy, where, as Subramanian (2006) points out, the social cognition of ragas themselves underwent discussion and revamping.

My respondents hence concluded that this decade seems to be the inflexion point for the construction of the idiom of what defines the "classical" and "aesthetic" in Carnatic music. The idea was perhaps how not to "sound" like a *devadasi* and move as far away from that sound. While it is tough to tangibly list out what these features of the *devadasi* "sound" were, as discussed in the section above, in these later recordings they refer to the profusion of *gamakas*, the attempt to make the music sound more "methodical," devotional, and a serious, seminal pursuit rather than a flippant exercise as the *devadasi* music was considered to be. The absence of genres associated with the *devadasi* also added to this component of the "new normal" of Carnatic classical music.

Analysis of Hindustani Music Recordings

Theoretical Background and Stylistic Parameters in Hindustani Music

As discussed earlier in this chapter, Indian classical music (both Hindustani and Carnatic) has two broad categories of musical forms: the *anibaddha* (open or unbound) and the *nibaddha* (closed or bound). *Anibaddha* refers to music that is not set within the limitations of a composition. It has no rhythmic structure or defined sectional arrangements.

Deva (1973: 36–38) records that the most important form of unbound music in the Hindustani tradition is the *aalaap*, where the raga is developed and elaborated slowly, note-by-note, and phrase-by-phrase. There is no rhythmic accompaniment for this elaboration. It is usually rendered with vowels, syllables, and meaningless words such as *aa, tere, dere, nom, tom,* and so on. Emphasis is laid on the emphatic notes, signifier phrases, and graces of the raga. Musicians usually begin with a lower pitch and gradually work it up. Unlike Carnatic music, which has a separate improvisatory portion (the *aalaapana)* preceding a composition, in the *khayal* genre of Hindustani music, improvisation is incorporated into the *bandish* (or composition). When this improvisation is done using words of the composition, it is known as a *bol aalaap* and is rendered with rhythmic accompaniment to coordinate a closure of melodic patterns with the rhythmic cycle. Musicians also incorporate within the composition, fast, improvisatory phrases known as *taans*. These are complicated patterns of notes coming in quick succession at moderate and quick tempos. When a *taan* is sung using the words of the composition, it is called *bol taan*. The *bol taan* is a fast phrase sung with the libretto or the *bol*. *Taans* usually form the climax of a composition's presentation. Similar to the *kalpana swarams* of Carnatic music, extempore solfa singing in Hindustani music is known as *sargam*.

Regarding the closed forms of Hindustani music, Deva (1973) mentions that there are several forms that included *dhrupad, khayal, thumri, tappa, tarana,* and *bhajan* (38–42). One of the more common and accepted forms is the *khayal*. The very word *khayal* in Persian means "idea" or "imagination." A *bandish* or composition in *khayal* is set to different ragas and has two parts: *sthayi* and *antara*. The *sthayi* has its movements generally in the lower and middle octaves, and all the melodic variations and improvisations end with the last few phrases of this section. In essence, it is the burden of the song or performance. The first line of the *sthayi* (also known as the *mukhra*) serves as a cadence, while the entire *sthayi* is the most important part of composition as it delineates the metre and the mode of the piece and usually forms the basis for subsequent improvisations. *Antara* is the second part of the composition with its progressions sung in a higher register focusing on the middle and upper octaves with a considerable amount of text manipulation and repeated forays into the *sthayi*. The two sections complement each other and together provide a holistic picture of the raga's framework.

There are two kinds of *khayal: bada* (big) and *chhota* (small). Both are similar, in that they have the *sthayi* and *antara*. Deva (1973: 40) mentions that the *bada khayal* is composed to suit slower tempos with a structure that can accommodate a leisurely *aalaap* and melodic movements in slow to medium tempo. A few melodic phrases that are enunciated before presenting the *bada khayal* are known as *auchar*. Then the *sthayi* is rendered in slow or medium tempo. The text is sung for one or two cycles of the tala and the *aalaap* or the *bol aalaap* commences, where the musician elaborates and improvises either with or without the lyrics of the composition. Similar pattern follows the *antara* too. The rendition of a *bada khayal* is usually followed by a *chhota khayal* in the same raga, though not the same tala. This is rendered in medium and fast tempos, with no detailed *aalaap* but *taans*, *bol taans*, *sargams* and cross -rhythmic patterns to create a climactic finish. In all the renditions of *bada* and *chhota khayal*, the nucleus of attention is the *sam* (or the first beat of the rhythmic cycle) to which the melody must repeatedly return.

Different *gharanas* in Hindustani music have different approaches to enunciation, musical idioms and accents in presentation of the *khayal* format outlined above, though the structure and grammar of the ragas remain the same in all the *gharanas*. The prominent *gharanas* include Gwalior, Agra, Kirana, Jaipur-Atrauli, Rampur, and Patiala to name a few and are referenced by the town of origin.

The *thumri* form that is associated with the *tawaifs*, and of which they made several recordings, is discussed in detail later in this chapter.

Recording Analysis in Jaunpuri

As per Bhatkhande's (1999) classification, this raga belongs to the Asavari *Thaat*. It uses the notes S R M P D N in the ascent and S N D P MG R in the descent and is performed in the late morning (645). In terms of scales or modes, the Asavari *Thaat* is akin to the Aeolin mode of Western classical music. Jairazbhoy (1995) states that Dha and Ga are the important notes, treated as

> ...parallel in the descending conjunct tetrachords, *Sa'- Pa* and *Pa-Re*... *Dha* is an extremely dissonant note and has, in addition, a very high dynamic function since it is the penultimate note in the descending tetrachord *Sa'-Pa*. It therefore acts as a powerful 'leading note' to the *Pa*. The longer *Dha* is sustained, the more urgently it needs to resolve on *Pa*, and correspondingly the more satisfying is the resolution. (169–170)

One of the respondents, musician Sounak Chattopadhyay states:[15]

> Some people refer to this raga as Asavari with a natural *Re* (or second note). The usage of the flat *Ni* in ascent distinguishes it from Asavari. While *Ga* is omitted in the ascent, it is used in the descent. *Ga* and *Dha* are important notes in this raga and are oscillated, and *Pa* is a resting note.

Zohra Bai of Agra

I first analyse the recording of Zohra Bai of Agra (1868–1913). As discussed earlier, she was an artist of great virtuosity particularly in *khayal* renditions

Table 6.7 Structure of Zohra Bai's recording

	Begins at (in sec)	Duration (in sec)
Zohra Bai of Agra – matki mori re – khayal in raga Jaunpuri – 1909 recording		
START	0	
Tonic	4	2
Sthayi- Iteration 1	6	18.5
Sthayi- Iteration 2	24.5	8
Antara- Iteration 1	32.5	19.5
Antara- Iteration 2	52	7.5
Mukhra /refrain	59.5	7.5
Sargam 1	67	12.5
Mukhra /refrain	79.5	3
Sargam 2	82.5	7
Mukhra /refrain	89.5	2
Bol Taan 1	91.5	13
Mukhra /refrain	104.5	4
Bol Taan 2	108.5	14
Mukhra /refrain	122.5	5
Bol Taan 3	127.5	11.5
Mukhra /refrain	139	4.5
Antara	143.5	5
Bol Taan 4	148.5	7
Mukhra /refrain	155.5	5
Taan	160.5	11
Mukhra /refrain	171.5	3
Announcement *"Zohra Bai Agrewaali"*	174.5	2
END	176.5	
Total Recorded		**172.5**

and was an exponent of the Agra *gharana*. Sampath (2010) states that her *khayal* renditions were counted among the best during her times and she could elaborate a raga in a structured fashion for several hours (57).

In the 1909 recording of a *khayal, Matki Mori Re* in raga Jaunpuri set to rhythmic cycle of slow tempo *(vilambit) teental* (16 beats) by Zohra Bai of Agra, I find the following structure in the rendition; refer Table 6.7.

Zohra Bai begins with the tonic for a few seconds. This leads her into the refrain *(mukhra)* of the initial part *(Sthayi)* of the fixed *khayal* composition *(bandish) Matki Mori Re*. The word *Re* in the lyrics coincides with the *sam* (or start of the rhythmic cycle) and that seems to be a departure from contemporary *Jaunpuri* renditions. As musician Sounak Chattopadhyay mentions in my interview with him:

> The *"Re-Pa"* combination almost sounds like it is the raga *Kafi* and this recurs time and again in the composition. Among the recordings analysed in *Janupuri*, this is the only recording which has a *Re-Pa* phrase in addition to the regular *Re-Ma* phrase that is typical of *Jaunpuri*.[16]

Table 6.8 Structural components of Zohra Bai's recording

Component	Duration (in sec.)	Percent of recording
Composed component	53.5	31
Improvised component	76	44
Refrains + pauses	39	2
Miscellaneous (announcement, tonic)	4	2
Total	**172.5 seconds**	

The *sthayi* forms the base because the musician returns to it repeatedly after every portion of the composition. Zohra Bai sings the entire *sthayi* once and establishes the plaintive mood of the raga. Only a portion of the *sthayi* is repeated in the second iteration. A similar format of singing the entire line and then a small portion of it is followed for the *Antara*.

She spends almost equal amounts of time on each of the two iterations of the *sthayi* and *antara* and together this composed section takes up a minute of the recording.

Zohra Bai then begins the improvisation portion in the recording. The improvisation is composed of two sets of extempore solfa notes (*sargam*), three sweeping melodic phrase manipulations on the *mukhra* (*bol taan*) and one sweeping melodic phrase (*taan*). These improvisations form the core of the recording and consume the maximum time. At the end of every improvisation there is a return to a compressed version of the *mukhra*. She concludes the recording with the announcement of her name *Zohra Bai Agrewali*.

Various structural parts of the recording are detailed in Table 6.8.

The two improvisatory *sargams* (or solfa phrases) that Zohra Bai uses are:

1 s r m p D,, n s' r' s' n d n s' n d n d p M,, M, P, D,,,
   n s' r' s' n dn S' r s' n d n s d n d p m p r m p d m p ggrs (*Mori*) — *12.5 seconds*
2 r m p D, p m p r m p D,,
   n s r' s' n d n s' r' s' n d n s' n d p m p r m p d m p ggrs (Mori) — *7 seconds*

The two are spectrographically represented in Figure 6.16.

The spectrogram shows that in accordance with the rules of the raga, Zohra Bai has confined the presentation to the upper tetrachord; there are not too many oscillations visible and the patterns are stable. The elongated portions of the spectrogram are where she places the emphasis on *Dha*, again in accordance with the grammar of the raga.

Zohra Bai's gramophone recording of a musical form such as the *khayal* is important from the view point of understanding how Indian classical music (Hindustani, in this case), might be reconciled to the three-minute capsule that the recording technology offered. Within its own terms and definition, the recording is well structured and has an inherent sense of balance by adhering to the aesthetic aspects of the musical form and giving equal

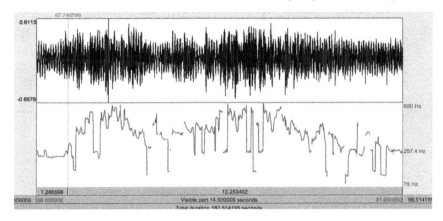

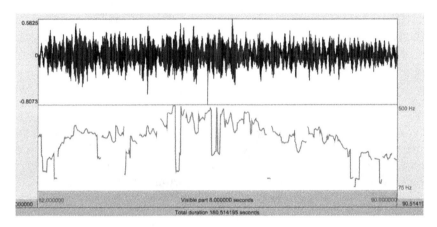

Figure 6.16 Spectrogram of the *sargam* sung by Zohra Bai in the 1909 *khayal* recording in raga *Jaunpuri*.

weight to both composed and improvised sections of the music. As Farrell (1993) states:

> The analysis of performance in terms of the proportions of composed to improvised sections is particularly valid in the context of recording where the musician has to decide what to include or leave out. Such decisions have a different meaning in the unfolding of a temporally open-ended live performance. (51)

In my interview with the stalwart contemporary musician of the Agra *gharana* Lalith J. Rao, she notes:

> But what is significant about this recording is that in this very short capsule Zohra Bai still manages to show us a glimpse of the *gharana*

that she belonged to: the Agra *gharana*. It is a feature of the *gharana* of using phrases in the composition to expand the raga. Using this technique the sentiment of the raga becomes clearer and more powerful. We Agra *gharana* musicians also use vocal techniques such as *Deergha Meend* (prolonged sliding notes), *Suron ki aas* (reverb effect of notes) and *Andolan* (vibration in notes) in their singing, particularly of *taans*. I observe Zohra Bai showing us a glimpse of this as well in the unitary *taan* (sung more as a *behlaawa*)[17] that she manages to sing within the limited time of this recording. The other unique feature of the Agra *gharana* that Zohra Bai portrays is the generous usage of the *bol taans*, an improvisation technique where words and rhythmic *taans* are combined together. That she uses 47 seconds of the recording (nearly one third of the time available) on essaying four *bol taans* is to depict the importance of this improvisation technique in her *gharana*. In the *sargams* too (which interestingly are not a typical component of the Agra style of singing) she succinctly gives us a glimpse of the raga *swaroop* or feature of the raga by using characteristic phrases of *Jaunpuri* like M,P D,, and ggrS, and using the elongated note *Dha* sliding to the note *Pa* in order to paint a characteristic picture of the raga.[18]

Faiyaz Khan

I compare the *Matki Mori Re* recording of Zohra Bai analysed in the earlier section, with that of *Ustad* Faiyaz Khan (1886–1950), the foremost male doyenne of the Agra *gharana*. The recording of the *khayal*, *Phoolwana ki gendana* in raga *Jaunpuri* belongs to late 1930s or early 1940s and is set to medium tempo rhythmic cycle of *madhyalaya teental* (sixteen beats).

The structure of the recording is detailed in Table 6.9.

The structure of this recording is simpler than that of Zohra Bai's and yet it conveys several features that will be discussed subsequently. The quality of the recording and the enunciations are much better than Zohra Bai's possibly because of the advanced technology, the use of the microphone (that was beginning to be used from 1925) and the familiarity with the recording technique. The recording begins with the tonic, which meanders into a brief *aalaap*. Faiyaz Khan then starts the *mukhra* of the *sthayi* and makes improvisatory repetitions for four times before singing the second line of the *sthayi*. The recording is punctuated at regular intervals by brief but powerful full-throated vocal bursts, which in a way also punctuate the transition to another part of the composition or towards the improvisation. Faiyaz Khan does one elaborate *bol taan* and *bol aalaap* in medium tempo and as the *tabla* picks up speed he does an extensive *bol taan* in fast tempo for one minute and fifteen seconds before concluding the recording. The tempo increases again around two minutes and forty-three seconds into the recording.

Table 6.9 Structure of Faiyaz Khan's recording

	Begins at (in sec)	Duration (in sec)
Ustad Faiyaz Khan of Agra – phulwana ki gendana – khayal in raga Jaunpuri – 1930–40 recording		
START	0	
Tonic followed by an aalaap	2.5	11.5
Sthayi- Iteration 1	14	11
Sthayi- Iteration 2	25	5
Sthayi- Iteration 3	30	6
Sthayi- Iteration 4	36	16.5
2nd line of sthayi	52.5	4.5
Mukhra refrain	57	10
Bol Taan/Bol Aalaap 1	67	26
Mukhra refrain	93	5
Antara	98	20
Increase in tempo	118	4.5
Bol Taan 2	122.5	70.5
End	193	
Total Recorded		**190.5**

Senior musician of the Agra *gharana, Pandit* Vijay Kichlu observes, in my interview with him:

> Ustad Faiyaz Khan has eschewed elements such as *sargams* and conveys a perfect picture of the style of the Agra *gharana*. He is in fact considered as the very embodiment of the Agra *gharana* style of singing and most of us Agra *gharana* artists post-Faiyaz Khan era have performed mostly within the framework, mannerisms and stylisations as defined by him. We Agra *gharana* singers place stress upon cultivating a powerful voice through the practice of bass, where a full-throated voice is gradually increased towards the lower octave to achieve a special grandeur and breadth to the voice. This vocal power and resonance is amply visible in this recording. The *behlaawas*, long *meends*, extensive, full-throated and breathless *bol taans* and aggressive vocalisation inspired by some streams of the *dhrupad* vocalism bear a distinctive Agra *gharana* stamp. The *gharana*, especially during the time of Faiyaz Khan, was perceived as "masculine" because of its aggressive vocalisation[19] and use of bold forms of melodic execution.[20]

Gopalrao Kelkar (2015) mentions that the approach to voice production and delivery biased the *gharana* "towards staccato intonation" and a "marked angularity of melodic contours" (67). A sense of drama is created in the renditions of several Agra singers and this is perceived even in this recording of Faiyaz Khan.

Kesarbai Kerkar

Just as in the case of the recordings analysed of Zohra Bai and Faiyaz Khan in the preceding sections, I find a similar adherence to *gharana* traditions in the recording of a stalwart of the Jaipur Atrauli *gharana:* Kesarbai Kerkar (1892–1977). The recording of the *khayal,* "*Hun to jaiyyo piya ke desh*" possibly belongs to the 1930s. The three-minute recording is made up entirely of *akaars* (elongated phrases produced by the syllable "*aa*") and *taans.* Kesarbai does not even sing the whole *sthayi* or the *antara* even once and just uses the *mukhra* "*hu to jaiyyo*" as the refrain. Some of the *taans* are sung in a breathless manner. Mukherji (2006) quotes musician Shrikrishna Haldankar speaking about this aspect of the Jaipur *gharana*:

> When a Jaipur *gharana* artiste takes a *sam* and begins his rendition in a new *aavartan*, he takes care that he does not pause in his *aalaap* or break his *aalaap* before he sings the *mukhda* again to reach the *sam.* The old records of Kesarbai or Moghubai will amply prove this point... This kind of presentation also requires a continuous thought pattern or process, or the building up of a macro composition. Thus a massively structured improvisation (*deergha rachana*) facilitated by astounding breath control could be said to be the intrinsic feature of this *gharana.* The impact of this kind of presentation on the audience is such that the listener reacts to the music with awe. (226)

This sense of awe is very evident in this three-minute recording of Kesarbai and her presentation of *Jaunpuri*. Haladanakara (2001) states that in the Jaipur style those compositions that facilitate the "tenet of ceaselessness emanating from long breath" are selected (64). The words of the composition mean little for the musician and are usually "spread out over the range of the rhythmic cycle to create this expansiveness" and to connect the words the *aa* syllable is used, thus making a long-winded and continuous presentation. At the risk of making the rendition monotonous to a listener, the *gharana* insists on the *akaara*. Usage of long t*aans* is also another prominent feature of this *gharana*. The *taans* are delivered in a "long breath but they are also intricately ornamented and spectacularly designed"(81).

Most of Kesarbai's *taans* in this recording are ten to fifteen seconds long and delivered in one breath. A visual representation of the *taans* she performs in the recording at 40, 50, 130, 152 and 168 seconds is shown in Figure 6.17.

The above spectrograms show the range of the pitch and also the speed of her *taans*. The lack of gaps between the various portions of the spectrogram depict that they have been rendered in one long breath that was her characteristic. The spectrograms demonstrate that not only were the *taans* long and delivered in one breath, but also were of intricate patterns, offering, as Mukherji (2006) states "bejeweled patterns, each different from the other, rendered in *shuddh akaar*"[21](255).

Describing the style of Kesarbai, Mukherji (2006) who had heard her live concerts and gramophone recordings writes:

> Her 78-RPM records of *Gauri, Kafi Kanhra, Bihagada, Nand, Durga, Maru Bihag, Lalita Gauri* and *Tilak Kamod* (ragas) are absolute gems which aspiring female students of *khayal* must hear repeatedly. But her recitals seemed like elongated versions of these records and ran the risk of sounding monotonous to a fastidious ear after a while. Her limitations of course, are the limitations of the Jaipur *gaayaki*. Without *bol-vistar, bol-banao, bol-bant*[22] and with a somewhat limited imagination, her treatment of raga, like that of other members of her *gharana*, could not last more than half an hour without repetition. (203–204)

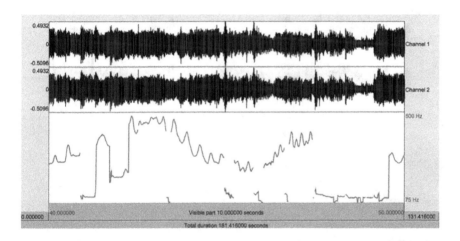

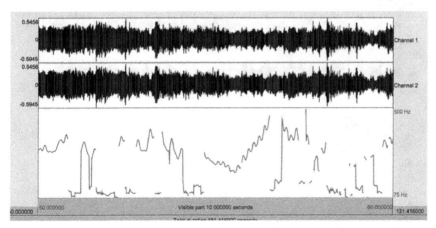

Figure 6.17 Visual spectrograms of Kesarbai Kerkar's *taans*. *(Continued)*

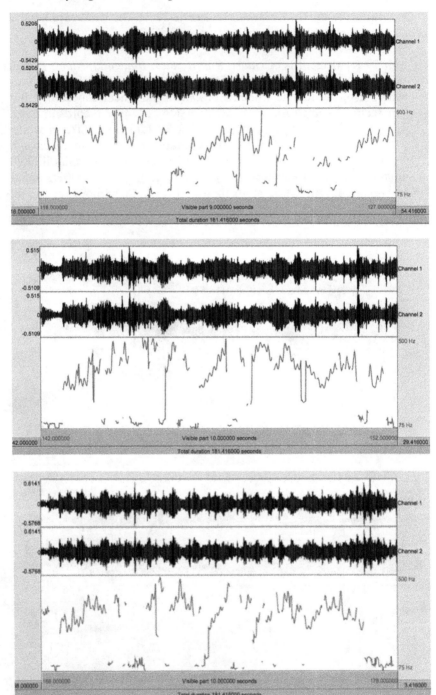

Figure 6.17 (Continued)

Sampath (2010) writes that Kesarbai was an exception to the trend of women singers from the courtesan community to record on the gramophone readily. She was quite wary of the medium and also very particular about the representation of her work. Consequently she recorded very few gramophone discs for The Gramophone Company and Broadcast labels.

Master Krishnarao Phulambrikar

Interestingly, a synthesis of both the styles discussed above: the Agra and Jaipur *gharanas* is visible in the 1920s recording of a *bada* (big *khayal*), *Baaje Jhanan paayaliya mori* in raga *Jaunpuri* and set to *Jhoomra* tala. The recording is of Master Krishnarao Phulambrikar (1891–1974). This recording appears to have been so popular that musician Pushkar Lele says in my interview with him: "His 78-RPM record of raga *Jaunpuri* was so popular, he was known as *Baaje Jhanan Master Krishna* in (the) 1920's."[23] The synthesis of *gharanas* in Krishnarao's singing is not surprising because he was the disciple of Bhaksarbuwa Bakhle (1869–1922). Bakhle was among the earliest vocalists to learn from stalwarts of the Kirana, Gwalior, Agra and Jaipur *gharanas* and thereby create a new and synthesised style of several *gharanas*. See Table 6.10 for the structure of the recording.

After singing the entire *sthayi* once, Krishnarao begins the *Bol vistaar* (expanding the words of the lyrics) in typical Agra style by using *bol aalaap* and a bit of *bol taan*. In the second *bol aalaap* he interestingly uses the Jaipur

Table 6.10 Structure of Krishnarao's recording

Master Krishnarao – baaje jhanan – khayal in raga Jaunpuri – 1920s recording		
	Begins at (in sec)	*Duration (in sec)*
START	0	
Sthayi- Iteration 1	1	36
Mukhra refrain	37	4
Bol Aalaap and Bol Taan	41	20
Mukhra refrain	61	4
Bol Aalaap	65	30
Mukhra refrain	95	9
Taan series	104	14
Laykari	118	11
Mukhra refrain	129	3
Antara	132	28
Mukhra refrain	160	4
Taan series	164	8
Mukhra refrain	172	5
End	177	
Total Recorded		**176**

Table 6.11 Break-up of recording of Krishnarao into composition and improvisation

Component	Duration (in sec)	Percent of recording
Composed component	65	37
Improvised component	3	48
Refrains + pauses	25	14
Miscellaneous	1	1
TOTAL	**174**	

style of elongation using "aa" (*akaar*) in the *aalaap*. In my interview with him Pushkar Lele mentions:

> True to the Agra style, he presents a brief *Layakaari*, which are cross-rhythmic variations of words of the *mukhra* to fit into the rhythmic cycle of the tala. The series of *taans* that he sings are reminiscent of the Jaipur style and in fact some of them are more intricately ornamented than the Jaipur singers and rendered in lightning speed and with great vocal flexibility.[24]

A break-up of the recording into sections again demonstrates the emphasis given to improvisation; see Table 6.11.

My observations from the *khayal* renditions of the singers mentioned (Zohra Bai, Faiyaz Khan, Kesarbai and Krishnarao) who recorded across various decades of the twentieth century, refutes the claim made by Farrell (1993) who states:

> I suggest that one possible effect of the duration on early recordings was to lead artists to give greater weight to the composed or fixed parts of the performances than they would normally have done in live recitals. This is particularly true of forms like the *khayal*. To verify this point, however, requires further research with a larger sample. (51)

Improvisation continues to be the main component of recordings too as they were (and are) in live performances of Hindustani classical music. Composition elements such as the *sthayi*, *mukhra* or *antara* are presented only to the extent that it is required in a rendition format. In a way the presentation of composition elements is a microcosm of what it is in a live performance, just as the improvisation too is an abridged version.

Gauhar Jaan and Malka Jaan of Agra

I briefly analyse two earlier recordings in *Jaunpuri*: Gauhar Jaan's *Chanana Bichuwa* from the second recording expedition of 1904–05 and Malka Jaan of Agra's *Bhor bhayi Milan bailawa* from the 1906–07 recording expedition.

Table 6.12 Structure of Gauhar Jaan's recording *Chhum Chanana Bichuwa*

	Begins at (in sec)	Duration (in sec)
Gauhar Jaan – chhum chanana bichuwa – khayal in raga Jaunpuri – 1904–05 recording		
START	0	
Sthayi	2	4.5
Sthayi- entirely sung	6.5	18
Sthayi- Iteration 2	24.5	13
Taan	37.5	3
Mukhra refrain	40.5	1.5
Taan	42	7
Mukhra refrain	49	2
Bol Taan 1	51	6.5
Sthayi	57.5	22.5
Taan	80	6
Mukhra refrain	86	4
Antara	90	15
Mukhra refrain	105	2
Taan and aalaap	107	23
Mukhra refrain	130	4
END	134	
Total Recorded		**132**

Gauhar Jaan learnt from several *Ustads* belonging to various *gharanas* but she is most closely associated with the Banaras *gharana*, which is better known for its "light-classical" *thumris* than the *khayal* style. A lack of any specific *gharana* stamp is evident in her recording, as we do not find any distinctive *gharana's* features

Table 6.12 shows the structure of the recording.

One has to keep in mind that this was the very second recording expedition in India (i.e. in 1904–05). The technology and the manner of adapting a *khayal* to fit into the three minute capsule was still being experimented with by artists, including Gauhar Jaan. Hence, I observe a more scattered, unstructured and repetitive rendition. The same lines of the *sthayi* are repeated several times with not too many imaginative improvisations.

This repetition leads to a dominance of the composed component in the recording vis-à-vis the improvised component. One, however, sees a rather unique *uthaan* or ascent of the *antara* that sounds such as MPnS, which occurs at 1.30 minutes (Table 6.13).

In the very next recording expedition in 1906–07, I find a *khayal* recording of Gauhar Jaan in raga *Bhoopali Itna Joban* where the improvised content accounts for 75 seconds (56%), the composed component for 40 seconds (30%) and refrains for 20 seconds (14%) in a total recording time of 2 minutes and 35 seconds.

Table 6.13 Break-up of recording of Gauhar Jaan *Chhum Chanana Bichuwa* – composition and improvisation

Component	Duration (in sec.)	Percent of recording
Composed component	73	55
Improvised component	45.5	34
Refrains and pauses	13.5	10
Miscellaneous	0	0
Total	**132**	

However, the recording of Malka Jaan, who is also considered a musician of the Agra *gharana*, is marked by a complete lack of creative expression. She appears uncomfortable with the *khayal* structure, and the recording lacks musical virtuosity. It tends to be very repetitive with the same lines of the *sthayi* and *antara* being repeated without any improvisations done over them. Her recordings of *thumris* are more popular and Sampath (2010) says she is credited with developing a new full-throated *thumri* singing style (57). But the *khayal* recording of 1906–07 certainly has no indication of the Agra style or of her virtuosity.

Inferences

Figure 6.18 shows the mapping of the Hindustani music recordings chronologically.

The inference that emerges from the recording analysis of the musicians (Gauhar Jaan, Malka Jaan, Zohra Bai, Kesarbai, Faiyaz Khan and Krishnarao) is that the gramophone recordings actually reinforced the *gharana* traditions and styles even within the limitations of time. In a way the limited time duration available for recording compelled the musician to distil the features of their singing (*gaayaki*) and their *gharana* and present the most important elements that set their style apart. My deduction from this analysis is that although the male *Ustads* might have been wary of recording initially, the popularity of the gramophone and also their own introspection about how effectively this new medium could be used to present a succinct picture of their individual and the *gharana* style, made them take to recording more readily by the end of the second decade of the twentieth century.

The Thumri Recordings of Hindustani Music

I now analyse a sub-genre of Hindustani classical music that was specifically associated with the *tawaif* – *thumri*. Just as the status of the *tawaifs* was ambiguous in society, so was their musical repertoire. While they learnt the regimented classical (*maargi*) forms of *dhrupad* and *khayal*, their performances and certainly recordings have a surfeit of sub-genres such as *thumri*,

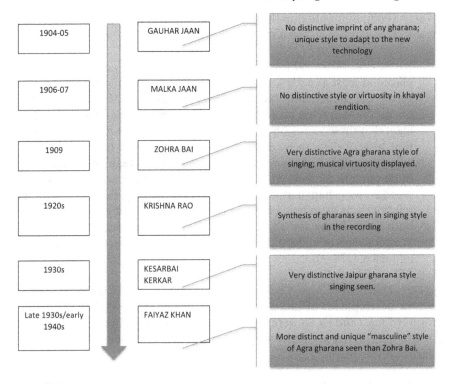

Figure 6.18 The chronological journey of Hindustani music recordings and the inferences.

chaiti, kajri, hori and *dadra* that are associated more as *desi* (regional/folk/semi-classical). The *thumri* has an ancient past and musicologists are divided about when it exactly originated and crystallised into the form that we know of today. Musicologist Thakur Jaideva Singh traces its origins to mythology and also references it to the *Natya Shastra* of Bharatha. He states:

> The *thumri* is a form of *nritya* music of which *abhinaya* or acting was an indispensable component. I am using the word *nritya* advisedly, for it is untranslatable in any other language. *Nritta* is simply gestures and movements of definite patterns based on laya and tala. *Nritya* combines with this *abhinaya*, which means communication of *bhaava* and *rasa*, and may be roughly translated as acting...the English word 'dance' may be a synonym for *nritta* but cannot do justice to the connotation of nritya. Some scholars have suggested 'representational dance' as an equivalent for *nritya*. French Indologists have suggested '*danse communicante*' or '*danse communicatrice*' as equivalents for *nritya*. (1961:10)

Rao (1996) opines that in the patriarchal world of Hindustani genres, the *thumri* represents the "feminine voice." She states:

> In the case of *thumri* it seems that the 'authentic' style is theoretically placed at least as early as the tenth-century A.D. while practically, the *gaayaki* is modeled on the recordings of voices of Moizuddin Khan, Girija Shankar Chakravarthy, Gauhar Jaan and Jaddan Bai. It is significant that these voices sing, shape the 'authentic' form for us at precisely that historical moment when a Western world-view (notions of class, culture, morality, women's status, aesthetics and realism) had already burst upon the Indian scene. It seems to me that *thumri*, as we imagine it today, was shaped at a time when Indian history, culture and social relationships were being reformulated and performing traditions were both assimilating and contesting Western ways of seeing and hearing, Western ways of understanding the relationship between performer and audience. (278–315)

Devi (1985) states that Lucknow, Banaras and Gaya were the main centres of development of the *thumri*. It was in Banaras and Gaya that folk forms of *kajri* and *chaiti* were stylised and became a part of *thumri gaayaki* or singing (15). In my interview with one of the living legends of *thumris*, Girija Devi explains:

> The delicacy of expression is the most important feature of *thumri* rendition and the main stress in *thumri* singing is upon the expressive aspect of the song and not on the intricacies of the technique. The worth of an artist rendering this form is determined by how well a true musical portrayal of the lyric is made and is dependent on the temperament and mood of the artist too. Various embellishments such as *murki, khatka, kan, zam-zama, meend* and *pukaar* are used in rendering a *thumri*. The *thumri's* essential *rasa* or emotion is that of *shringara*. *Shringara* is a complex term that fails to have a direct English equivalent and romance is far from what the term actually conveys.[25]

Sampath (2010) writes that the *naayika* (or protagonist) of a *thumri* is always a woman, even though the lyrics might be composed or sung by men. He writes that there are several kinds of heroines in a *thumri*. There is the *naayika* who is all decked up and ready for union with her lover; then there is one who is suffering deep anguish at being separated from her beloved. One *naayika* represents a woman who has parted from her lover after a bitter quarrel. Then there is one who is enraged at her beloved's infidelity and his flirtations with other women. Allied to this theme is the plight of the *naayika* deceived by her lover. Sometimes the memory of a husband who is on a journey or in a foreign land evokes loneliness while in other cases the heroine moves towards her lover's abode, her heart aflutter with excitement and anticipation. In some rare cases the woman is in control and has sub-jugated her beloved. The pangs of unrequited love, agony of separation, the ecstasy of union and the anger coupled with sorrow at being deceived thus form the thematic content of *thumris*. It is usually Radha and Krishna around whom these themes are woven, but sometimes it is also anonymous men and women who are the heroes and heroines of these stories in verse. Themes of *thumris* revolve around these different protagonists (104).

Girijia Devi mentions in my interview with her:

> There are two main types of *thumris*: *Bol Baant* or *Bandish ki thumri* that focuses on elaborate rhythmic play. *Bol Banao thumris* or *Khayal ang ki thumri* or *Khayalnuma thumri* are typical of Banaras style. Here the leisurely tala or rhythmic framework and treatment give it expan-siveness akin to a *khayal* rendition. At the same time, it also focuses on the exploration of the multi-layered meanings of the *bol* or word and hence it derives this name. They are set in typical 'light' or semi-classi-cal ragas such as *Kaafi, Piloo, Ghara, Khamaj, Sindhura, Dhaani, Manj Khamaaj, Tilang, Jhinjhoti, Zilla* and so on. The talas that are typically associated with the *thumri* are *Deepchandi, Addha, Ikwaai, Sitarkhani* and those derived from folk music such as *Keharwa, Dadra, Khemta* and *Chaachar*. The rustic nature of the lyrics, the free rhythmic character and open-endedness impart to the *thumri* the ability to create multiple patterns that gives the artist the scope for improvisation. For instance, a single line of a *thumri* such as *Kaun gali gayo Shyaam?* (Which road has Krishna taken?) can be demonstrated by an able *thumri* singer using innumerable varieties of emotions just with a shift of emphasis in the lyrics or by varying the rhythmic pattern.[26]

On the openness and ambiguity of the text or lyric of a *thumri*, Manuel (1989) states:

> A good *thumri* text is 'incomplete'; in that its expression of emotion is sufficiently broad, simple and general so that the singer can interpret it in innumerable ways. At the same time, each line is 'complete' and autonomous in that the emotional thought, however simple, is expressed within that one line, and does not require two or more lines in order to be clear. (112)

This ambiguity of text is explored and negotiated at several levels: the textual, at the malleability of the raga, the changing patterns of rhythm or tala and the theme. Rao (1990) elaborates on this concept:

> A *thumri* singer would revel in the points of danger and explore just how far and how much otherness can be introduced into the body of the raga. A *swar* in the raga becomes the door that leads to other ragas; a

swar as it is heard in one raga is deliberately punned upon to give it the meaning in another raga. (157)

It is not so much that the ragas of a *thumri* are mixed to create a third new raga with its own identity and personality. Instead, the points of weakness, and the boundaries in a raga's structure are used as points at which other ragas are allowed to enter into the body of the main raga. Rao (1996) also suggests that in performances of *thumris*, particularly in the *kothas* or salons of *tawaifs*, the intimacy of the performance where she performed only to a select few in a room making eye contact with them as she sang and danced lent an erotic element to the *thumri*. It thus had a "strong visual aspect: the *tawaif*'s body is ineradicably present in the performance (283)." In the salon, a musical performance invariably was accompanied with dance, performed by the *tawaif* in a seated position. Rao (1996) therefore indicates that the *tawaif*'s body and emotions are therefore "displayed and consumed as much as are the body and emotions of the *naayika* who is evoked through the performance" (283).

The above discussion suggests that the intimacy between the performer and the audience is essential for the performance of a *thumri* to be complete. The emotion needs to be evoked, expressed and communicated through the voice and body gestures. The exploration of the ambiguities of meaning, raga, and tala required leisure and time. This was possibly the biggest challenge that the *tawaifs* who recorded on the gramophone faced. They were used to salon performances where they used hand gestures, facial expressions, dance movements, erotic and sensuous expressions, glittering jewelry, and clothing in addition to their vocal prowess to evoke the right kind of emotion in the performance. In the gramophone recording studios they had to sing into a horn and the audience was unknown. The restricted time limit of three minutes constrained them from bringing about all these multiple emotions and ambiguities to an unknown and unseen audience. Yet, we find as discussed earlier that these semi-classical genres (such as the *thumri*) formed the bulk of the recorded repertoire of the first two decades of the twentieth century.

Thumri Recordings in Raga Bhairavi

One of the most commonly recorded ragas on gramophone records was *Bhairavi*. *Bhairavi* is a heptatonic melody and belongs to the Bhairavi *thaat* of Hindustani music. It is usually performed as the concluding piece in contemporary concerts.

Pakad is the shortest note combinations to identify a raga and a *chalan* is one of the many basic signifier phrases that define a raga. The *chalan* is a combination of phrases that illustrate the general movement of a raga. As a raga is open to interpretation (within certain bounds) by musicians, multiple *chalans* are possible for a given raga. Many *chalans* constitute a raga.

Bhairavi is a raga that is normally employed more by the semi classical genres of Hindustani music such as *thumris, dadras,* and *bhajans,* although classical genres such as *dhrupad, dhamar,* and *khayals* in the raga do exist. During my interview with Hindustani musician and musicologist Lalith J. Rao, she mentioned: "Traditionally there have been two main ways of rendering this raga, one in which the *Madhyam* or *Ma* is *pradhaan* or the chief note and another with *Gandhaar* or *Ga* as *pradhaan*."[27]

As discussed in the section about *thumris,* while singing *thumris* in this raga, small phrases from other ragas and different notes that are normally not associated with notes of *Bhairavi* are also used very often. Since there is a scope for including notes/phrases from other ragas, raga *Bhairavi,* especially in *thumri* and allied forms are also referred as *Mishra* (mixed) *Bhairavi.* This is an accepted nomenclature convention in Hindustani music. However, for purposes of simplicity, in this section I refer to the raga as *Bhairavi* only.

I have analysed some of the recordings of *Bhairavi* by various artists starting from the first recorded artist, Gauhar Jaan by listening to these recordings in the presence of Lalith J. Rao, contemporary Hindustani musician Sounak Chattopadhyay, and record collectors Suresh Chandvankar and Vikrant Ajgaonkar.

Gauhar Jaan's own composition, a *thumri, Ras ke bhare tore nain* is a recording of the 1904–05 vintage. *Ras ke bhare tore nain* literally translates to "Your seductive eyes that are full of elixir" and the poet makes her entreaties to her beloved to come and embrace her and his image is etched in her heart and without his presence she finds no peace. The mood therefore is one of longing and desire, which Gauhar Jaan manages to convey. Unlike most *thumris* that have just a few lines of lyrics, this recording has her recite long passages, which she might have done to ensure that her lyrics were preserved for posterity. However, my respondents[28] told me that contemporary musicians seldom know that this is Gauhar's composition, nor do they sing all verses of the *thumri* in a concert or recording. Gauhar Jaan begins the recording with *teevra* (augmented or sharp) *Madhyam* (Ma) transposing the tonic to the fourth or the sub dominant. In line with the musicological acceptance of the *pancham* (Pa) as the dominant note of the raga, she provides a lot of prolonged sustain (*nyaas*) on this note. In between the lyrics she also does improvisations in the form of taans, which use certain characteristic phrases of *Bhairavi,* sung in varied speeds and in different octaves. For instance she creates *taan* patterns incorporating signifier phrases such as S,,sRG,, and NS GM, PD,,P,,

Overall, all my respondents agreed that a complete musicological picture of *Bhairavi* is presented in this early recording, much in line with the way the raga is presented today and at the same time managing to convey the emotional content of the lyrics within the limited time span.

We then analysed the recording of the same song by another contemporary of Gauhar Jaan, the male musician Peara Saheb. My respondents[29] opined that this recording of Peara Saheb is sung in a folk format and lacks the emotional content and spirit that Gauhar Jaan's recording of the same song had. It is sung in a very high feminine pitch and his voice cracks and gives in at many places. The lyrics are kept limited and the same lines of the lyrics are repeated with limited improvisations. *Taan* patterns are repetitive but they indicate the signifier phrases including NSGM, P, of *Bhairavi*. About one minute thirty-nine seconds into the recording, Peara Saheb prominently uses a point of departure in that the extraneous note of *Shuddha Rishab* (natural variant of *Re*) is utilised. *Teevra madhyam* note of the raga is used in the rendition of ascent phrases. Similar to Gauhar Jaan's rendition, Peara Saheb also begins from the *madhyam* by shifting the tonic. Despite the poor vocal quality of the recording, my respondents felt it did give a succinct picture of the raga, though lacked the emotional appeal of Gauhar Jaan's recording.[30]

Gauhar Jaan's recording of another *thumri* dating to 1905–06 vintage *Raseeli Matwaliyon ne Jaadoo Daala* (literally meaning – "What a seductive magical spell he has cast on me!") is strikingly similar to the *Ras ke Bhare* recording in terms of the emotion conveyed of intense desire by utilising long chromatic *meend* or glides over notes. *Teevra madhyam* is used often, so is the signifier phrase g R r S; the *taan* patterns are very similar to the other recording.[31]

An important concept in Hindustani rhythm is that of the s*am*, which typically is a stress point and the first beat of the tala cycle. As a counterpart to the *sam*, *Khaali* can be understood as the release point of the tala cycle and is mid-way between the beginning (*sam*) and the end of the tala cycle. Lalith J. Rao explains in my interview with her:

> *Sam* literally translates to "coming together" or "conjoining". It has a special significance in both Hindustani musical performance and theory as it establishes a point of resolution. The lead artist is free to create improvisations and also begin a fixed composition from any point of the cycle (*aavartan*), they eventually almost always resolve on the *sam* that acts as a pivotal point. At this point the artist and the rhythmic accompanist, the *tabla* player, would converge on the first beat of the cycle, which is usually greeted ecstatically by connoisseurs in the audience who understand the rhythm play going on.[32]

It was noticed that both recordings of Gauhar Jaan have their *sam* points at the tonic (*Shadaj*) or *Sa*, thereby creating a sense of completeness.

I then contrasted the recordings of Gauhar Jaan and Peara Saheb with that of another contemporary male singer Mauzuddin Khan of Banaras, along with my respondents.[33] He was supposedly a star of his times as Sampath (2010) quotes D.P. Mukherjee:

> The best *dhruvapadiyas*[34] and *khayaliyas*[35] would listen to him spell bound. In my own view, India has not produced another *thumri* singer like him. I have seen tears in the eyes of Gauhar Jan, Malka Jan,

Shyamlal Khatri, Girija Babu and many others when Mauzuddin improvised on a simple *Bhairavi*. (61)

According to Kinnear's (1994) catalogue the recording of Mauzuddin's *thumri*, *Baaju Band Khul Khul Jaaye* (meaning: "The armlet slips away") belongs to the 1908–10 vintage. My respondent Sounak Chattopadhyay noticed a distinct influence of the doyen of Kirana *gharana* Abdul Karim Khan.[36] Sounak explains in my interview with him:

> In this recording, Mauzuddin Khan uses his point of departure as the extraneous *shuddha nishaad* note (natural variant of *Ni*) in the descent phrases. The *sam* lands at the *pancham* (Pa) note giving a sense of musical anticipation rather than fulfillment or completion. His musical virtuosity is clear since the *thumri* is rendered in a pure classical style. He employs a lot of imaginative patterns of *aakaar taans* (usage of syllable 'aa' in the *taans*) in the *thumri*, more than *bol banao* as is more common and expected in a *thumri*. But it remains very much a *thumri*. Free and liberal use of *teevra madhyam* and *shuddha nishadh* certainly indicates that. He does not use a *taan* merely occasionally but they pervade almost throughout the performance. Nearly fifty seconds of *aakar taan* in a 2 min 38 sec *thumri* is a significant proportion.[37]

The *thumri* recording *Jaa main tose naahin boloon* (meaning "Go away! I will not speak to you") of Malka Jaan of Agra is true to the meanings of the lyrics. According to Kinnear's (1994) catalogue the recording belongs to the 1910–14 vintage. The song features a heroine annoyed with her lover and chides him saying she will not speak to him. It is hence rich in emotional content, passion, robustness and voice modulations that convey the heroine's annoyance and anger at possible betrayal with her lover. Around two minutes thirty seconds into the recording many beautiful ornamentations on the lyrics are performed in the true style of rendering a *thumri*. Lalith J. Rao explains in my interview with her

> Though the approach is more *thumri* oriented, one can notice the full-throated rendering style, which she was famous for and had acquired due to her training under the maestros of the Agra *gharana*.[38]

A late 1920s *thumri* recording *Lagat Karajwa Mein Chot* (meaning "My heart aches") of **Sawai Gandharva** (1886–1952) is a typical Kirana *gharana* presentation. Sawai Gandharva was one of the foremost disciples of Abdul Karim Khan, the founder of the Kirana *gharana*. In my interview with him, Sounak Chattopadhyay mentions:

> The strong use of the extraneous *shuddha nishaad* note seems to depict the indelible influence of his guru. He maintains long sustains (*nyaas*)

on *teevra madhyam* and *pancham* (Pa). Around one minute forty five seconds into the recording he uses a very unique phrase of *Bhairavi* n D, m g R. The *sam* occurs at the tonic or *shadaj* (Sa).[39]

All my respondents noted that almost two decades into recorded history of Hindustani music, the features of the raga *Bhairavi* had mostly remained consistent in the recordings of all the artists thus far, be it in the usage of the *vaad–samvad* (important and defining) notes of the raga, or complimentary notes from the lower and higher tetra chords, or in the usage of signifier phrases. Only slight departures occurred in individual performances and styles, such as the elongated *shuddha nishaad* in Sawai Gandharva's recording. This observation is at variance from the Carnatic music analysis appearing earlier in this chapter.

I then analysed the *thumri* recording of the late 1920s of Kesarbai Kerkar: *Kaahe ko Daare Gulaal* (meaning "Why do you throw colours at me?") set to the fourteen beat *Deepchandi* tala. It is masterly in its emotional content where the heroine is both angry and chides Krishna for throwing colours at her in the festival of colours, Holi and at the same time feels embarrassed at being drenched in colour. In my interview with him Suresh Chandvankar states:

> This recording has her typical flashes of brilliance, cyclical movements and her characteristic long elongation of notes. There is almost an architectural build up of the raga step-by-step in the form of a *khayal*, despite it being a supposed semi-classical genre of *thumri*. Though unlike some of the male singers, the emotional content is also equally maintained. She makes long breath elaboration mainly in an *akaar (aa)* format typical of the Jaipur *gharana*. She takes great liberties with notes and has several points of entry and departure into the raga in the true spirit of openness of a *thumri*. Usage of several extraneous natural variant notes such as *shuddha rishabh, shuddha dhaivat*, unusually long *shuddha rishabh* and *shuddha nishaad* in the *antara* section of the thumri, in addition to the usual *teevra madhyam*, helps create variations in the emotion and the moods of the heroine of the song.[40]

This is a two-sided record and hence there are six minutes of recording. The leisure of time has also possibly contributed to her expansiveness in improvisation. In an interesting adaptation of the Banaras *Bol Banao thumris*, Kesarbai also indulges in an interesting *laggi*.[41] In this recording the *laggi* interlude is for a rhythmic cycle of 4 + 4 after which she returns to the original 14 beat cycle of *Deepchandi* tala.

The 1930s *thumri* recording of **Narayanrao Vyas** (1902–1984) *Bahut Sahi Tori Gaari* (meaning: "A lot of abuses to you") is also set in the same *Deepchandi* tala. Vyas belonged to the Gwalior *gharana* and was a disciple of one of the renaissance men of Hindustani music, Vishnu Digambar

Paluskar. He cut several gramophone discs of *khayals* and semi-classical *thumris* and devotional *bhajans*. The advance in technology by then is clearly audible in the quality of recording. The rendition is melodious and steeped in emotion of a heroine who chides her lover. His rhythmic plays by changing tempos in the midst of the rendition add great beauty to the recording. In my interview with him, record collector Vikrant Ajgaonkar stated:

> The *sam* is on the tonic or *Shadaj* (Sa). I feel what however makes this recording distinctive and remarkable is the manner in which the *thumri* progresses. Like Kesarbai's rendition, I notice that the *badhat* or build up of the composition and the improvisations are a lot like a *khayal* is developed in phases through t*aans* rather than the *Bol banao* style of *thumris*. As you have noticed, at around two minutes into the record-ing he presents incredible and spiraling volleys of *taans* that sound like spinning tops. This can possibly be traced to his own birth place of Kolhapur in the Western Indian state of Maharashtra that had a unique classically inspired theatre music tradition called the Marathi *Natya sangeet* tradition. However the basic raga characteristics of *Bhairavi* and the Sa-Pa or Sa-Ma combinations between notes that are charac-teristic of the raga remain the same as it was in Gauhar Jaan's early recordings.[42]

Similar observations were made by analysing by a contemporary 1930s *thumri* recording of Mehboob Jaan of Solapur *Katat Naahin Piya Bin* (meaning: "The night does not pass without the beloved"). While musical virtuosity of the recording is not outstanding, what makes her recording interesting is that while she adheres to the raga characteristics of *Bhairavi*, at around two minutes twelve seconds she takes a strange departure point from *Bhairavi*. Sounak Chattopadhyay mentions in my interview with him: "With an unorthodox usage of *Shuddha dhaivat* or natural variant note of *Dha*, she gives a glimpse of another raga *Gunkali*."

Another undated recording of an unknown artist V.N. Thakkar is a devo-tional song *Govind ko Bhajana*. The recording shows an immense influence of Abdul Karim Khan and one of his legendary recordings in *Bhairavi: Jamuna ke Teer* that influenced many contemporaries and successive musi-cians. Sounak Chattopadhyay mentions in my interview with him: "The improvisatory patterns and the liberal use of both *teevra madhyam* and *shud-dha nishad* at twenty-two seconds bear the Abdul Karim Khan stamp. He also uses *shuddha dhaivat* for ornamentation at one minute fifteen seconds. The ascent phrases involve R n S R M and some typical signifier phrases of *Bhairavi* – N S G M P in the ascent and g S r S are employed."[43] Thakkar sings at a very high-pitched feminine voice. Based on this one could assume that the recording is of the first decade of the twentieth century as that was when male singers crooned at high pitched voices.

Summary of Carnatic and Hindustani Music Findings

Carnatic Music Findings

Critical Perspectives of Respondents

In the case of Carnatic music, the recordings of the women musicians of the early gramophone era (1904–1920) such as Salem Godavari, Salem Ammakannu, Bangalore Nagarathnamma, Dhanakoti Ammal of Kanchipuram and Coimbatore Thayi were heard and analysed in the presence of contemporary musicians and musicologists. The following inferences were drawn:

1 **Accelerated tempo and its effect on lyrical and emotional content:** Due to the limited time restraints of the gramophone recording technology, all the artists have adopted an accelerated tempo. Medium tempo or *madhyama kaala* is adopted even for compositions traditionally meant to be sung in a slow tempo (*vilamba kaala*). Barring the recordings of Dhanakoti, which seemed to lack emotional content, voice modulation and finesse, the recordings of the other artists were rendered in loud clear voice with no compromise on the lyrical or emotional content of a composition. The soft and supple voices of some of the artists such as Coimbatore Thayi and Salem Ammakannu was beneficial for the delivery of leisurely, erotic *padams* and *javalis* that were sung with the adequate emotional content of sensuality and longing.

2 **Quality of pronunciation:** Barring good Sanskrit diction of Bangalore Nagarathnamma, all other artists had very poor pronunciation, making it difficult to clearly understand the words that were being sung unless one already knew the song.

3 **Virtuosity displayed in improvisatory techniques:** The limited time of the recording offers little scope for improvisation within the recording of a composition. However, separate recordings of only *aalaapanas* are extant for artists such as Salem Godavari, Bangalore Nagarathnamma and Coimbatore Thayi. The improvisations are largely done with pyro-technic oriented, scalar phrases using long and fast paced cadences, and disjointed octave jumps in phrasing, unlike contemporary renditions. Phrase syntax used is different as compared to contemporary renditions. Artists such as Godavari have also rendered *neravals*, which demonstrate their virtuosity.

4 ***Gamakas* or note centric inflexions** are used minimally and are not the deep, scooping *gamakas* that are characteristic of contemporary Carnatic music. It is more of straight and scalar phrases that revolve around the most important note or notes of a raga.

5 **Changes noticed in raga grammar as compared to contemporary performance standards:** Several signifier phrases of a raga that are used in contemporary Carnatic music were absent in the early recordings. Some notes which

are essential for a raga too were missing; for instance: Dhanakoti's Raga *Keeravani* rendition lacked the *Kaakali Nishaadham* or augmented seventh note of the scale, an otherwise essential feature of the raga.

6 **Enunciation differences** were noted between the gramophone recordings and contemporary practice. Particularly in the rendition of *aalaapana*s well-rounded *akaaram* syllables used in place of the contemporary *Tha Dha Ri Na Na*. All the gramophone era singers displayed a very strict and sound adherence to pitch (*shruti shuddham*).

EMPIRICAL MUSICAL ANALYSIS

Recordings in ragas *Thodi* and *Kambodhi* were chosen for analysis, using the software PRAAT, as these were/are popular classical ragas that are amenable to extensive improvisation and also have a rich repertoire of compositions set in them. Recordings of three Carnatic music women singers: **Bangalore Nagarathnamma, T.N. Manickam and Mysore T. Chandra**, of the early gramophone era (1904–30) were contrasted with Carnatic music recordings of male musicians **G.N. Balasubramaniam and Ariyuakudi Ramanuja Iyengar** (1930–50 era recording), female musicians **M.S. Subbulakshmi and M.L. Vasanthakumari** (1950–1980 era recording) and a contemporary and popular female vocalist Bombay Jayashri. Following parameters were analysed and inferences drawn:

1 **Changes to raga specific behaviour:** Quantitative investigations revealed more richness in *valli gamakas* in contemporary recordings than in gramophone era recordings. This demonstrates a marked change in the understanding of a raga, its melodic content and pitching.
2 **Changes in the *aalaapana* structure or improvisatory syntax:** The critical perspectives offered by respondents about the profusion of scalar phrases in the gramophone recordings were reinforced through spectrogram analysis. The percentage of time of a recording of scalar cadences expressed as a ratio of the total time of a recording proved this point more substantively. Also, the appearance of artist-specific novel phrases was quantified. It was noticed that a higher quotient of unique phrases was used by the gramophone era singers than for those acquired pedagogically as raga grammar in contemporary practice. Modern renditions showed a stricter adherence to raga grammar in improvisatory phrases.
3 **Connections between improvisation and composition:** These connections in the gramophone era and signature phrases of the raga used in gramophone recordings vis-à-vis contemporary recordings were analysed quantitatively. It was noted that in the case of the gramophone era singers the melodic content of the *aalaapana* was more tightly linked to the compositions that they had memorised.
4 **Changes to performance schema and compositional structure:** These were explored using structural analysis and analysis of cyclic routines. The

recording of a popular composition in raga *Kambodhi* of *devadasi* singer Salem Godavari in 1906–07 was compared with a 1930s recording of the same composition by a male classical musician Chembai Vaidyanatha Bhagavathar. The glides of the raga were different, and Godavari's rendition was more instrumental and not vocal driven as Carnatic music is today. It was observed in Godavari's rendition that the elements of compositional restating, interpretation, small improvisatory forays, and distinct rhythmic modulations were collaged into a powerful rendition in the recording. In contrast, Chembai's rendition was seen to be more linear and presented with patterns or *sangatis* without too many flashes of improvisation or any form of modulation. This is similar to contemporary Carnatic music presentation where composition presentation is separated out from the improvisatory sections in time, space, and protocols. It was also noted that the structure of the compositions too has undergone a change. The number of patterns on phrases of the lyrics (*sangatis*) has increased in number, complexity, shape, and range in the scale of a raga. The recording of Chembai shows a more methodical development of phrase and pattern complexity across the same nodes. Also, his recording shows the usage of more than twice the number of *gamakas* or oscillations; thereby presenting a very different form of the raga and the composition.

Changes in raga presentation and the composition's performance schema were attributed to the social changes brought about with the abolition of the *devadasi* system and the attempts at standardisation of classical music. It must be noted here that during the early gramophone era (1904–20) there are no recordings in classical music of male musicians available and women largely dominated the classical repertoire. Hence, the only available recorded auditory material for the gramophone era is of the women singers. When one contrasts these recordings of Carnatic classical music to the recordings of the 1930s of men, one sees the changes stated above that are linked closely to the social cognition of ragas and compositions and how distinct and different they need to sound from the *devadasi's* repertoire and style. The disappearance of the erotic genres of *padams* and *javalis* from the Carnatic music catalogues beginning at the end of the first decade of the twentieth century and later from music pedagogy, due to their close association with the *devadasi*, also points to the sociocultural changes associated with the demonisation of the courtesan.

Hindustani Music Findings

Critical Perspectives of Respondents

In the case of Hindustani music, *thumri* recordings in raga *Bhairavi* were heard and analysed in the presence of contemporary musicians, musicologists and record collectors. The recordings of male and female musicians right from 1902 till the late 1940s: Gauhar Jaan, Malka Jaan, Peara Saheb, Mauzuddin Khan, Sawai Gandharva, Kesarbai Kerkar, Narayan Rao Vyas, V.N. Thakkar, and Mehboob Jaan were analysed. The following inferences were drawn:

1 It was observed that the presentation of the raga and its grammar were by and large consistent across all these recordings and also in comparison with contemporary Hindustani music practice.
2 The early recordings of all the artists managed to convey the emotional content of the lyrics within the limited time span.
3 The recordings varied in emotional content depending on the competence and virtuosity of a musician and barring these slight departures in individual performance styles there was no noticeable change in raga grammar, usage of signifier phrases, or composition structure.

Empirical Musical Analysis

Khayal recordings in raga *Jaunpuri* were chosen for this analysis in the case of Hindustani music. Along with critical perspectives from respondents on these recordings, a time-structure analysis of the recordings was also undertaken. Recordings from 1902 to the late 1930s/early 1940s of both male and female musicians Gauhar Jaan, Malka Jaan, Zohra Bai, Kesarbai Kerkar, Faiyaz Khan, and Master Krishnarao were analysed. The following inferences may be drawn:

1 The gramophone recordings actually reinforced the *gharana* traditions and styles even within the limitations of time.
2 In a way the limited time duration available for recording compelled the musician to distil the features of their singing (*gaayaki*) and their *gharana* and present the most important elements that set their style apart.
3 While the male *Ustads* might have been wary of recording initially, the popularity of the gramophone and also their own introspection about how effectively this new medium could be used to present a succinct picture of their individual and the *gharana* style, made them take to recording more readily by the end of the second decade of the twentieth century.

Notes

1 See Vishwanathan (1977) for details on each of the listed ten *gamakas* and their aesthetic value in Carnatic music.
2 Interview excerpts of author with Dr. Jayanthi Kumaresh.
3 Interview excerpts of author with Dr. Jayanthi Kumaresh..
4 Interview excerpts of author with Dr. Jayanthi Kumaresh.
5 Interview excerpts of author with Smt. Neela Ramgopal.

6 Interview excerpts of author with Dr. T.S. Sathyavathi.
7 These are part of the series of interviews undertaken by me to listen to the recordings along with musicians and musicologists, elicit their feedback, and also tally my own notes and inferences with their understanding of the musical value of the recordings. These included detailed discussions with Carnatic veena exponent Dr. Jayanthi Kumaresh in Bangalore, Carnatic vocalist Dr. S Sowmya in Chennai, and Carnatic vocalist, musicologist, and scholar, Neela Ramgopal in Bangalore.
8 Interview excerpts of author with Dr. Jayanthi Kumaresh.
9 Translations to the lyrics were provided by Dr. Jayanthi Kumaresh in my interview with her.
10 In the notation, the underlining of a phrase indicates that it has to be rendered in double the speed of the non-underlined segment.
11 Interview excerpts of author with Dr. Jayanthi Kumaresh.
12 Interview excerpts of author with Smt. Neela Ramgopal.
13 Interview excerpts of author with Dr. Jayanthi Kumaresh.
14 Interview excerpts of author with Smt. Neela Ramgopal.
15 Interview excerpts of author with Sounak Chattopadhyay.
16 Interview excerpts of author with contemporary musician Sounak Chattopadhyay.
17 *Behlaawa* is a play of combination of notes and phrases with the help of medium tempo heavy *taans* and *meends*. It is a specialty of the Agra *gharana* singers. *Behlaawas* slowly evolved into *taans* at a later stage.
18 Interview excerpts of author with Dr. Lalith J. Rao.
19 Usage of such forms as *meend, gamaka, gitkiri, khatka* etc., as opposed to gentler and delicate ornamentations such as *murki*.
20 Interview excerpts of author with Mr. Vijay Kichlu.
21 Implying the usage of purely open-throated "aa" syllables in the renditions.
22 All these are kinds of improvisation done on the *bol* or the words of the lyrics of a composition. It is also referred to as *Bol Ang* and the Agra *gharana* has ample amount of *bol ang.*
23 Interview excerpt of author with musician Pushkar Lele.
24 Interview excerpts of author with Pushkar Lele.
25 Interview excerpts of author with Smt. Girija Devi.
26 Interview excerpts of author with Girija Devi, where she demonstrated this with several improvisations.
27 Interview excerpt of author with Dr. Lalith J. Rao.
28 Interview excerpts of author with Lalith J. Rao, Sounak Chattopadhyay, and Suresh Chandvankar.
29 Interview excerpts of author with Lalith J. Rao, Sounak Chattopadhyay and Vikrant Ajgaonkar.
30 Interview excerpts of author with the above respondents.
31 Interview excerpts of author with Vikrant Ajgaonkar.
32 Interview excerpts of author with Lalith J. Rao.
33 Interview excerpts of author with Lalith Rao, Sounak Chattopadhyay, Vikrant Ajgaonkar and Suresh Chandvankar.
34 Singer of Dhrupad.
35 Singer of *Khayal.*
36 Sounak Chattopadhyay belongs to the same Kirana *gharana* tradition of Abdul Karim Khan, and he pointed out these specific musical inferences of the Kirana tradition.
37 Interview excerpts of author with Sounak Chattopadhyay.
38 Lalith Rao belongs to the same Agra *gharana* tradition of Malka Jaan and was able to point this out in my interview with her.

39 Interview excerpts of author with Sounak Chattopadhyay.

40 Interview excerpt of author with Suresh Chandvankar. His Society of Indian Record Collectors has brought out extensive discographic material on Kesarbai Kerkar and also a CD of her vintage recordings released. Being an admirer of her singing, he was able to bring out these facets of her style in my interview with him.

41 A *laggi* is a rhythmic interlude in the Banaras *thumri* tradition, which was a direct adaptation of folk rhythms. These are sequences of dense and fast tabla patterns built around repeated nuclei of two or four strokes and are usually set to 8 or 16 beat cycles irrespective of the tala that the preceding *thumri* is set in.

42 Inferences drawn from interview of author with Kushal Gopalka and Vikrant Ajgaonkar on the style of singing during the interview.

43 Interview excerpts of author with Sounak Chattopadhyay.

7 Conclusion

By the second half of the nineteenth century, the consolidation of British imperialism in colonial India brought with it a shift in patronage for the arts from princely courts, royal families, and aristocracies to newly developing urban centres. From ancient times, the courtesan in India had been a custodian of the traditional music and dance forms and was accorded a position of eminence in society, particularly by the patrons of the arts. With the shift of power and patronage to urban centres, the courtesan had to quickly adapt and reinvent herself and her art to a new salon audience.

The Gramophone Company came to India in 1902 to record native voices and commercially exploit the recordings. The advent of the gramophone heralded a completely different world of opportunities for musicians and connoisseurs.

The role of the women musicians becomes important in that they pioneered the recording process for Indian classical music through their ready adoption of this technology. Between the first three recording expeditions of The Gramophone Company, in 1902, 1904–05, and 1906–07, women's recordings of Indian classical music accounted for 80.95%, 83.51%, and 85.36% of the total recorded catalogue of Indian classical music. There were very few male classical musicians who recorded.

Between 1902 and 1920, courtesan women such as Gauhar Jaan of Calcutta, Malka Jaan of Agra, Janki Bai of Allahabad, Zohra Bai of Agra, Kali Jaan of Delhi, Mumtaz Jaan of Delhi, Binodini Dasi of Calcutta, Salem Godavari, Bangalore Nagarathnamma, Dhanakoti of Kanchipuram, Coimbatore Thayi, and several others were the chartbusters for The Gramophone Company. In the same period of 1902–20, with some exceptions (Abdul Karim Khan, Inayat Khan, Maujuddin Khan, and Peara Sahab in the North and Bidaram Krishnappa of Mysore, Rachappa, Vaidhyanatha Iyer, and Veena Sheshanna in the South), the male voices recorded were predominantly non-classical and included everything from comic songs and drama dialogues to poetry recitations and religious chanting.

The reluctance of the male musicians to participate in the recording expeditions of The Gramophone Company may be attributed to their unwillingness to making publically accessible the hitherto secretive musical

DOI: 10.4324/9780367822026-7

knowledge that was confined to musical lineages. The male musicians were possibly diffident about the three-minute recording format of the gramophone. They possibly saw the shortened recording format as a dilution of the classicism of an art form such as Indian classical music, which has always been expansive and improvisatory in nature. The courtesans overcame the existing social taboos and inhibitions about recording and the logistical challenges of the primitive technology. They saw an opportunity in this new technology and hence readily adapted to it. This is what makes the role of these women important.

As cultural custodians of a range of genres, the courtesan's recordings created an archive, which would have otherwise been lost to the world. Their records formed the bulk of the early-recorded catalogue of Indian classical music. Being unaware of what determined audience interests, the early catalogues have the widest possible range of genres recorded by the women in both Hindustani and Carnatic music. Many of these genres, such as *padams* and *javalis* in Carnatic music and *holi, chaiti, kajri, sawan,* and *geet* in Hindustani music, are rarely a part of modern performance repertoire. The recordings of the women thus give us a glimpse into genres of music that have been forgotten or excised from modern performance. Had it not been for the intervention of the women musicians, it might have taken a much longer time to create this vast repertoire of recorded Indian classical music.

At a distance of some hundred years, we can now only be grateful to these women for their initiative to preserve these valuable genres of Indian classical music for posterity. The women thus played a pioneering role in the establishment of the Indian recording industry.

Firstly, the gramophone recordings gave the courtesans an opportunity to reach out to middle-class families and newer audiences, which hitherto had no access to their music. Recording opened up new markets and opportunities for collaborations. Secondly, popular artists became iconic stars and won both fame and money that freed them from their exploitative patrons. Recording brought both financial independence and empowerment for the women who embraced this technology.

The disappearance of traditional patronage of royal houses and aristocracies forced the courtesans to reinvent themselves in modern urban salons. The gramophone brought for them an opportunity to break the confines of their salons and reach out to a larger audience. Indian middle-class families who would have hitherto never invited a courtesan to their homes for a performance were now comfortable listening to her voice at home, on a record. The records thus brought to the courtesan respectability – albeit briefly – by bringing her voice right into Indian middle-class households.

Pasler's (2007) narration of the interaction between Coimbatore Thayi and Maurice Delage and Delage's creation of Western music compositions called *Ragamalika*, inspired by Thayi's repertoire, is indicative of the new opportunities that were made available to the courtesan through recording technology (277–279).

Recording technology brought with it great fame and brand recognition. The success and widespread sale of these records made icons of many of the women musicians. Gauhar Jaan became a star of her times with her pictures routinely appearing on postcards, advertisements, and matchbox covers. This work brings to light several stories of the contemporaries of Gauhar Jaan who achieved fame and wealth through the agency of the gramophone. The substantial monetary benefits that the women acquired through recording freed them from exploitative patronage to become women of independent means. The monetary benefits led many of the women to lead hedonistic lifestyles. This theme of how recording empowered the women to question status quo and contest popular notions of power structures is a constant theme of many women musicians of this era. Huge monetary costs were attached to recording popular women musicians such as Gauhar Jaan, Janki Bai, Salem Godavari, and Coimbatore Thayi. Special recordings sessions called "Coimbatore Thayi Sessions" (1908) were made in Madras by George Dillnut of The Gramophone Company. An artist such as Bangalore Nagarathnamma fought a bitter war against the proscription of her book *Radhika Santhvanamu*, banned on the charge of being obscene. This sense of empowerment, possibly bolstered through the agency of recording, enabled a common *devadasi* singer such as Dhanakoti Ammal to refuse to be accosted discourteously by a patron, whom she would have otherwise hitherto had to meekly surrender to. The participation of *tawaifs* such as Husna Jaan of Banaras and Vidhyadhari Bai and their recordings and performances in live concerts of songs of protest against the colonial British government further illustrate this sense of empowerment that recording brought to the lives of these women, changing their social status, and their music.

Even as this revolution was silently taking place in the Indian music industry, the anti-nautch campaign to abolish performing women too was gaining momentum from the last decade of the nineteenth century. It was launched at the behest and backing of the British government, Christian missionaries, Social Purity movements, and members of the neo-educated Indian elite. There were competing motivations for each of these players.

First, the banning of performing women and branding them as prostitutes and the revival of the arts were perceived as key measures of a nationalistic agenda. Second, the popularity, wealth, and empowerment that the women gained in the wake of recording stirred a sense of envy in their detractors. Finally, the anti-nautch movement against the women was aimed at their vilification and their excision from the performance arena in the name of social purification.

On the one hand, the movement of arts revival was perceived as being as important as gaining freedom for the country from British colonial rule. It was driven by a sense of nationalism. Bakhle (2005), Subramanian (2006), Sampath (2010), and Soneji (2012) argue how the arts were perceived to be the best way of creating a sense of identity and self-respect in an emerging free nation. Hence, the construction of antiquity for Indian classical music and dance was considered necessary.

In parallel, and in what appears as a contradictory action, these movements were also reinforcing the opinions of the British colonial masters on social reforms and Christian values and morality for Indian society. The narrative of decadence and fall from grace of the arts in the hands of allegedly debased and immoral courtesan women necessitated reform movements to rescue the arts from the courtesans and revive the arts. Purist voices across India censored creative works of courtesans, citing alleged harm to morality and social interests. The protagonists and antagonists of the anti-nautch movement brought about vibrant debates in the press on the pros and cons of abolition. The references made in this work to original documents from the archives of Dr. Muthulakshmi Reddy, Krishna Aiyar, representations from late nineteenth century made to the British governments, viceroys, and governors general to stop patronising courtesans, and the *devadasi* and *tawaif sabhas* or associations campaigning against the demonisation of their community are illustrations of the social tensions that the anti-nautch campaign created in Indian society in the first three decades of the twentieth century.

The 1930s also saw the advent of radio technology. All-India Radio, which came to be known as *Aakashvaani* after Indian Independence in 1947, was the national broadcaster. The mass medium of radio continued and amplified the social and aesthetic processes that were initially motivated by the gramophone recording industry and that have led, at least in part, to present-day conceptions and understandings of Indian musical traditions. Dr. B.V. Keskar was the Minister of Information and Broadcasting in independent India from 1950 to 1962. Lelyveld (1994) argues that it was Keskar who was the formulator of the musical ideologies and policies of All-India Radio. Keskar was a purist and, in a way, continued the nationalistic project that had begun in Hindustani music by Bhathkhande and Paluskar. Lelyveld contends that Keskar believed that Indian music was damaged by the attitude of the colonial British masters and the many royal families of India, who had mere "wandering attention" and not a guided policy towards strengthening the musical traditions of India and propagating it (117). In particular, his ire was directed at the Muslim musicians who, he believed like Bhathkhande, had "appropriated and distorted the ancient art, turning it into the secret craft of exclusive lineages, the *gharanas*, and ignorant of Sanskrit, divorced it from the religious context of Hindu civilisation (Lelyveld, 1994: 117). In the Muslim hands, this music had fallen from its pedestal of pristine glory and was no longer spiritual, but reduced to eroticism, having become the preserve of "dancing girls, prostitutes and their circles of pimps" (117). Music, according to Keskar, regulated both human emotions and the social order and, hence, it became the responsibility of the State to intervene in creating the ideal musical tradition by preventing the entry of what was considered as harmful to the morality of society. In fact,

Keskar's predecessor, Sardar Vallabhai Patel, who was also the Minister of Home, firmly believed that courtesans "whose private life was a public scandal" were to be barred from entering the studios of All-India Radio (Lelyveld, 1994: 119). This attitude was further institutionalised by Keskar who monitored every aspect of programming minutely, set up an elaborate audition and grading mechanism for artists, along with scrutiny of their backgrounds, their diction, and musical aesthetics. While the dynamics of the radio culture are beyond the scope of this work, it is important to note that the same nationalist project that led to the excision of women from the gramophone industry by the 1930s was total and complete with government sanction in free India. This sounded the eventual death knell to the final cultural traces of the courtesan community in India.

It is speculated that given the incredible public acclaim and monetary benefits accrued by recording technology that led to financial independence for several courtesan women, the envy of their wealth and visibility in society was another driver for the reform movements against the women. Vijaisri (2004) and Soneji (2012) postulate that while social reformers such as Muthulakshmi Reddy had genuine concerns about the trafficking of young girls in the name of dedication to temples as *devadasis*, the movement was soon hijacked by men belonging to the same caste as these women whose aims seemed to be both the displacement of the women musicians from the performing space and a capture of their wealth.

It is speculated in the wake of evidence put forth by Bakhle (2005) that many reformers believed that the women were not really contributing to the advancement of musical knowledge or its documentation, but merely replicating music in a condensed format and making money in the process. This could be another reason why the reformers deemed it proper to prohibit the women from the performance space. Hence, contemporaneous to the movement to ban the women performers was also the drive to create new knowledge and codify and systematise rules for Indian classical music.

The banning of courtesans from the performing space was accompanied by a renaissance and an arts revival movement that aimed at expunging every trace of the courtesan from Indian music and dance. This renaissance brought with it a standardisation and universalisation of Indian classical music. Memories associated with the courtesan, the genres she popularised (*padams* and *javalis* in Carnatic music or sanitisation of lyrics of *thumris* and *dadras* in Hindustani music), and the musical instruments (the *sarangi*) that came to be linked with her were also obliterated. The recorded catalogues began to illustrate these new musical sensibilities and cultural politics.

Following this prohibition, a vacuum was created in the performing arts space. To address this, a vigorous renaissance and arts revival was undertaken. Reformers such as Vishnu Narayan Bhatkhande and Vishnu Digambar Paluskar for Hindustani music and institutions such as the Madras Music Academy for Carnatic music, strove towards a national project of standardisation, universalisation, systematisation, and institutionalisation of Indian classical music. The outcome was that Indian classical music was made more accessible to learn in a university context and perform in a modern, urban proscenium, and "safe" for boys and girls belonging to upper caste and middle-class Indian households to pursue. This could not have been imagined in the late nineteenth century or the first two decades of the twentieth century.

All these initiatives of standardisation, systematisation, and sanitisation of Indian classical music (both Carnatic and Hindustani) with the excision or dilution of genres associated with the courtesan, resulted in the creation of a new "classical" idiom that sounded different from that of the courtesan's music. The accompanying instrument of *sarangi* in Hindustani music associated with the *tawaif* was replaced by the harmonium as a symbolic gesture of erasure of all traces of the *tawaif* from modern musical performance.

In all these sociocultural changes, The Gramophone Company played a major role as the vehicle facilitating firstly the women's prominent role in the recording industry and secondly, in a passive way, their excision from the same industry after they were turned *persona non grata* in the arts space by reinforcing the "new normal." This "new normal" was to become homogenised and further normalised by the new medium of mass communication and dissemination, the All-India Radio.

In this entire process, The Gramophone Company was to emerge as a monopoly player in the Indian recording industry. The Gramophone Company understood the conditions of the Indian market and built a vast repertoire of popular artists. Unlike its competitors in India, The Gramophone Company clearly understood the minds and tastes of their target audience. They accordingly created a communication plan and messaging that appealed to Indian religious, historical, cultural, and nationalistic sensitivities. It was quick to realise the needs as well as the taboos of an average Indian listener of music. Despite being the first player in the Indian market, it understood that being the first mass medium for consumption of Indian classical music, the gramophone had caught the attention and fancy of the average Indian music lover who hitherto might not have had access to live performances. The novelty of listening to an artist of one's choice, in the comfortable confines of one's homes and the absence of taboo associated with the music of courtesans that was now heard at home without the physical presence of the performer added to the popularity of the gramophone. The Gramophone Company seized on this opportunity and created a market for the records based on innovative pricing and advertising strategies and the choice of popular artists and genres that were recorded.

Despite The Gramophone Company being a British multinational firm, Indians who were boycotting all foreign goods in their struggle for freedom from imperialism, readily bought both the machines and the records because of the focused and targeted advertising strategy of The Gramophone Company. Finally, the favourable British Government and market conditions, the adverse impact in European markets due to the two World Wars,

and the shrinkage in the markets of their competitors led to the entrenchment of The Gramophone Company as a monopolistic player in the Indian
market.

Given its wide reach, the gramophone played an important role in popularising classical music across India. Despite the handicap of a three-minute
time limitation that did not allow for a complete and leisurely exposition by
the artist, the gramophone records created awareness about Indian classical music and possibly made people interested in attending live concerts.
Hearing the records inspired future generations of musicians, who were
not only enamoured by the cult status achieved by some of the celebrated
recorded musicians, but also used these recordings as a learning tool.

Given the limitation of time, smaller musical pieces were recorded in
large numbers. These lesser known genres or forms within Indian classical
music had been relegated as "light" or "semi-classical" and usually associated with the courtesan. The gramophone played an important role in
popularising these genres and creating a mass appeal for them in the initial
years of recording. The early recording expeditions of The Gramophone
Company thus offered women artists the freedom to negotiate genres and
explore those that normally were forbidden to them due to the social distinctions that determined musical hierarchies. Recasting of musical identities
thus became a possibility for the women artists and this was the space that
recording offered to them.

The reverse was true as well. Due to the sale of records and their popularity the lighter musical forms became well known, and this prompted the
male musicians to negotiate them as well. This forced even traditional and
orthodox musicians to pick up these genres and popularise them in their
own recordings and in live concerts. With the arts revival project, however,
while these musical pieces might have been sanitised and changed, but their
mass appeal remained.

From the musical analysis done in this work, it was observed that the
gramophone recordings played a more disruptive role in the case of Carnatic
music, than in Hindustani music where presentation of the raga, its grammar
and an overall adherence to *gharana* rules, were by and large consistent with
contemporary practice. On the one hand, the early recordings (1904–25) displayed the distinctive style and the genres of the *devadasi* and demonstrate
what mainstream/classical Carnatic musical tradition possibly was before
the anti-nautch debates culminated in the abolition of women performers.
The early recordings became examples of poor, unsophisticated, and unau-
thentic versions of Carnatic music in the emerging tradition; this is evident
in the later recordings of the late 1920s and 1930s. The new classical idiom in
Carnatic music following the debates and discussions in music conferences
of the Music Academy and other such institutions was then propagated and
popularised by The Gramophone Company, which reinforced sociocultural
demands, thereby creating a new appeal and aesthetic for the new form of
music.

In the gramophone recordings of Carnatic music, a marked difference with contemporary practice was noticed in terms of raga presentation and grammar, minimal use of *gamakas* and performance schema in compositions. In Hindustani music, recordings managed to convey the emotional content of the lyrics within the limited time span. The recordings varied in emotional content, depending on the competence and virtuosity of a musician. Barring these slight departures in individual performance styles, there was no noticeable change in raga grammar, usage of signifier phrases or composition structure.

Finally, this work builds a case for evolving a multi-dimensional comprehensive and scientific methodology for empirical musical analysis for Indian classical music.

GLOSSARY

Aalaap   Note-by-note delineation of a raga in Hindustani classical music, bound by slow tempo but not necessarily by any rhythmic cycle. This is extempore music and depends on the artist's creativity.

Aalaapana   Same as above, in the case of Carnatic classical music.

Aarohan   Ascending scale of notes in a raga.

Aavartan   The complete rhythmic cycle of a tala.

Anibaddha   Not bound, meaning music that is not set within the limitations of a song or within the limitations of rhythmic cycles or sectional arrangements. The improvised portions of Indian classical music: *Aalapana, Neraval, Kalpana Swaram, Taanam* etc. in Carnatic music; *Aalaap, Taan* etc. in Hindustani music are *Anibaddha*.

Antara   The Second part of a *khayal* composition or *bandish* whose progressions are in the middle and upper octaves. Is sung after the *Sthayi*, the first part of a *Bandish*.

Anti-Nautch   Campaign launched against courtesan women in India, starting the 1890s branding them as common prostitutes and seeking their complete abolition in the performance space.

Anupallavi   Literally means that which follows the *Pallavi*. Like the *Antara*, it is the second part of the *kriti* or composition in Carnatic music and follows the first part or *Pallavi*.

Arulpa   Tamil devotional compositions of Ramalinga Swamigal, a nineteenth-century mystic who grew up in Madras. The *devadasis* sung these routinely to please the Gods of the temples to which they were attached.

Avarohan   Descending scale of notes in a raga.

Badhat   Orderly development of musical ideas in the form of *aalap* and *taan* within the *khayal* composition.

Bai   The suffix given to a *tawaif* who only sang and did not dance. With respect they were known as *Bai-ji*.

Bandish   A musical composition in Hindustani music. The lyrics are usually composed in Hindi/Hindustani or local dialects of North India such as Brij Bhasha, Bhojpuri etc. They provide spaces for musical elaboration. Instrumental compositions are called *Gat Bandish*.

Bandish ki Thumri   A type of *thumri* that focusses on elaborate rhythmic play.

Behlaawa   A play of combination of notes and phrases with the help of medium tempo heavy *taans* and *meends* (glides). *Behlaawas* slowly evolved into taans at a later stage.

Bhajan   A devotional composition in praise of Gods and Goddesses.

Bhakti   Devotion.

Bharatanatyam   The classical dance form originating from South India, earlier known as *Dasi Attam* or *Sadir* performed by *devadasis*. It was reformed after the anti-nautch campaign to form a more sanitised version.

Bhriga   Phrases in the raga sung in a very fast tempo.

Bol Baant ki Thumri   Same as *Bandish ki Thumri*. See above.

Bol Banao Thumri   A type of *thumri* where the leisurely tala or rhythmic framework and treatment gives it an expansiveness akin to a *khayal* rendition. At the same time, it also focuses on the exploration of the multi-layered meanings of the *bol* or word and hence it derives this name.

Bol Taan   Word sallies. Specific melodic figures, note-patterns showing the characteristic phrases of a raga are known as *Taan*. There are sixteen varieties of *taans* in *khayal*. *Taans* with note sequence rendered with the words or lyrical passages of a composition are called *bol taans*.

Bol-Baant   Division of words. Lyrical and melodic lines of a vocal composition rendered in short and various divisions within rhythmic variants.

Bol-vistaar   An elaborate expansion of the words of the lyrics.

Chaiti   Traditional seasonal songs belonging to the North Indian State of Uttar Pradesh sung in the months of *Chaitra* (March-April). They relate to the love between Radha and Krishna and the season of spring. Ragas such as *Pahadi, Maand, Piloo* enhance the romantic beauty of the *Purabia* dialect in which these are set.

Charanam   Literally means the feet. The final part of a *kriti* or composition in Carnatic music.

Chinna Melam   The group of men who lived off the *devadasis* and accompanied them in ritual performances in temples by playing on their drums known as *muttu*.

Dadra   There is a tala in Hindustani music consisting of six beats in two equal divisions of three, called *Dadra*. There is also a genre of Hindustani music called *dadra*, which is a light classical form performed in the Agra and Bundelkhand regions of the North Indian State of Uttar Pradesh. They are set to either the *dadra* tala or to another tala called *Keherwa*.

Dashavidha Gamaka   Ten different types of archetypal inflexions on musical notes prescribed in ancient Indian music treatises: *Arohana, Avarohana, Ahata, Pratiyahata, Sphurita, Tripuscha, Dhalu, Andolita, Kampita,* and *Murchana*

Deredaar Tawaif   Highest in the hierarchy of *Tawaifs*. They were descendants of the dancing and singing girls who were originally tent owners and moved from town to town, fair to fair entertaining people. These women were highly accomplished and were well-versed in music, dance and also poetry. They usually kept one or two patrons all their lives and remained committed to their patron (s). It was the patron's duty to maintain the *deredar tawaif* and provide for her expenses and livelihood, and also the children she bore him. They were allowed to invite other patrons to their salons to watch their performances, but physical relationships or commitments were kept up only with their chosen patron, who was the only man allowed to stay back in a salon after the performance while the rest of the guests had to leave.

Desi   Refers to regional or folk or semi classical genres of Indian music.

Devadasi   Courtesan in the South Indian context who was dedicated at a young age to the deity of a temple.

Devaranama   Devotional songs in the South Indian language of Kannada composed by mystic saint poets since the thirteenth century called the *Haridasas*.

Dhrupad   Derived from the words *Dhruva* (immovable or permanent) and *pada* (verse). One of the oldest forms of composition in Indian classical music and a genre of the Hindustani style. Themes include spirituality, heroism, thoughtfulness, and virtuosity and the music is largely in praise of Hindu Gods and Goddesses. It has four parts – *Sthayi*, *Antara*, Sanchari, and *Abhoga*. Performed to the rhythmic accompaniment by a *Pakhawaj*. The four schools of styles of *Dhrupad* are: *Dagar Bani*, *Gauhar Bani*, *Khandar Bani*, and *Nauhar Bani*.

Dhrut   Fast tempo.

Domni   *Tawaifs* who were in the lowest strata of social hierarchy and came from tribal communities.

Durita Kaalam   Increased tempo.

Gaayaki   Singing. Means styles of improvisations in classical Hindustani vocal music.

Gamaka   Musical ornamentation or graces or embellishments used in both styles of Indian classical music. See *Dashavidha Gamaka*.

Gharana   Schools of Hindustani *khayal* music with distinctive features related to voice throw, style of singing, and approach to music. They have names of towns and cities of India where the originator of the style lived. eg. Gwalior, Agra, Jaipur, Kirana, Bhindibazar, Rampur, Indore, Sham Chaurasi, Bishnupur, Banaras etc. Sons and family members carried the tradition forward. Gradually mentor-pupil mode or *guru shishya parampara* started welcoming outsiders into the fold.

Ghazal   An amatory sonnet, a popular form of Urdu poetry that is sung as light-classical form in Hindustani music.

Guru   Teacher, who is revered as a veritable incarnation of God in the Indian context.

Guru Shishya Parampara   The tradition of mentor-pupil where the latter stayed at the house of the mentor and learnt the art form and also performed household chores.

Holi   Hindu festival of colours. Also a light form of Hindustani music with songs of Radha and Krishna celebrating the festival.

Isai Velalar   The erstwhile teachers of *devadasis* who were known as *melak-kaarars* and *nattuvaanars (chinnamelam)* and ritual musicians in temples *(periyamelam) and* lived or worked as part of the *devadasi* community. With time, they felt a need to develop a closed patriarchal tradition for themselves within the *chinnamelam*, independent of their illustrious womenfolk and formed the *Isai Velalar* community.

Javali   Erotic compositions associated with the *Devadasis*. A light classical form of Carnatic music. Unlike *padams*, which are also associated with the *devadasi* and where the love portrayed between humans is sought to be explained as a euphemism for the love of the soul and super soul, *javalis* are more direct descriptions of human love and considered non-allegorical. They are sung in a fast tempo.

Kaala Pramaanam   Tempo.

Kacheri   Concert in South Indian context. Literal meaning is a court or office, the allegory being the musician is put to test in the court of the afficianados.

Kaikolan   Community of traditional weavers in The South Indian state of Tamil Nadu, from where most of the *devadasis* originated.

Kajri   A folk song in the North Indian state of Uttar Pradesh sung during the rainy season and draws upon the tales of Krishna.

Kalpana Swaram   Singing of the melodic line using the signatures of notes or impromptu solfa singing. Part of the improvisation portion of Carnatic music.

Kalpita Sangeetha   Composed music or the *nibaddha* form. Bound or set within a frame of lyrics and rhythm.

Kathak   The classical dance form originating from North India, earlier known as Naach and performed by *tawaifs*. Was reformed post the anti-nautch campaign to form a more sanitised version.

Khatka   A form of embellishment or grace in Hindustani music (one among the triad of *Khatka, Murki* and *Gitkiri*). Two-note span giving edge, sharpness, and speed to the figure.

Khayal   The most popular form in Hindustani classical music. Derived from the Persian word meaning "idea" or "imagination," it relies heavily on improvisation. It has two parts – *Sthayi* and *Antara*. There are two kinds of *khayal*: *Bada* (Big) and *Chhota* (small). The former is composed to suit slower tempos with a structure that can accommodate aalaap and movements in medium tempo. *Chhota khayal* is in medium and fast tempos, no detailed aalaap but improvisatory *taans, bol taans, sargams* and cross-rhythmic patterns predominate to end in a crescendo.

Kotha   The Salon of a *tawaif* where performances called *Mujras/Mehfils* were held every evening for the rich patrons of the town.

Kriti   Composition in Carnatic music. Has three portions: *Pallavi, Anupallavi*, and *Charanam*. Several great composers of Carnatic music have bequeathed a wealth of compositions. The most prominent of these are termed the Trinity of Carnatic music: Thyagaraja, Mutthuswami Dikshitar, and Shyama Shastri.

Laya   Tempo of a piece of music. *Vilambit, Madhya*, and *Dhruta* indicate Slow, Medium, and Fast tempi, respectively.

Layakari   The play of multiples of the three basic layas or tempos. This could be double, triple and quadruple measures. The *aad* (1 1/2 *matras* or beats), *kuaad* (1 1/4 beats) and *biaad* (10 1/4 beats) are known *vikrita layakari*.

Maargi   Refers to the regimented classical forms within Indian music.

Madhyalaya   Medium tempo (Term used more commonly in Hindustani music).

Madhyamakaala   Medium tempo (term used in Carnatic music).

Mandra Sthaayi   Lower octave.

Manniyam   Huge grants of lands given to *devadasis* who were attached to prominent temples of South India.

Manodharma   Literally means the path taken by the mind. It refers to the *anibaddha* or unbound improvisatory aspects of Indian classical music.

Meend   Smooth, uninterrupted glide from one note to another connecting them by using shrutis or microtones, one of the most important forms of *Gamakas* in Hindustani music.

Mehfil   An assembly, a congregation, an intimate musical gathering.

Melakarta   Parent ragas (*Janaka* ragas) from which other ragas are generated. Carnatic music has an elaborate classification of ragas into seventy-two *Melakartas* from which all other ragas are derived. The equivalent in Hindustani are ten groupings called *Thaats*.

Mridangam   South Indian instrument, the Drum that is used to keep time and provide rhythmic accompaniment.

Mujra   Performance of song and dance by *tawaifs* in their salons or *kothas*.

Mukhra   The first line of the *sthayi* of a *khayal* that serves as a cadence.

Murki   A short sharp twisting figure of two or three notes with high decorative power mostly used in light classical idioms of Hindustani music.

Muttu   The small drum used by the *chinna melam* or the musicians accompanying the *devadasi* in ritual performances in South Indian temples.

Naayika   The heroine on whose theme the compositions such as *thumri, dadra, padams* and *javalis* are composed in both styles of Indian classical music.

Nagaswaram   A reed pipe used by musicians in temples and for ritualistic performances (also called *nadaswaram*).

Nath Utharana or missi   Ritual of passage for the *deredar* related to their initiation into the professional world of performance. The literal meaning of *nath uthaarna* is removal of the nose ring, which actually symbolised the loss of virginity. On a girl coming of age, the female matron of the *kotha*, who was known as *chaudhrayan*, would formally advertise for the *nath babu* or the man who would undertake to pay a sizeable dowry and maintain the girl. It was a kind of contract-based union. The ceremony was accompanied by a lot of gaiety, music, dance and merriment.

Nattuvanar The dance teacher of a *devadasi*.

Neraval A typical open form/improvisatory pattern in Carnatic music where certain sections of the song are chosen and the words of these phrases are sung with more and more complex melodic and rhythmic emphasis and variations.

Nibaddha Bound, set within a frame. Refers to the closed forms within Indian classical music, set to lyrics and rhythm.

Nityasumangali The ever-auspicious. The title given to the *devadasi*. Being "married" to the deity of a temple where she was dedicated, she was considered free from the scourge of widowhood. Widowhood is considered inauspicious by patriarchal systems of Indian tradition. Being able to never be a widow by virtue of her marriage to God, the *devadasi* was hence considered to be ever- auspicious.

Nritta Gestures and movements in Indian classical dances, of definite patterns based on *laya* and tala.

Nritya *Nritya* is when the dancer combines with the *Nritta, abhinaya*, which means communication of *bhaava* and *rasa (emotions)* and may be roughly translated as acting.

Padam A closed form of Carnatic music, erotic in content and associated with the *devadasi*. Their texts and music are more lyrical than *kritis*, and they deal with romantic and erotic themes. The common themes dealt in *padams* and *javalis* are the pangs of separation or the joys of union of two lovers, misunderstandings that arise between them, uncertainty of anticipation, and the nostalgia of memory of union. *Padams* are allegorical and the human love is usually a euphemism or reference to the yearning of the human soul for the Supreme Being. *Padams* are rendered in a slow tempo.

Pakad Certain phrases in a raga, which are signifiers and characterise the raga, giving it its melodic form. They have to be repeated and emphasised so that the uniqueness of the raga is made clear to the listener. These are called *Pakad*. They are the shortest note combinations to identify a raga

Pallavi Derived from the word *Pallava*, which means to Blossom. It is the opening section or the first part of a *kriti* or composition in Carnatic music.

Periya Melam The group of musicians who performed on the professional basis in temple rituals in South India, on the *nagaswaram* and *thavil* comprised the *periya melam* or large band.

Pottukkattutal A young girl born into the *devadasi* community would be "dedicated" to the deity of a temple. This dedication or rite of passage took place when the girl was between six and nine years of age. She would be married to God and the priest of the temple officiated as the intermediary by conducting the rituals on behalf of the deity. This rite of passage was known as the *pottukkattutal* ritual or the tying of the sacred emblem or *pottu* around the girl's neck. Her formal training in dance and music would be followed immediately thereafter.

Pukaar   Melodic expression that is mainly used in *thumri*.

Purdah   Veil with which women from respectable houses would cover themselves with in the presence of outsiders or men of the family other than their husbands.

Quwwali   Originated from the word *qawl*, mystical Sufi sayings. It was sung by the followers of Khwaja Moinuddin Chisti of Ajmer and became popular in the thirteenth century.

Raag Chalan   Collection of phrases indicating general way to move within a specific raga.

Raga   The melodic structure that forms the bedrock of Indian classical music. May be broadly defined as a melodic scheme, characterised by a definite scale or notes, order of sequence of these notes, melodic phrases, pauses and stases, and tonal graces. It needs to be pleasing to the ear and have an emotional appeal. Derived from the Sanskrit word *Ranj*, which means to please. Its general lexical meaning is also emotion, colour, etc.

Raga Bhava   Underlying emotion of a raga.

Raagdari   The technique of delineation of a raga.

Raga Chaaya Sanchara   Characteristic phrases of a raga.

Ragam Tanam Pallavi   It is a form of singing in Carnatic music, which allows the musicians to improvise to a great extent. It is one of the most complete aspects of Indian classical music, demonstrating the entire gamut of talents and the depth of knowledge of the musician. The *Ragam* portion of the presentation is pure melodic improvisation where the musician starts with a refrain to create the mood of raga and lays a foundation for composition to follow. *Taanam* is the second component of this composite form of improvisation. Originally developed for the *veena*, it consists of expanding the raga with syllables from the phrase "*Ananta Anandam Ta*" (Means "Oh Lord, Give me happiness"). *Taanam* is a rhythmic version of the raga aalaapana. The word *Pallavi* is derived from the three syllables *Pa – Pada* (words), *La – Laya* (rhythm) and *Vi – Vinyasam* (variations). *Pallavi* is the equivalent of a refrain in Western music. The *Pallavi* is usually a one-line composition set to a single or more cycle(s) of a tala. The tala could range from the simple to the complex and there may also be different gatis or speeds/tempo being employed. The *Pallavi* ends with an expansive *kalpana swaram* or extempore solfa singing. The entire exercise takes more than an hour and displays the virtuosity and creative talents of a musician

Ragamala Paintings   Series of illustrative paintings from medieval India based on *Ragamala* or the "Garland of Ragas," depicting various

Indian musical modes called ragas. They stand as a classical example of the amalgamation of art, poetry and classical music in medieval India. *Ragamala* paintings were created in most schools of Indian painting, starting in the sixteenth and seventeenth centuries, and are today named accordingly as *Pahari Ragamala, Rajasthan* or Rajput *Ragamala, Deccan Ragamala,* and Mughal *Ragamala.* In these s each raga is personified by a colour, mood, a verse describing a story of a hero and heroine (*nayaka* and *nayika*), it also elucidates the season and the time of day and night in which a particular raga is to be sung; and finally most paintings also demarcate the specific Hindu deities attached with the raga, like *Bhairava* or *Bhairavi* to Shiva, *Sri* to Devi, etc. The paintings depict not just the ragas, but also their wives, (*raginis*), their numerous sons (*ragaputra*) and daughters (*ragaputri*).

Ragamalika   Literally, a garland of ragas, is a very popular form of composition in Carnatic music. Also called *Ragamala* in Hindustani music. These are delightful compositions, where the various segments are set to different ragas, with a smooth and melodious flow of music during the transition from one raga to the next. The choice of ragas, as well as the order in which they appear in a *Ragamalika*, are based solely on aesthetic considerations. The main point is that a feeling of abruptness or a gap should be avoided when shifting between ragas and the flow of music should be very smooth. Also, closely allied Ragas do not generally appear in the same composition. Ideally, consecutive ragas should possess distinct melodic character.

Rakti Prayoga   The evocative phrases of a raga.

Rasika   An aesthete or connoisseur of music. Derived from Sanskrit word meaning full of Passion, elegant; with discrimination. An expert who is able to appreciate a field; especially in the fine arts.

Sabha   Musical assembly. In modern Carnatic parlances, these are the urban salons or proscenium where concerts are performed.

Sahitya   Lyrics of the composition.

Sam   First beat of the rhythmic cycle.

Samadhi   A memorial, usually of a saint or an important personality.

Sangati   Improvised patterns on phrases of the lyrics of a composition.

Sarangi   A bowed, short-necked string instrument from India as well as Nepal, which is used in Hindustani classical music. It is the most popular musical instrument in Western part of Nepal and said to most resemble the sound of the human voice – able to imitate vocal ornaments such as *gamaks* (shakes) and *meends* (sliding movements).

Sargam   Improvisatory solfa singing in Hindustani *khayal* renditions.

Shadja   Refers to the tonic in the octave.

Shehnai   Musical instrument similar to the oboe, made out of wood, with a double reed at one end and a metal or wooden flared bell at the other end. Its sound is thought to create and maintain a sense of auspiciousness and sanctity. As a result, is widely used during marriages, processions and in temples although it is also played in concerts. The *shehnai* is similar to South Indian *nadaswaram*.

Shringara   Is one of the nine rasas or *nava rasas*. Usually translated as erotic love, romantic love, or as attraction or beauty. *Rasa* means "flavour," and the theory of rasa is the primary concept behind classical Indian arts including theatre, music, dance, poetry, and sculpture. Much of the content of traditional Indian arts revolves around the relationship between a man and a woman. The primary emotion thus generated is *shringara*. The romantic relationship between lover and beloved is a metaphor for the relationship between the individual and the divine.

Shruti   A Sanskrit word, found in the Vedic texts and means musical intonation and "what is heard" in general. It is also an important concept in Indian music, where it means the smallest interval of pitch that the human ear can detect and a singer or musical instrument can produce. The musical shruti concept is found in ancient and medieval Sanskrit texts such as the *Natya Shastra, Dattilam, Brihaddesi*, and *Sangitaratnakara*. The *swara* differs from *shruti* concept in Indian music. A *shruti* is the smallest gradation of pitch representing the quality of frequency (timbre), while a *swara* is the selected pitches from which the musician constructs the scales, melodies and ragas. The *Natya Shastra* identifies and discusses twenty-two *shruthis* and seven *swaras* per octave.

Shruthi Shuddham   Adherence to pitch. Pitch perfect rendition.

Sitar   A plucked stringed instrument used in Hindustani music. The instrument is believed to have been derived from the *veena*, an ancient Indian instrument, which was modified by a Mughal court musician to conform with the tastes of his Mughal patrons.

Sthayi   The first portion of a *bandish* or composition in *khayal* with movements generally in the lower and middle octaves, and all the melodic variations and improvisations ending with the last few phrases of this section. In essence it is the burden of the song or performance. The first line of the *sthayi* (also known as the *mukhra*) serves as a cadence, while the entire *sthayi* is the most important part of composition as it delineates the metre and the mode of the piece and usually forms the basis for subsequent improvisations.

Swara   Sanskrit word that connotes a note in the successive steps of the octave. More comprehensively, it is the ancient Indian concept about the complete dimension of musical pitch. The Seven notes In Indian Classical system are *Shadja (Sa), Rishabha (Ri), Gandhara (Ga), Madhyama (Ma), Panchama (Pa), Dhaivata (Dha)*, and *Nishadha (Ni)*.

Swara Sthana   Pitch position assigned to each note in the octave.

Taan   Virtuoso technique used in the vocal performance of a raga in Hindustani classical music. It involves the singing of very rapid melodic passages using vowels, often the long "aa," and it targets at improvising and to expand weaving together the notes in a fast tempo.

Taar Saptak   Upper octave.

Tabla Hindustani musical instrument, pair of drums, used to maintain rhythm/time in a performance.

Tala Term used in Indian classical music to refer to musical metre, that is any rhythmic beat or strike that measures musical time. A recurring arrangement of rhythmic patterns.

Tappa It is said that the songs of camel drivers in North Western India in the deserts got refined into a semi classical form called *tappa*. Usually composed in the Punjabi language, they are composed of quick turns of phrase with no slower elaborations. Even in the Eastern State of Bengal, *tappas* were composed in the nineteenth and twentieth century.

Tawaif Courtesan in the North Indian context.

Thaat The ten basic scales from which all ragas are derived in the Hindustani system. According to *Pandit* Vishnu Narayan Bhatkhande, the ten thaats are *Bilawal, Kalyan, Khamaj, Kafi, Bhairav, Marwa, Poorvi, Asavari, Todi,* and *Bhairavi.*

Thavil A barrel (drum) shaped heavy percussion instrument from South India used in temple, folk and Carnatic music, often accompanying the *nadaswaram*. The *thavil* and the *nadaswaram* are essential components of traditional festivals and ceremonies in South India.

Theka The bare structure of the tala played on the *tabla* with simple bols or words.

Thevaram Denote the first seven volumes of the *Tirumurai*, the twelve-volume collection of Tamil Shaiva devotional poetry. All seven volumes are dedicated to the works of the three most prominent Tamil poets of the seventh century, the Nayanars – Sambandar, Tirunavukkarasar, and Sundarar. The singing of *Thevaram* is continued as a hereditary practice in some Shiva temples in Tamil Nadu.

Thillana A rhythmic piece in Carnatic music that is generally performed at the end of a concert and widely used in classical Indian dance performances. A *thillana* uses tala-like phrases/mnemonics (*jatis*) in the *pallavi* and *anupallavi*, and lyrics in the *charanam.*

Thumri Originally associated with the ankle bells or the dance this idiom later captured, occupied an important place in light classical music. Composed in dialects such as Brij Bhasha and Bhojpuri, the romantic lyrics demand all the skills of a classical musician along with a delicate, emotive appeal obtained by a judicious mix of ragas. The style flourished in Lucknow and Banaras. The two types of *thumris* are *Bandish ki thumri* and *Bol Banao thumri.*

Ustad A male expert or maestro in music in the Hindustani context. Honorific used for a Muslim maestro; *Pandit* is the Hindu counterpart.

Vaggeyakara Poet-Composer.

Valli Gamaka Deep scooping oscillations on notes that characterise contemporary Carnatic music.

Vallinam – Thallinam Vocal dynamics and modulation.

Varnam Basic type of composition in Carnatic music, usually the start-ing piece of a modern Carnatic concert. It is composed in such a way that it shows the characteristic phrases, states, melodic movements, and graces of a raga and an insight into the structure of the varnam leads to the insight of the structure of a raga. It has two parts *Poorvanga* (which further has *Pallavi, Anupallavi* and *Muktaayi Swaras*) and *Uttaranga* Or *Etthukadai* (Having a *charanam* and *swaras*). Types of *Varnams* include *Pada varnams/Chowka varnams*, which have meaningful texts in the composition, and *Tana varnams* and *Dharu varnams*, which have part text and part solfeggio passages.

Veena A multistringed chordophone of the Indian subcontinent. It is an ancient musical instrument that evolved into many variations, such as lutes and arched harps. The many regional designs have different names such as the *Rudra veena*, the *Saraswati veena*, the *Mohan veena*, *Chitra veena*, *Vichitra veena*, and others.

Vidwan A male expert or maestro in music in the Carnatic context.

Vilambit Slow tempo.

Vishesha Prayoga Special phrases of a raga.

Zam Zama An Urdu word meaning "addition of notes." Like a *khatka*, it is once again a cluster of notes, used to embellish the landing note. Unlike a *khatka*, notes in a *zam zama* are rendered in progressive combinations and permutations. The end result sounds like a complex *taan* pattern with sharp *gamaks*. *Zam zama* forms an integral part of the Hindustani form known as *Tappa*, where it is applied on the *bols* or lyrics of the song and must be applied in *khayal* renditions with great caution.

APPENDIX 1
COMPLETE TEXT OF SELECTED
ARCHIVAL MATERIAL

**Memorandum Signed by 2000 Signatories to the Governor
of Madras, Wenlock, in 1893, Appealing to the Viceroy
and Governor Not to Attend Nautch Performances
and Thereby Give It a Modicum of Credibility**

The humble memorial of the undersigned members of the Hindu Social
Reformer Association of Madras and others most respectfully sheweth:

1 That there exists in Indian community a class of women commonly
  known as nautch girls.
2 That these women are invariably prostitutes.
3 That countenance and encouragement are given to them, and even a
  recognized status in society secured to them, by the practice which pre-
  vails among Hindus, to a very undesirable extent, of inviting them to
  take part in marriage and other festivities, and even to entertainments
  given in honour of guests who are not Hindus.
4 That this practice not only necessarily lowers the moral tone of society, but also tends to destroy that family life on which national soundness depends, and tends to bring upon individuals ruin in property and
  character alike.
5 That this practice rests only upon fashion and receives no authority
  from antiquity or religion, and accordingly has no claim to be considered a National Institution, and is entitled to no respect as such.
6 That a strong feeling is springing up among the educated classes of this
  country against the prevalence of this practice, as is evinced among the
  other things by the proceedings at a public meeting in Madras, on the
  5th of May 1893.
7 That so keenly do your Memorialists realize the harmful and degrad-
  ing character of this practice, that they have resolved neither to invite
  nautch girls to any entertainments given by themselves, nor to accept
  any invitation to an entertainment at which it is known that nautch girls
  are to be present.

8 That your Memorialists feel assured that, your Excellency, desires, to aid, by every poor means, those who labour to remove any form of social evil.

9 That your Memorialists accordingly appeal to your Excellency, as the official and recognized head of society in the Presidency of Madras, and as the representative of Her Most Gracious Majesty, the Queen-Empress, in whose influence and example, the cause of purity has ever found support, to discourage this pernicious practice by declining to attend any entertainment at which nautch girls are invited to perform, and thus to strengthen the hands of those who are trying to purify the social life of their community.

Letter of Muthulakshmi Reddy in *The Hindu* Dated 3 July 1928 to Create Public Opinion in Favour of a Ban on Performing Women

It is not possible for anyone to give adequate expression to the feelings of horror and righteous indignation that are aroused in one's mind by the sad reports of young innocent minor girls having been set apart for an evil profession even from their infancy and actually trained with the full knowledge and consent of our society that on attaining their womanhood they may administer to the vile and baser passions of the other sex. Could anyone picture to himself or herself a worse perversion of the human mind or an act more inhuman and unjust?

I have received a most touching letter from a public-spirited and right-minded citizen and a trustee of a temple in Madras informing me of the sad lot of a minor girl aged 10, an orphan who having been adopted by a Devadasi, is being trained for that horrid life that inevitably awaits such girls. When the writer had the goodness to point out to the other trustees the iniquitous nature of such an act on the part of the old Devadasi, the latter not only paid not heed to his just remonstrance but what is much more revolting to our moral sense the trustees went seeking for precedents in support of such a heinous crime from the previous history of the temple. Naturally this just minded individual would not be satisfied with their wrong logic. He has been good enough not only to inform the Police Commissioner of this unjust deplorable event, but he had also sent me a copy of that letter. Could any of us imagine a more unholy act than the practice of training children within the sacred pecincts of a holy temple to lead the prostitute's life? Is it not a most regrettable fact that some of our university graduates should come forward to defend such a pernicious practice in the name of religion and hoary traditions?

I take this opportunity to inform the public that I have been receiving several letters from the mofussil as to how the trustees of most of our temples encourage the old Dasis in the evil practice of dedicating their own or adopted children to a life of vice, and how the public in those parts encourage such acts and what is much worse still even raise obstacles in the way of those righteous individuals who try against odds to dissuade these Dasis from victimizing those innocent girls to this most cruel and inhuman of acts...

Two girls aged 10 and 9 respectively were brought to me two days before from the mofussil who had already been made to undergo the ceremony of dedication and who were too young and innocent to understand the real significance of 'Pottu' tying and the horrors of a prostitute's life.

Again I have been getting information from reliable quarters that some of the zamindar women, to kill time and to please their fancy, purchase children from poor but good families paying a heavy price for them, bring them up in luxury and the dedicate them to their family deities so that they may become the concubines of their male relations because in the public mind the Devadasi prostitute differs from the brothel prostitute in more than one respect, that is the Devadasis having received the sanction of the holy temple to practice vice would monopolize the profession of prostitution to herself and to her clan, outcaste though she may be, she is not a sinner as she is supposed to work and her past formed by the practice of her present life and hence some attempts to rescue her from such a life nor any member of the other sex who associates with her need carry the blame of his neighbours or the censure of Gods, as the Gods themselves have created the Devadasis to serve the human needs and thus save her married sisters from being tempted by evil men and led astray into an immoral life.

As the proverb says 'Evil to him who evil thinks', so this wrong procedure on the part of our society has wrought havoc and ruin on all concerned....so is it not high time that following the good example of the League of Nations, we of this Presidency should appoint a committee of experts to go into this question of trafficking women and children and educate the ignorant...? As Mrs Sarojini Naidu so aptly put in her speech during the last Social Reform Conference, 'the degradation of one woman is the degradation of the whole manhood and the womanhood of the country.'

We have fortunately for Madras the Children's Protection Act in force by which the minor girls who are found in brothels are rescued and safely lodged in the Children's Aid Society but the police have no power to remove young girls from the company or association of Devadasi prostitutes because the general public even to this day hold firmly in the belief that it is the Devadasis' privilege to lead a prostitute's life as they are but implicitly obeying the dictates of hoary customs and traditions and as such are indispensable to society. I feel most strongly that the Hindu community cannot afford to be any longer indifferent to this all important question of allowing the sacred rights of the children to be violated in the name of religion and their innocence abused by this cruel and meaningless custom. I am further of opinion that vigorous propaganda is necessary both to reform the Devadasis and to educate the public. Devadasis have to be told that the original high ideal of dedication of virgin girls to pious and religious service in the temples having been lost sight of their present day habits do not entitle them to any place in the holy temple where all kinds of humanity resort for light and guidance. The misguided and ignorant public have to be taught that the only path and the sure path too to a moral and well-regulated happy and peaceful life is to deal out equal and just treatment to both the sexes and both men and women should be taught the right principles of life and the sacred laws of nature that they may fulfil the primary and sacred function of life, which is nothing but the propagation of a healthy and virile race. It is a good sign of the times that some of us are deeply conscious that till now we have not been administering the right remedy to the most fell disease that ever has afflicted humanity interfering with its healthy growth and right development.

So in the name of outraged humanity and in response to the sacred call of those innocent and helpless children, I appeal to our young men and women imbued with high moral and spiritual ideals, not to put up any longer with such soul-killing emotions and practices, and rising in revolt against them boldly, face the situation without fear or favour and thus save society from one of its deadliest enemies.

The Anti-Devadasi Stance Was Opposed by Several Men of the Upper Castes. One Such Instance Is of E. Krishna Aiyar Writing to *The Hindu* in His 'Letters to the Editor' Dated 7 December 1932

Sir, Dr. Mrs. Muthulakshmi Reddi's article in *The Hindu* of yesterday concerning Dance and Devadasis in connection with an entertainment at Willigdon raises certain important considerations for lovers of Art. I am not concerned with the said function or the appropriateness or otherwise of the entertainment therein. But as one who has had something to do with the arts of Dancing, Music and Drama, I would be failing in my duty, if I do not draw pointed attention to some practical aspects of art and social reform.

At the outset, I may say few can quarrel with the learned Doctor in her noble view that the Devadasi class as such should not be encouraged and that the girls should not be allowed serve merely as an advertisement for the person of the lady artist for immoral purposes. But on account of a conscious or unconscious over-emphasis merely on the social reform aspect of the matter, the arts themselves are made to be mistaken for the medium by which they are represented. The learned Doctor says that 'they must be dissociated from various associations and restored to their original purity and grandeur so that respectable, good and virtuous women may come forward to learn and to practice them." No doubt a noble sentiment! But when one looks at the practical steps taken to realize this object, one cannot congratulate the anti-nautch social reformers on their achievement. Fifty years of work—says the Doctor—has achieved wonderful success in killing nautch parties and made the only cultivators of the art to give it up. What a tragedy in success! 50 years had been long enough to produce three generations of lady artists of cultured and virtuous class in Carnatic dance. Yet, one may look and look and rub his eyes and look and may not find one single respectable lady to have taken to Bharatha Natyam. There is nothing now and it needs no great effort to have the mind to take to it as it is an art followed by the names of Goddesses, and Royal ladies, Parvati, Usha, Uttara, Malavika etc. If side by side, with the crusade against Devadasi Art, respectable ladies also have taken to it they could have easily driven the undesirables to the wall and the art would have been in their hands by now. On the contrary, the art is even now just like a minor girl of a very respectable family who has been callously neglected and driven out to fall somehow into the hands of undesirables and who is shivering and yearning to be rescued and fed properly, but still cruelly neglected without even a rescue home.

To take another instance of the interest of social reformers in Art: Anybody who knows anything about the development of music in South India for the last four or five years may be aware of the huge efforts made by some of us to have music introduced from the school and college levels, in B.A. Classes, especially in the Queen Mary's College for women. What a splendid chance there was to restore the Art to its original purity and grandeur for respectable ladies to take to it. And yet, the educational authorities on the pretext of retrenchment have stopped admission into the B.A. course for music from 1933 (after only two years' existence of the course). May I know whether Mrs. Muthulakshmi Reddi and her Women's Association have moved their little finger to prevent that tragedy? Do they also know at all that some of the girls who have taken up music in the Intermediate Classes are now blinking as to their future course of studies on account of this unceremonious kicking out the Muse from her pedestal?

Again with regard to the Cinema, I have got a straight and practical proposition to make. A certain respectable film Company—desirous of producing at least one Tamil Talkie of a high standard is on the look-out for cultured and respectable actors and actresses and have also requested me to help them in their search. They are willing to provide the necessary facilities and safeguards to make the players feel at home without any violence to their sentiments of a higher nature. I have mooted the latter to some of the respectable and high-placed ladies. As yet no one has come forward. Will the learned Doctor and her reformer friends move in the matter and help in a desirable reform to rescue the art from unworthy hands?

One can understand and appreciate the Doctor if she says that private morality ought to be a primary concern in all walks of life including art. But she says with pride that certain classes in the South have successfully been made to give up even teaching of the art to their girls; and conferences have been urging for legislation to prohibit even teaching of the art—as that training inevitably leads them into a life of prostitution. What a confusion of purpose and means! Should the art be penalized for a defect of society? Can not social reform take the shape of making girls become regular wives and family women by giving up prostitution and at the same time cultivate the art. Is it really the arts that lead them to concubinage? If that is so, how is the learned Doctor going to solve the general problem of the relation of art and morality, even when respectable classes take to it, according to her wish. Again have the reformers set their faces against the type of mixed dances exhibited by westerners in balls in very high quarters in the country?

The fact of the matter is, that the arts must thrive somewhere. They could not and would not die. Nor can they thrive merely on the hopes and pious wishes of reformers of the destructive type. They cannot recognize or live in a vacuum between the abolition of the Devadasi class as a whole and the doubtful coming up of respectable ladies to take to them. The arts need not be blamed if for want of better persons they thrive, where they are or occasionally submit themselves to the not very enviable spectacle of stiff limbed males vainly attempting to imitate women's graces-

I do not know whether the learned Doctor is aware of one ether sad phenomenon- Devadasi art is condemned and respectable women would not touch it. 50 years of destructive work has been done; and you see the spectacle of foreign artistes occasionally sweeping the country with advertisements of the perfect Yankee type, professing to interpret our own art for as—with the result that it is neither Indian nor foreign. They nibble at the Art here and there, make sweeping generalisations of a patronising type; and there, is no end of young leaders and cultural associations—of a type very common- in the south—to sing hallelujahs and fill newspapers with encomiums of a thing -which neither they nor the artistes themselves really understand. When in very many of the Western countries people are introducing dancing in the shape of rhythmic exercises, in schools and colleges, our reformers are still content with merely crying down the association of the art with undesirables.

It is easy to destroy a culture, that is a legacy of ages; but not so to build it up. If India lives today and can hold up her head proudly even in these degenerate days, it is more on account of her culture and art than by her kings, ministers, or legislators. The legacy of the art, hallowed by the names of Gods and Royal ladies, is too precious a treasure to be destroyed or dimmed by the confusion of purpose and method of over-enthusiastic reformers with no proper perspective of Indian life and its amenities.

Reply of Muthulakshmi Reddy to Krishna Aiyar's Letter in *The Hindu* Dated 10 December 1932

Sir—In the article of Mr. E. Krishna Aiyar dated 7th, Mr. K. Krishna Aiyar has mixed health and social purity activities with those of social reform. Trying to save girls and boys from a life of infamy and vice is no social reform. This idea is nothing new to any civilized society. It is universally recognized elementary code of morality that all creeds and all nations have accepted and have to observe in the interest of the race itself and hence laws exist in every country to educate the ignorant on the right principle of life and conduct. That is why the League of Nations, the International Assembly, has taken up this question of combating the evils arising from immoral traffic in women and children. I am glad to note that Mr. Krishna Aiyar appreciates this aspect of question in his letter. Under these circumstances, surely no fair-minded person will advocate that any art, however great and unique, should be cultivated and encouraged at the expense of this universally recognized principles of social purity. As the teaching of music and dance to girls of particular communities has become at the present day identical with the training of such girls for a life of promiscuity, those communities themselves in their mass conferences of men and women have not only condemned the practice but have also demanded effective legislation to put down the evil. It is a fact that the girls among those communities who are taught music and dance do not marry and are not respected by their own people as the learning and practice of the art has become inseparable at the present day from a life of prostitution and none, even Mr. Krishna Aiyar inclusive, will deny that the public also holds the same opinion that the Devadasis who dance in public are prostitutes and none but they would learn and practice the art. As I have stated in my previous letter, if good and virtuous women are to learn and cultivate the art of music and dance, the prevalent notion that only women of questionable character could take to this art, has to be changed. How can we bring about the change? The change is possible only when lovers of art firmly set their faces against disreputable women-performers, so that women of culture may take their place, learn and cultivate the art and restore it to its high status.

I do not share in the fear of Mr. Krishna Aiyar that our fine arts will die out if we do not encourage the present day nautch-girls. While a few years ago, there was strong opposition even from the parents to the teaching of music in girls' schools, now it has become very popular subject in our schools. I regret that Mr Krishna Aiyar has ignored the work of women's associations 'and women's conferences in this connection. The introduction of music in the B.A. classes in the Queen- Mary's College was no less due to the; representation of women as to that of the men. In the new Central Training College for women to be soon opened at Delhi through the activities of the All-India Women's Conference, music and fine arts find a prominent place. The Women's Indian Association has strongly recommended the retention of music in the Queen Mary's College and the public knows that under the present retrenchment scheme many useful and essential activities have suffered.

Now, in Northern India Indian dance is taught in girls' schools and colleges and Tagore dance has become very popular. No doubt, in the South, I do admit that we are still backward in this matter which is due to the fact that the art of music and dance is even today associated with a life of impurity, As I have stated, good women will take to it only when the public mind has been educated so as to dissociate the art from a life of infamy.

Therefore the duty of all lovers of art is to help the work of social purity by encouraging the cultivation and the practice or the art by the establishment of a school of music and dance by attracting women of culture and character to the noble profession with special scholarships, in the same way as women have been attracted to the profession of medicine, teaching and nursing, and as the Indian School of Medicine has been established to keep alive, the Ayurvedic and the Unani systems of medicine.

Therefore, I still-strongly urge on the public that no art or learning should be cultivated and encouraged at the expense of the health and the morality of the individual and the race. Any art or culture worth surviving will certainly hold its own against all times and against all conditions. Our attempt should be to free it from the ugly associations and the incrustations of ages which now keeps it dim and repulsive to many so that the divine art may be learned, practiced by royal ladies and by all good and noble women—as goddesses of old. Then only India's art, the rich legacy of ages, will shine brighter and will command the respect and admiration of the world.

A Letter from Berliner to Hawd, Dated 13 January 1900, Available in the EMI Archives (London)

My dear Jack,

In the first place, every man who knows anything about the situation there says the field for our machines in India is beyond any realization, without having been in the country and knowing its resources. For instance, Calcutta has one and a half millions of inhabitants and is called 'The city of palaces' meaning that there is scarcely any city in the world which contains so many people who are able to spend a fair amount of money for an article like ours. It has been a desire on my part for some time to start our business in that territory and I am very seriously thinking of the wisdom of doing it. Your work in Hanover has been a good one and has brought order out of chaos; the results which you have shown are such that you have a good right to feel very proud. Now, what I propose as to Calcutta and Bombay is this: That within 3 or 4 weeks, I make all preparations as this is the best time of the year, and if you will undertake it start by steamer with at least 500 machines and say, 30,000 records and go and stay long enough in Calcutta and Bombay to prove the possibility of making a business there and then after that has been done, in 3, 4 or 5 months turn the business over to some large House on the basis of wishing to start the work in different localities of that region. You must go prepared with all sorts of advertising matter and the most perfect preparations that can possibly be planned, and I do this with a belief that knowing well how all our methods have succeeded here that you will adopt the same methods and come out of it with great success, and that it will prove a fine market.

Elaborate Account of Recording Process by Recording Expert T.J. Theobald Noble Is Available in The *Talking Machine News and Side Lines***, Vol 8, No 10, October 1912, pp. 331/334. A Copy of This Was Accessed by the Author at the British Library, London**

Though it is the business of the dealer to vend records, still, I venture to remark, few even pause to consider how master records are obtained and transferred to disc or cylinder as the case may be. The skill required to secure the natural tone quality of the artiste, the great amount of labour required to produce the multitudinous records which are sold in every corner of the globe, the fees paid to artistes, which alone runs into many thousands of pounds per month, and other similar incidentals with which the record producer has to be au fait.

Before going any further it is as well for me to state that I do not propose to give a detailed description of the various technicalities encountered in the actual recording of the human voice, but what I will give is sufficient date to enable the reader to understand how the result is obtained—just a concise account of how a voice is recorded.

Primarily trials are heard and made of several artistes to secure what may be termed a recording voice. Not all voices are suitable; some of our most popular artistes fail to make a satisfactory commercial record. There are many reasons for this. A voice may be too weak or too nasal and in another the enunciation too bad and so on, but if an artiste is selected as entirely satisfactory, he will receive a song or two to study prior to making a record. The musical director of the company then ascertains the key which suits the artiste best and proceeds to orchestrate for however many musicians are considered necessary. This is usually twelve, and then a date is arranged for making the record.

We will now suppose the artiste and musicians to be in the recording room in the hands of the recording expert. The musicians are all, of course, men well-versed in recording and require little or no instructions from the recorder. The artiste, however, providing he is not an old hand at the game, requires such advice and attention of the recorder.

Artiste and orchestra proceed to rehearse and time the selection and this over the recorder places his artiste a few inches in front of the horn. Immediately behind and around are the musicians arranged as the recorder may desire. In all cases the reed instruments are nearer to the horn than the brass. All instruments have to be carefully focused to the mouth of the horn, otherwise the result would not be properly balanced. The orchestra now plays the introduction, during which the artiste leans away in order to enable the bandsmen to play right into the horn without the vocalist's head obstructing, as is the case when he is singing. This over, the artiste commences to sing, with the recorder in close attendance to ensure evenness in strength. The voice—or sound waves—travels down the horn, through the special rubber attachment, through the trunnion supporting the dia-phragm, on to the diaphragm itself, thereby vibrating the recording glass, which in turn vibrates the sapphire, cutting the indentations or sound-waves into the fast revolving disc or cylinder.

Such in brief outline is what goes on when a voice—or for that matter any other series of sound waves—is recorded. And this, I hope, will be intelli-gible to the reader...Now, as I said before, the recorder has to lightly hold place his hand on the singer's shoulder—during the singing, for on a loud note it is sometimes necessary to take the artiste a few inches back from the horn, and on a subdued, or low note nearer to it. After the completion of a selection the record is scrupulously cleaned of wax chips, and tested in the presence of the recorder, musical director, conductor and artiste. Faults are found and remedied and suggestions made as to improvement, after which another record is usually made of the same selection. If there should be faults after the second attempt, the process as again gone through until a satisfactory record is obtained.

We will now assume that a good record has been obtained. The next step in the process is its passing. When a record is passed as being good techni-cally and artistically, it is numbered and carefully packed away preparatory for transit to the factory, and the next selection taken.

Several tests are made by the recorder of the artiste's voice with separate diaphragms and horns for the purpose of securing the diaphragm and horn which I most appropriate for the particular artiste. Each horn gives a dif-ferent tone, and each diaphragm possesses a particular quality. Horns are used which can make a voice sound thin, tubby, or weak; diaphragms, too, appear to have their idiosyncrasies. One may be excellent for an orchestra, but useless for a soprano. Another good for a soprano and bad for a tenor, and so on. This, however, is not the case with the few good experts who are making records. A diaphragm should be made to record all selections, even as the human ear hears all sounds in its proximity.

The diaphragm is the chief item in recording, and the most infinitesimal raising or lowering of a sapphire in its holder will alter the whole tone of a record. The diaphragm which cuts exactly in the centre of a record may result in obtaining a thin tone, whilst cutting 1/16th in front or behind the centre will produce a fine round tone.

Such are but a few technicalities a recorder should know. For recording a military or full-band selection the orchestra is augmented, and a band of 20–24 men as usual for such numbers. I have, however, recorded as many as 50 instrumentalist abroad, and in some cases one hundred musicians have been recorded at one time. In the instances a much larger horn is used and the machine generally lowered to obtain a fuller tone.

The same difficulties are encountered as with vocalists, for several tones can be obtained, therefore trials have to be made to ascertain the most nat-ural of them. One of the most difficult tasks, however, is the placing of the musicians to obtain a good balance. The musicians chosen for the talking machine, by the bye, are the best possible to find in the town where one may be recording. Ordinary musicians are of little use, for it is a severe test to play such selections as "Tannhauser" repeatedly before a satisfactory record is secured. Furthermore, the slightest mistake made will damn the record, and the whole selection has to be played through again and again until it is made without error.

In the theatre should a mistake occur it is passed, and soon forgotten, but on a record, it is always there, an irremediable flaw which is repeated on each occasion that the record is played. I have known musicians to play for three consecutive hours such selection s 'Introduction to the Third Act of Lohengrin' and other numbers, several times over.

After having secured a number of master records they are sent to the factory, where they are placed in an electric bath; for the purpose of having matrices made from them. From these matrices are printed the commercial records. The first print made is sent to the recorder to test as to whether it is to pass or be condemned, for after a record is sent to the factory, a matrice made, and a print obtained, it may lose some of its quality. The surface may be too rough, the matrice overpolished and so has erased a considerable amount of tone, or the matrice may be scratched. All these multifarious faults are carefully attended to, and another matrice then made, or should the original master wax record be spoiled, the selection will have to be recorded again until satisfactory prints are obtained for selling purposes. I have endeavoured to explain in rough outline the duties of the Recorder at home. His duties, however, do not always end there. Often he has to travel the wide, wide world, as I did, in search of his quarry.

Account of Theobald Noble in the *Talking Machine World*, pp. 48–49, 15 May 1913. I Accessed a Microfilm of This at the British Library, London

The weather was so oppressively hot in Madras that I was compelled to record with only my pajamas on, and those of the thinnest silk obtainable. I was to record only native artists, and there was no fear of 'shocking' their modesty. Of the artists, I will mention but one; the one that I had come to Madras to record, Miss Godavari, the first artist in the Tamil language. We visited the woman's house for the purpose of discussing terms (this is always a tedious and worrying business). The house was a great surprise, for the interior was constructed of marble and a faint glimmer of a blue-shaded light cast an interesting and warm sensation over the interior that was at once fascinating and seductive. It was presented to her by an admirer and had cost 180,000 rupees ($60,000). We were compelled to pay two visits before ultimately coming to terms. We secured her for 16 titles for the sum of 300 rupees per song. I may add that she held out consistently for 2 days for 900 rupees per record. The trouble we discovered was through the agents, who are a most arbitrary set of men. They persuade most of the artists to ask for large fees in order to swell their commission and at the same time advise us that such and such a price is usual for a particular artist.

She came to the hotel to record, accompanied by a retinue of seven servants, including two accompanists. One of the instruments for accompanying was the most extraordinary musical instrument, I should imagine, in the world; it is best described as a large earthernware pot, which is held in the lap of a man who plays it by beating a series of taps on the periphery, certain parts of which give out various tones. The accompanist's fingers have to be particularly hard and dexterous for to continually beat on such a hard surface sufficiently loud for recording purposes requires an appreciable amount of strength and adroitness. The other accompanist was a young girl playing the harmonium, whilst the artist herself was playing another instrument bejeweled in most elaborate fashion. The instrument was valued at 12,000 rupees. She was covered with gold and precious stones of great value. It was for the express purpose of guarding these jewels that she possessed a guard of four men. An Indian artist by-the-by invariably dons her finest jewelry in the presence of a white. Round her throat she wore a necklace of English sovereigns, the clasps holding each to the other were studded with diamonds. There being in all fifty sovereigns and fifty clasps, the value can be appreciated. On the toes she wore platinum and gold rings. I secured a photograph but she insisted on removing from her person all jewels, for what reason I was never able to comprehend. In the photograph nevertheless, can be seen the rings on her toes and the large diamonds in the ears. She sang exceptionally well, her high cadenzas being particularly loud and clear, which is always a great necessity and advantage for recording. It may be interesting to state here that the broker present was so enraptured with the singing that he immediately ordered 3000 of each title. She, herself, ordering from the broker 50 of each title for distribution amongst her friends. Having made records before, she was little troubled and in fact was a great assistance, for it was she who instructed the accompanists exactly what to do and where to sit, explaining to me that the position in which she placed the men was the best position, for the so-and-so company had already experimented with the placing and had lost two days before ultimately succeeding. I therefore left it to her and the result proved eminently satisfactory.

APPENDIX 2
LINKS TO GRAMOPHONE
RECORD TRACKS ANALYSED
IN CHAPTER 6

1 **RAGA THODI CLIPS (CARNATIC):** https://soundcloud.com/archive-of-indian-music/sets/raga-thodi-clips
2 **RAGA KAMBODHI CLIPS (CARNATIC):** https://soundcloud.com/archive-of-indian-music/sets/raga-kambodhi-clips
3 **RAGA JAUNPURI CLIPS (HINDUSTANI):** https://soundcloud.com/archive-of-indian-music/sets/raga-jaunpuri-clips
4 **RAGA BHAIRAVI CLIPS (HINDUSTANI):** https://soundcloud.com/archive-of-indian-music/sets/raga-bhairavi-clips
5 **SALEM AMMAKANNU CLIPS (CARNATIC):** https://soundcloud.com/archive-of-indian-music/sets/salem-ammakannu
6 **BANGALORE NAGARATHNAMMA CLIPS (CARNATIC):** https://soundcloud.com/archive-of-indian-music/sets/bangalore-nagarathnamma-1
7 **DHANAKOTI AMMAL CLIPS (CARNATIC):** https://soundcloud.com/archive-of-indian-music/sets/dhanakoti-ammal
8 **COIMBATORE THAYI CLIPS (CARNATIC):** https://soundcloud.com/archive-of-indian-music/sets/coimbatore-thayi-1
9 **SALEM GODAVARI CLIPS (CARNATIC):** https://soundcloud.com/archive-of-indian-music/sets/salem-godavari-1

BIBLIOGRAPHY

List of References[1]

Acharekar, B. *Bharatiya Sangit ani Sangitashastra*. Bombay: Maharashtra Rajya Sahitya Sanskriti Mandal, 1974. Print.

Ackoff, Russell. *Redesigning the Future*. New York/London: Wiley, 1974. Print.

Adorno, Theodor. "The Form of the Phonograph record" and "The Curves of the Needle." Trans. Thomas Levin. October 55: 48–56, 1934. Print.

———. *Negative Dialectic*. New York: Seabury Press, 1973. Print.

All-India Music Conference Proceedings. 1916–18. Baroda: All-India Music Conference. Print.

Ahmad, Najma Perveen. *Hindustani Music: A Study of its Development in Seventeenth and Eighteenth Centuries*. New Delhi: Manohar Publications, 1984. Print.

Ahobala, P. *Sangita Parijata* (3rd ed.). Ed. Kalindji. Hathras: Sangeet Karyalaya. 1971. Print.

Aliviztou, M. "The Paradoxes of Intangible Heritage." *Safeguarding Intangible Cultural Heritage*. Eds. M. Stefano, P. Davis and G. Corsane. Woodbridge, UK: Boydell Press, 2012. Print.

Allen, A. "Ecomusicology: Music, Culture, Environmental Studies and Change". *Journal of Environmental Studies and Sciences* 2.2 (2009): 192–201. Print.

Ammaiyar, Ramamirtham. *Dasigalin Mosaavalai Alladhu Matiperra Mainar*. Madras: Pearl Press, 1936. Print.

Anandhi, S. "Representing Devadasis: Dasigal Mosavalai" as a Radical Text." *Economic and Political Weekly* 26.11–12 (1991): 739–46. Print.

———. "Caste and Gender in Colonial South India." *Economic and Political Weekly*, April 9 (2005): 1518–22. Print.

"Annual Report." *Gandharva Mahavidyalaya*, Lahore, 1904–5. Print.

Appadurai, Arjun. *Worship and Conflict under Colonial Rule: A South Indian Case*. Cambridge: Cambridge University Press, 1981. Print.

Archer, W.K. "On the Ecology of Music". *Ethnomusicology* 8.1 (1064): 28–33. Print.

Armbrust, Walter. *Mass Culture and Modernism in Egypt*. Cambridge: Cambridge University Press, 1988. Print.

ARSC (Association for Recording Sound Collections Journals): 1982–2010. Web.

Ashby, Arved Mark. *Absolute Music, Mechanical Reproduction*. California: California University Press, 2010. Print.

Atkinson, Paul and David, Silverman. "Kundera's Immortality: The Interview Society and the Invention of the Self." *Qualitative Inquiry* 3 (1997): 304–325. Print.

Attali, Jacques. *Noise: The Political Economy of Music.* Trans. Brian Massumi. Minneapolis: University of Minnesota Press, 1985. Print.

Aubert, Lament. *The Music of the Other: New Challenges for Ethnomusicology in a Global Age.* Trans. Carla Ribeiro. VT: Ashgate, 2007. Print.

Auerswald, E.H. "Thinking about thinking in family therapy." *Family Process* 24 (1985): 1–12. Print.

———. "Epistemological Confusion in Family Therapy and Research." *Family Process* 26 (1987): 317–330. Print.

Ayyangar, Rangaramanuja. *History of South Indian (Carnatic) Music: From the Vedic times to the present.* Bombay: Vipanchi Cultural Trust, 1972. Print.

Ayyar, C. S. *The Grammar of South Indian (Karnatic) Music.* Madras: Ananda Press, 1951. Print.

Babbitt, Susan E. "Feminism and Objective Interests? The Role of Transformation Experiences in Rational Deliberation." *Feminist Epistemologies.* Eds. Linda Alcoff and Elizabeth Potter. New York: Routledge, 1993. Print.

Bai, C. Banni. *Srimati Vidya Sundari Bangalore Nagarathnam Ammayarin Suyacharitai.* Madras: Sami Printers, 1953. Print.

Baier, Susan. "The Need for More than Justice." *Science, Morality, and Feminist Theory.* Eds. Marsha Hanen and Kai Nielsen. Minneapolis: University of Minnesota Press (1987). Print.

Bakhle, Janaki. *Two Men and Music: Nationalism in the Making of an Indian Classical Tradition.* New Delhi: Permanent Black, 2005. Print.

Ballahatchet, Kenneth. *Race, Sex and Class Under the Raj: Imperial Attitudes and Policies and Their Critics, 1793–1905.* London: Wiedenfield and Nicholson, 1979. Print.

Bandopadhyay, Debojit. *Beshya Shongeet, Baiji Shongeet.* Calcutta: Subornorekha Publications, N.d. Print.

Bangre, Arun. *Gwalior ki Sangeet Parampara.* Hubli: Yashoyash Prakashan, 1995. Print.

Banerjee, Sumanta. *The Parlour and the Streets: Elite and Popular Culture in Nineteenth Century Calcutta.* Calcutta: Seagull Press, 1989. Print.

Barlow, Jon and Lakshmi Subramanian. "Music and Society in North India." *Economic and Political Weekly* 42.19 (2007): 1779–1787. Print.

Baskaran, S. Theodore. *The Message Bearers: The Nationalist Politics and the Entertainment Media in South India, 1880–1945.* Madras: Cre-A, 1981. Print.

Basic Texts of the 2003 Convention for the Safeguarding of the Intangible Cultural Heritage. France: UNESCO, 2016. Web 12 December 2016.

Baxter, Pamela and Susan Jack. "Qualitative Case Study Methodology: Study Design and Implementation for Novice Researchers". *The Qualitative Report* 13.4 (2008): 544–559. Print.

Bayley, A. Ed. *Recorded Music: Performance, Culture and Technology.* Cambridge: Cambridge University Press, 2010. Print.

Bautze, Joachim K. 2006. "The Dancing Girl ('Devadasi') of South India in Actual Early Photographs." *Sahrdaya: Studies in Indian and South East Asian Art.* Ed. Bettina Baumer et al. 201–25. Chennai: Tamil Arts Academy, 2006. Print.

Beauvoir, Simone De. *The Second Sex.* Constance Borde and Sheila Malovaney-Chevallier. *(trans).* New York: Vintage Press, 2011. Print.

Bel, B. "Musical Acoustics: Beyond Levy's Intonation of Indian Music." *ISTAR Newsletter* 2 (1984): 7–12. Web 12 August 2017.

———."Pitch Perception and Pitch Extraction in Melodic Music." *ISTAR Newsletter* 3–4 (1984–85): 54–59. Web. 12 August 2017.

Bendrups, Dan and Katelyn Barney. Eds. "Musicology Australia: Special Issue": *Sustainability and Ethnomusicology in the Australian context* 35.2 (2013): 153–158. Print.

Benhabib, Seyla. "Sexual Difference and Collective Identities: The New Global Constellation." *Signs* 24 (1999): 335–361. Print.

Benjamin, Walter. *Illuminations*. New York: Schocken Books, 1973. Print.

Berry, Wallace. *Musical Structure and Performance*. New Haven: Yale University Press, 1989. Print.

Besant, Annie. *Wake Up, India: A Plea for Social Reform*. Adyar, Madras: Theosophical Publishing House, 1913. Print.

Bharata. *Natya-Sastra*. Ed. Manmohan Ghosh, 2 Vols. Calcutta: Manisha Granthalaya, 1967. Print.

Bharathi, Suddhananda. *Saint Thyagaraja: The Divine Singer*. Madras: Yoga Samaj, 1968. Print.

Bhaskaran, Theodore. *The Message-Bearers: Nationalist Politics and the Entertainment Media in South India, 1880–1945*. Madras: Cre-A, 1981. Print.

Bhatkhande, V. N. *A Comparative Study of Some of the Leading Music Systems of the 15th, 16th, 17th, 18th Centuries*. Lucknow, 1916. Print.

———. "A Short Historical Survey of the Music of Upper India." (Lecture presented at the first All-India Music Conference, Baroda, India, 1916). Bombay: Bombay Samachar, 1917. Print.

———. Ed. *Hindusthani Sangeet Paddhathi*. Bombay: Popular Prakashan, 1999. 5 vols. Print.

Bhattacharya, Rimli. Ed. and trans., *Binodini Dasi: My Story and My Life as an Actress*. New Delhi: Kali for Women, 1998. Print.

———."Promiscuous Spaces and Economies of Entertainment: Soldiers, Actresses, and Hybrid Genres in Colonial India." *Nineteenth Century Theatre and Film*." 41.2 (2014): 50–75. Web. 21 March 2016.

Bhattacharya, Sudhirbhushan. *Ethnomusicology and India*. Calcutta: Indian Publishers, 1968.

Bhole, Keshavrao. *Majhe Sangeet Rachana ani Digdarshana*. Bombay: Marg Prakashan, 1964a. Print.

———. *Vasant Kakachi Patre*. Pune: First Edition, 1964b. Print.

———. *Je Athavate Te*. Pune: Prestige Prakashan, 1974. Print.

———. *Sthayi*. Pune: Prestige Prakashan, 1996. Print.

Blaikie, N. *Approaches to Social Enquiry* 1st ed., Cambridge: Polity Press, 1993. Print.

———. *Designing Social Research*1st ed., Cambridge: Polity Press, 2000. Print.

Blaukopf, Kurt. *Musical Life in a Changing Society*. Trans. David Marinelli. Portland, OR: Amadeus, 1992. Print.

Bloomberg, L. D. and Volpe, M. *Completing your Qualitative Dissertation*. Thousand Oaks, CA: Sage, 2012. Print.

Bohlman, Philip. "Musicology as a Political Act." *Journal of Musicology*. 11 (1993): 411–36. Web. 7 March 2015.

Bor, Joep. "The Voice of the Sarangi." *National Centre for Performing Arts Quarterly Journal* 15/16 (1986/1987). Print.

———.The Rise of Ethnomusicology: Sources on Indian Music c. 1780–c.1890. *Yearbook for Traditional Music* 20 (1988): 51–73. *JSTOR*. Web 20 December 2015.

Bor, Joep and Kai Reschke. *Masters of Raga*. Berlin: Haus der Kulturen der Walt, 1992. Print.

Boghossian, Paul A. *Fear of Knowledge: Against Relativism and Constructivism*. Oxford: Clarendon Press, 2006. Print.

Brady, Erika. *A Spiral Way: How the Phonograph Changed Ethnography*. Jackson: University Press of Mississippi, 1999. Print.

Braun, Hans Joachim. Ed. *Music and Technology in the Twentieth Century*. Baltimore/London: Johns Hopkins University Press, 2002. Print.

Brecht, B. *Brecht on Theatre*. Trans. and Ed. J. Willet. New York and London: Hill and Wang (1978). Print.

Bresler, L. Embodied Narrative Inquiry: A Methodology of Connection. *Research Studies in Music Education*. (27 Dec 2006): 27(1): 21–43. Print.

Brihaspati, Acharya. *Musalman Aur Bharatiya Sangeet*. Delhi: Rajkamal Publications, 1974. Print.

Brinda, T. *Javalis of Patnam Subrahmanya Iyer, Tiruppanandal Pattabhiramayya, Dharmapuri Subbaraya, Tirupathi Narayanaswami and Others*. Madras: Music Academy, 1960. Print.

Brown, Wendy. *Manhood and Politics: A Feminist Reading in Political Theory*. Totowa: Rowman and Littlefield, 1998. Print.

Bryman, A. "The Debate about Quantitative and Qualitative Research: A Question of Method or Epistemology?" *The British Journal of Sociology* 35.1 (1984): 75–92. Print.

Burr, V. "Overview: Realism, Relativism, Social Constructionism and Discourse." *Social Constructionism, Discourse and Realism*. Ed. I. Parker. London: Sage Publications, 1988. 13–26. Print.

Burton, Antoinette. *Burdens of History: British Feminists, Indian Women and Imperial Culture, 1865–1915*. Chapel Hill: University of North Carolina Press, 1994. Print.

Butler Brown, K. "The Social Liminality of Musicians: Case Studies from Mughal India and Beyond." *Twentieth-Century Music* 3.1 (2007): 13–49. Web 10 August 2017.

Butler, Judith. "Gender Trouble, Feminist Theory, and Psychoanalytic Discourse." *Feminism/Postmodernism*. Ed. Linda Nicholson. New York: Routledge, 1990. Print.

———.*Gender Trouble: Feminism and the Subversion of Identity*. New York: Routledge, 1990

Byrne, Michelle M. "Hermeneutics as a Methodology for Textual Analysis." *AORN Journal*. 73.5 (1996): 968–970. Print.

Candy, Catherine. "Relating Feminisms, Nationalisms, and Imperialisms: Ireland, India, and Margaret Cousin's Sexual Politics." *Women's History Review 3*, no. 4 (1994): 581–594. Print.

Cerulo, K.A. "Social Disruption and its Effects on Music – An Empirical Analysis". *Social Forces*. 62 (1984): 885–904. Print.

Chakraborty, Mridula Nath. "Wa(i)ving it All Away: Feminists of Colour." *Third Wave Feminism: A Critical Exploration* (2nd ed.). Eds. Stacy Gillis, Gillian Howie, and Rebecca Munford. Basingstoke: Palgrave Macmillan, 2007. Print.

Chakroborty, Somnath. *Kolkata Baiji Bilas*. Calcutta: Bookland Private Limited, N.d. Print.

Chakravorty, Pallabi. *Bells of Change: Kathak Dance, Women and Modernity in India*. Calcutta: Seagull Books, 2008. Print.

Chanan, M. *Repeated Takes: A Short History of Recording and Its Effects on Music*. London and New York, Verso, 1995. Print.

Chandvankar, Suresh. *Poorvasureenche Soor*. Pune: Swanandi Prakashan, 2007. Print.

———."Centenary of Indian Gramophone Records". 2002. Web. 14 April 2016.

Charmaz, K. *Constructing Grounded Theory: A Practical Guide through Qualitative Analysis*. Thousand Oaks, CA: Sage, 2006. Print.

———. "Grounded Theory Methods in Social Justice Research." *The SAGE Handbook of Qualitative Research*. Eds. N. K. Denzin and Y. S. Lincoln Los Angeles, CA: Sage, 2011. 359–380. Print.

Charter on the Preservation of the Digital Heritage. Paris: UNESCO, 17 October 2003. Web. 12 December 2016.

Chatterjee, Partha. *The Nation and Its Fragments: Colonial and Postcolonial Histories*. Princeton: Princeton University Press, 1993. Print.

Chatterji, P.C. *The Adventure of Indian Broadcasting: A Philosopher's Autobiography*. Delhi: Konarak Publishers, 1998. Print.

Chatterjee, Santosh. *Devadasi (Temple Dancer)*. Calcutta: Book House, 1945. Print.

Chaudhuri, Sukanta. *Calcutta: The Living City: Vol 1: The Past*. New Delhi: Oxford University Press, 1990. Print.

Chawla, Rupika. *Raja Ravi Varma Painter of Colonial India*. Ahmedabad: Mapin Publishing, 2010. Print.

Chelladurai, P.T. *The Splendour of South Indian Music*. Dindigul: Vaigarai Publishers, 1991. Print.

Chetti, P. S. Ramulu. *Gandharvakalpavalli: Being a Self-Instructor in Music*. Madras: India Printing Works, 1912. Print.

Chitragupto. *Gahar Jaan*. Calcutta: Sashadhar Prakashon, 1994. Print.

Clark, L. "The Journey from Post-Positivist to Constructivist Methods." *Media, Home, and Family*. Eds. S. Hoover, L. Clark, D. Alters, J. Champ, and L. Hood. New York: Routledge, 2004. 19–34. Print.

Clarke, Eric. "Generative Principles in Music Performance." *Generative Processes in Music*. Ed. John Sloboda. Oxford: The Clarendon Press, 1988: 1–26. Print.

Clarke, Eric and Nicholas Cook, Eds. *Empirical Musicology: Aims, Methods, Prospects*, Oxford: OUP, 2004. Print.

Clary-Lemon, Jennifer. "Analyzing Discourses of Political Elites: Discourse of Irish Emigration in the 1970s." *Discourse and Society* 25 (2014): 619–639. Print.

Clayton, Jay. "The Voice in the Machine: Hardy, Hazlitt, James." *Language Machines: Technologies of Literary and Cultural Production*. Eds. Jeffrey Masten, Peter Stallybrass, and Nancy Vickers. New York: Routledge, 1997. 209–32. Print.

Clayton, Mark. "Arthur Henry Fox-Strangways and the Music of Hindostan: Revisiting Historical Field Recordings." *Journal of Royal Music Association* 124 (1999): 88–118. Print.

Clayton, Martin and Laura Leante. "Role. Status and Hierarchy in the Performance of North Indian Classical Music." *Ethnomusicology Forum* 24.3 (2015). Print.

Clements, Ernest. *Introduction to the Study of Indian Music*. Chandigarh: Abhishek Publications, 1992. Print.

Cook, Nicholas. *A Guide to Musical Analysis*. New York: George Braziller, 1987. Print.

———. "Analysing Performance and Performing Analysis." *Rethinking Music*. Eds. N. Cook and M. Everist. New York: Oxford University Press, 2001. 239–261. Print.

———. "Between Process and Product: Music and/as Performance."*Music Theory Online* 7.2 (2001): n.p. Web. 22 April 2016.

————.Ed. et al. *Cambridge Companion to Recorded Music*. Cambridge: Cambridge University Press. 2009. Print.

————. "The Ghost in the Machine: Towards a Musicology of Recordings". *Musicae Scientiae*. 14.2 (2010): 3–21. Web. 18 October 2016.

Coomaraswamy, Ananda K. 1909. *Essays in National Idealism*. New Delhi: Munshiram Manoharlal, 1981: 166–200. Print. [First publ. as *Indian Music*.]

————. 1909. *Essays in National Idealism*. New Delhi: Munshiram Manoharlal, 1981: 201–6. Print. [First publ. as *Gramophones — and Why Not?*]

Corn, A. "National Recording Project for Indigenous Music in Australia." 2011. Web. 15 March 2017.

Coulter, Neil R. *"Music Shift: Evaluating the Vitality and Viability of Music Styles Among the Alamblak of Papua New Guinea."* Ph.D. dissertation. Kent, Ohio: Kent State University, 2007. Print.

————. "Assessing Music Shift: Adapting EGIDS for a Papua New Guinea Community."*Language Documentation and Description* 10 (2011): 61–81. Print.

Coulter, C. and Smith, M. "The Construction Zone: Literary Elements in Narrative Research." *Educational Researcher*. 38.8 (2009): 577–591. Print.

Cousins, Margaret. *Music of the Orient and the Occident: Essays Towards Mutual Understandings*. Madras: B.G. Paul, 1935. Print.

————. 1940. *Uttara Mandra* 1.1 (March 1970): 142. Print. [First publ. as *The Late Maharaja of Mysore's Patronage of Music*].

Craig, Edward. Ed. *Routledge Encyclopedia of Philosophy*, Volume 3. New York: Routledge, 1998. Print.

Crespin, Régine. *On Stage, Off Stage: A Memoir*. Trans. G.S. Bourdain. Boston: Northeastern University Press 1997. Print.

Daniel, E. V. and J.M. Peck. "Culture/Contexture: an Introduction." *Culture/ Contexture: Explorations in Anthropology and Literary Studies*. Eds. E. V. Daniel and J.M. Peck. Berkeley, CA: University of California Press, 1996: 281–286. Print.

Dang, Kokila. "Prostitutes, Patrons and the State: Nineteenth Century Awadh." *Social Scientist*. 21: 9–11 (September-November 1993). Print.

Dasgupta, Amlan. *Music and Modernity: North Indian Classical Music in an Age of Mechanical Repreoduction*. Kolkata: Thema, 2007. Print.

Davidson, Jane. "Music as Social Behaviour." *Empirical Musicology: Aims, Methods, Prospects*. Eds. Eric Clarke and Nicholas Cook. Oxford: OUP, 2004. Print.

Day, Charles. *Music and Musical Instruments of Southern India and the Deccan*. London and New York: Novello, Ewer, 1891. Print.

Day, Timothy. *A Century of Recorded Music: Listening to Musical History*. New Haven, Conn.: Yale University Press, 2000. Print.

Dean, Jonathan. *Rethinking Contemporary Feminist Politics*. Basingstoke: Palgrave Macmillan, 2010. Print.

De Bruin, Hanne. "The Devadasi Debate and Public Sphere." *Folklore, Public Sphere and Civil Society*. Eds. M.D. Muthukumaraswamy and Molly Kaushal. New Delhi and Chennai: Indira Gandhi National Centre for the Arts and National Folklore Support Centre, 2004. 103–111. Print.

de Lauretis, Teresa. "Feminist Studies/Critical Studies: Issues, Terms, Contexts." *Feminist Studies/Critical Studies*. Ed. Teresa de Lauretis. Bloomington: Indiana University Press, 1986. Print.

De Nora, T. *Music in Everyday Life*. Cambridge: Cambridge University Press, 2000. Print.

Deodhar, B. R. "*Pandit* Vishnu Narayan Bhatkhande: Vyaktitva tatha Karya." *Sangeet Kala Vihar* 10 (1947): 24–34. Print.

———. *Gayanacharya Pandit V.D. Paluskar*. Bombay: Akhil Bharatiya Gandharva Mahavidyalaya Mandal, 1971. Print.

Denzin, N. and Lincoln, Y, eds. *The Sage Handbook of Qualitative Research*, Second Edition. Thousand Oaks, CA: Sage Publications, 2000. Print.

Denzin, N. K. *Interpretive Interactionism*. Thousand Oaks, CA: Sage, 1989. Print.

Deva, B. Chaitanya. *An Introduction to Indian Music*. New Delhi: Publications Division, Government of India, 1973. Print.

Deshpande, Vamanrao. *Maharashtra's Contribution to Music*. Bombay: Popular Prakashan, 1972. Print.

———. *Indian Musical Traditions: An Aesthetic Study of the Gharanas in Hindustani Music*. Bombay: Popular Prakashan, 1973. Print.

Devi, Naina. "Thumri, Its Development & Gayeki." *ITC Sangeet Research Academy Journal* (1985): 13–17. Print.

Devi, Savita and Vibha, S. Chauhan. *Maa Siddheshwari*. New Delhi: Roli Books, 2000. Print.

Dewey, J. "Experience and Philosophic Method." *Complementary Methods for Research in Education* (2nd ed.). Ed. R. Jaeger. Washington, DC: American Educational Research Association, 1997. Print.

Dickerson, Victoria C. and Jeffrey L. Zimmerman. "Myths, Misconceptions, and a Word or Two about Politics." *Journal of Systemic Therapies*. 15.1. (1996). Print.

Doan, R. "The King is Dead: Narrative Therapy and Practicing What we Preach." *Family Process* 37.3 (1997): 379–385. Print.

duPerron, Lalita. "Thumri: A Discussion of the Female Voice of Hindustani Music." *Modern Asian Studies* 36.1 (2002): 173–193. Print.

———. "Sonic Performativity: Analysing Gender in North Indian Classical Vocal Music." *Ethnomusicology Forum*. 24.3 (2015): 349–379. Print.

Dunsby, J. "Guest Editorial: Performance and Analysis of Music." *Music Analysis* 8.1.2 (1989): 5–20. Print.

Durga, S.A.K. *Research Methodology for Music*. Chennai: Centre for Ethnomusicology, 1991. Print.

Dixit, K.D. "Abdul Karim Khan and the Kirana Gharana of Hindusthani Music." *NCPA Periodical* 2.1 (1973): 37–43. Print.

Eck, Diana. *Benares: City of Light*. Columbia: Columbia University Press, 1998. Print.

Edison, Thomas Alva. "The Phonograph and its Future." *North American Review*, 126/262 (1878): 527–536. Print.

Enos, Richard Leo. "Recovering the Lost Art of Researching the History of Rhetoric." *Rhetoric Society Quarterly* 29.4 (1999): 7–20. Print.

Ethnomusicology Newsletter 6 (January 1956): 5. Print.

Eisenberg, Evan. *Recording Angel: Explorations in Phonography*. New York: McGraw-Hill, 1986. Print.

———. *The Recording Angel: Music, Records and Culture from Aristotle to Zappa*. London: Yale University Press, 2005. Print.

Farrell, Gerry. *Indian Music and the West*. New York: Oxford University Press, 2004. Print.

———. "Images in Early Indian Gramophone Catalogues." *Music in Art*. 12. 1–2 (1998). Print.

———. "The Early Days of the Gramophone Industry in India: Historical, Social and Musical Perspectives." *British Journal of Ethnomusicology*. 2 (1993): 31–53. Print.

Feld, S. "Acoustemology". *Keywords in Sound*. Eds. D. Novak and M. Sakakeeny. Durham, NC: Duke University Press, 2015. Print.

Ferreira-Buckley, Linda. "Rescuing the Archives from Foucault." *College English* 61.5 (1999): 577–83. Print.

———. "Serving Time in the Archives." *Rhetoric Review* 16.1 (1997): 26–28. Print.

Forte, A. *The Structure of Atonal Music*. New Haven: Yale University Press, 1973. Print.

Fischer, Clara. *Gendered Readings of Change: A Feminist-Pragmatist Approach*. New York: Palgrave MacMillan, 2014. Print.

Flyvbjerg, B. "Five Misunderstandings about Case Study". *Qualitative Inquiry* 12.2 (2006): 219–245. Print.

———. "Case Study." *The Sage Handbook of Qualitative Research* (4th ed.). Eds. N.K. Denzin and Y. S. Lincoln. Thousand Oaks, CA: Sage Publications, 1994. 301–316. Print.

Gadamer, H. "Classical and Philosophical Hermeneutics." *Theory, Culture And Society*. *23*.1. (2006). 29–56. Print.

Ganguly, Rita. *Ae Muhabbat: Reminiscing Begum Akhtar*. New Delhi: Stellar Publications, 2008. Print.

Gaisberg, Frederick William. *Music Goes Round*. New York: Arno Press, 1942. Print.

———. *Music on Record*. London: Northumberland Press, 1947. Print.

Garg, Lakshminarayan. *Hamare Sangeet Ratna: Part 1*. Hathras: Sangeet Karyalaya, 1957. Print.

Gautam, Kailash. "Mera Naam Janki Bai Allahabad." *Dharamyug* 15 March 1987. Print.

Gautam, M.B. *Bhagyodayam: MadariBhagyareddi Varma, Life Sketch and Mission*. Hyderabad: Adi Hindu Social Service League, 1991. Print.

Gayathri, J.V. and R.K. Raju. *Selections from the Records of the Mysore Palace: Vol 1: Musicians, Actors and Artists*. Mysore: Divisional Archives Office Publication, 1993. Print.

Gelatt, Roland. *The Fabulous Phonograph*. London: Cassell, 1956. Print.

George, T. J. S. *MS: A Life in Music*. New Delhi: Harper Collins India, 2004. Print.

Gendrin, D. M. "Homeless Women's Inner Voices: Friends or Foes?" *Hearing Many Voices*. Hampton Press, 2000. Print.

Ghose, Rajeshwari. *The Tyagaraja Cult in Tamilnadu: A Study in Conflict and Accommodation*. New Delhi: Motilal Banarsidass, 1996. Print.

Ghosh, Suman. "Impact of the Recording Industry on Hindustani Classical Music in the Last Hundred Years." *IASA Journal* 15 (June 2000): 12–17. Print.

Gillis, Stacy et al. *Third Wave Feminism: A Critical Exploration*, 2nd Ed. Basingstoke: Palgrave Macmillan, 2007. Print.

Gjerdigen, R. "Categorization of Musical Patterns by Self-Organizing Neuronlike Networks." *Music Perception*. 7(1990). 339–369. Print.

Glesne, C. and Peshkin, A. *Becoming Qualitative Researchers: An Introduction*. White Plains, NY: Longman, 1992. Print.

Gould, Glenn. "The Prospects of Recording." *The Glenn Gould Reader*. Ed. Tim Page. New York: Knopf, 1966; 1984. Print.

Grant, Catherine. *Music Endangerment: How Language Maintenance Can Help*. New York: Oxford University Press, 2014. Print.

———. Endangered musical heritage as a wicked problem. *International Journal of Heritage Studies.* 21.7(2015): 629–641. Print.

Gronow, Pekka and Ilpa Saunio. *An International History of the Recording Industry.* London: Cassel, 1997. Print.

Gronow, Pekka. *The Recording Industry: an Ethnomusicological Approach.* Finland: University of Tampere Press, 1996. Print.

———. "The Record Industry Comes to the Orient." *Society for Ethnomusicology* 25.2 (May, 1981). *JSTOR.* Web. May 27 2016.

Gruber, H. "Acquisition of Expertise."*International Encyclopedia of the Social & Behavioral Sciences.* Vol. 11. Amsterdam, The Netherlands: Elsevier Science, 2001. 5145–5150. Print.

Grumet, M. "On Daffodils that Come Before the Swallow Dies." *Qualitative Inquiry in Education: The Continuing Debate.* Eds. E. Eisner and A. Peshkin. New York: Teachers' College, 1990: 316–329. Print.

Guba, E. G. and Lincoln, Y. S. "Competing Paradigms in Qualitative Research." *Handbook of Qualitative Research.* Eds. N. K. Denzin and Y. S. Lincoln. Thousand Oaks: Sage, 1994: 105–117. Print.

Guha, Ranajit. *Dominance without Hegemony: History and Power.* Cambridge, MA: Harvard University Press, 1997. Print.

Guha-Thakurta, Tapati. *The Making of a New "Indian" Art: Artists, Aesthetics, and Nationalism in Bengal, c. 1850–1920.* Cambridge: Cambridge University Press, 1994. Print.

Gullickson, Anna. "Sex and Gender Through an Analytic Eye: Butler on Freud and Gender Identity." *Honors Projects* (2000). Paper 7. Web. 10 August 2015.

Gupta, Charu. *Sexuality, Obscenity and Community: Women, Muslims, and the Hindu Public in Colonial India.* New Delhi: Permanent Black, 2001. Print.

Habibullah, Jahan Ara. *Zindagi ki Yaadein: Riyasat Rampur Ka Nawabi Daur.* Karachi: Oxford University Press, 2003. Print.

Haladanakara, Babanarava. *Aesthetics of Agra and Jaipur Traditions.* Mumbai: Popular Prakashan, 2001. Print.

Halverson, W. *A Concise Introduction to Philosophy* (4th ed.). New York: Random House, 1981. Print.

Harris, Robin. *"Sitting 'Under the Mouth': Decline and Revitalization in the Sakha Epic Tradition Olonkho."* Ph.D. dissertation. Athens, Georgia: University of Georgia, 2012. Print.

Harvith, John and Susan Edwards Harvith. *Edison, Musicians, and the Phonograph: A Century in Retrospect.* New York: Greenwood Press, 1987. Print.

Hatch, J. *Doing Qualitative Research in Educational Settings.* Albany, NY: State University of New York, 2002. Print.

Hatano, G. and Oura, Y. "Culture-Rooted Expertise: Psychological and Educational Aspects". *International Encyclopedia of the Social & Behavioral Sciences.* Vol. 11. Amsterdam, The Netherlands: Elsevier Science, 2001. 3173–3176. Print.

Haynes, Douglas and Gyan Prakash. *Contesting Power: Resistance and Everyday Social Relations in South Asia.* New Delhi: Oxford University Press, 1991. Print.

Held, Virginia. "Feminism and Moral Theory." *Women and Moral Theory.* Eds. Eva Feder Kittay and Diana T. Meyers. Totowa: Rowman and Littlefield, 1987. Print.

Henry, J. "Discovering Subjective Meanings: Depth Interviewing." *Doing Social Psychology.* Eds. D. Miell and M. Wetherell. London: Sage, 1998. 85–96. Print.

Hesmondhalgh, David. *Western Music and Its Others: Difference, Representation, and Appropriation in Music.* Berkeley, CA: University of California Press, 2000. Print.

Hoffman, L. "A Reflexive Stance for Family Therapy." *Therapy as Social Construction.* Eds. S. McNamee and K.J. Gergen. London: Sage, 1991. 7–24. Print.

Hood, Mantle. "The Challenge of 'Bi-Musicality.'" *Ethnomusicology* 4.2 (1960): 58. Print.

Horkheimer and Adorno Theodor. *Dialectic of Enlightenment.* New York: Herder and Herder, 1969.

Howard, K. "Introduction: East Asian Music as Intangible Cultural Heritage." *Music as Intangible Cultural Heritage: Policy, Ideology, and Practice in the Preservation of East Asian Traditions.* Ed. K. Howard. Farnham, UK: Ashgate, 2012. Print.

Hughes, D. M. "Significant Differences: The Construction of Knowledge, Objectivity and Dominance." *Women's Studies International Forum* 18.4 (1995): 396–406. Print.

Hughes, J. *The Philosophy of Social Research.* Essex: Longman Group, 1980. Print.

Hughes, Stephen Putnam. "Music in the Age of Mechanical Reproduction: Drama, Gramophone, and the Beginnings of Tamil Cinema." *The Journal of Asian Studies* 66.1 (2007): 3–34. *JSTOR.* Web. 20 April 2016.

———. "The 'Music Boom' in Tamil South India: Gramophone, Radio and the Making of Mass Culture." *Historical Journal of Film, Radio and Television* 22.4 (2002): 445–473. *JSTOR* Web. 21 June 2016.

Huron. D. *Music Research Using Humdrum: A User's Guide.* Stanford, CA: Centre for Computer Assisted Research in the Humanities, 1999. Print.

———. "Tone and Voice: A Derivation of the Rules of Voice-Leading from Perceptual Principles. *Music Perception.* 19 (2001): 1–64. Print.

ICTM-ANZ (International Council for Traditional Music Australia-New Zealand Regional Committee). "Statement on Indigenous Australian Music and Dance." 2011. Web. 16 March 2017.

Jackson, William J. *Tyagaraja and the Renewal of Tradition.* New Delhi: Motilal Banarsidass, 1994. Print.

Jairazbhoy, Nazir Ali. *The Raags of North Indian Music: Their Structure and Evolution.* Bombay: Popular Prakashan, 1995. Print.

Jairazbhoy, N.A. and A.W. Stone. "Intonation in Present-day North Indian Classical Music." *Bulletin of the School of Oriental and African Studies*, 26 (1963): 119–132. Print.

Janesick, V. J. "The Choreography of Qualitative Research Design: Minuets, Improvisations, and Crystallization." *Handbook of Qualitative Research* (2nd ed.). Eds. N. K. Denzin and Y. S. Lincoln. Thousand Oaks, CA: Sage, 2000. 379–399. Print.

Jariwalla, Jayantilal. *Abdul Karim: The Man of the Times, Life and Art of a Great Musician.* Bombay: Balkrishnabua Kapileshwari, 1973. Print.

Jeffreys, Sheila. *The Spinster and Her Enemies: Feminism and Sexuality 1830–1930.* London: Pandora, 1985. Print.

Jha, Shweta Sachdeva. "Eurasian Women as Tawa'if Singers and Recording Artists: Entertainment and Identity-making in Colonial India." *African and Asian Studies* 8.3 (2009): 268–287. Print.

———. "Tawaif, Urdu Poetry and Self-Fashioning: Rethinking Women's History and Vernacular Modernity." *European Conference on Modern South Asian Studies* (2010): n.p. Web. 30th November 2015.

Johnson, R. and Omwuegbuzie, A. "Mixed Methods Research: A Research Paradigm whose Time has Come." *Educational Researcher 33*.7 (2004): 14–26. Print.

Jonassen, D. H. "Objectivism Versus Constructivism: Do we need a new Philosophical Paradigm?" *Educational Technology Research and Development* 39.3 (1991): 5–14. Print.

Jones, Andrew F. *Yellow Music: Media Culture and Colonial Modernity in the Chinese Jazz Age*. Durham, NC: Duke University Press, 2001.

Jones, Geoffrey. "The Gramophone Company: An Anglo-American Multinational, 1898–1931." *The Business History Review*, 59.1: (1985) 77. *JSTOR* Web. 16 January 2016.

Jordan, Kay Kirkpatrick. "Devadasi Reform: Driving the Priestesses or the Prostitutes Out of Hindu Temples." *Religion and Law in Independent India*. Ed. Robert Baird. New Delhi: Manohar, 1993. Print.

Joshi, G.N. "A Concise History of the Phonograph Industry in India." *Popular Music* 7.2 (1988): 147–156. *JSTOR* Web. 10 August 2015.

Journal of the Madras Music Academy. Madras: Music Academy, 1930: 79–80. Print.

———. 1935: 161. Print.

Kapileshwari, Balkrishnabua. *Abdul Karim Khan yaanche Jeevan Chitra*. Bombay, 1972. Print.

Kannabiran, Kalpana and Vasanth Kannabiran. *Muvalur Ramamirthammal's Web of Deceit: Devadasi Reform in Colonial India*. New Delhi: Kali for Women, 2003. Print.

Katrak, Ketu. "Indian Nationalism, Gandhian 'Satyagraha' and Representations of Female Sexuality." *Nationalisms and Sexualities*. Ed. Andrew Park. New York: Routledge, 1992. 395–406. Print.

Katz, Mark. *Capturing Sound: How Technology has Changed Music*. Berkeley, LA/ London: University of California Press, 2004. Print.

Kavale, Vasanta. *Naadayatra*. Bangalore: Karnataka Sahitya Parishat, 1976. Print.

Kenney, William Howland. *Recorded Music in American Life: The Phonograph and Popular Memory*. 1890–1945. New York: Oxford University Press, 2003. Print.

Kersenboom, Saskia C. "Virali: Possible Sources of the Devadasi Tradition in the Tamil Bardic Period." *Journal of Tamil Studies* 19 (1981): 19–41. Print.

———. *Nityasumangali: Devadasi Tradition in South India*. New Delhi: Motilal Banarsidas Publishers Private Limited, 1987. Print.

Kalki [R. Krishnamoorthy]. *Isai Thattu*. Kalki (1 September 1945): 47. Print.

Keeney, B. P. *Aesthetics of Change*. New York: Guilford Press, 1983. Print.

Kenwood, A.G. and A.L. Lougheed. *The Growth of the International Economy 1820–1960*. London: Allen & Unwin, 1971. Print.

Keskar, B.V. *Indian Music: Problems and Prospects*. Bombay: Popular Prakashan, 1967. Print.

Kidwai, Saleem. *Song Sung True: A Memoir*. New Delhi: Zubaan, 2002. Print.

Kinnear, Michael S. *The Gramophone Company's First Indian Recordings, 1899–1908*. Bombay: Popular Prakashan, 1994. Print.

———. "Reading Indian Record Labels: Part 1." *The Record News: Journal of the Society of Indian Record Collectors*. 1 (January 1991): 7–10. Print.

———. "Reading Indian Record Labels: Part 2." *The Record News: The Journal of the Society of Indian Record Collectors*. 2 (April 1991): 9–12. Print.

———. "Reading Indian Record Labels: Part 3." *The Record News: The Journal of the Society of Indian Record Collectors*. 3 (July 1991): 11–19. Print.

Kirsch, Gesa E. and Liz Rohan, eds. *Beyond the Archives: Research as a Lived Process*. Carbondale: Southern Illinois UP, 2008. Print.

Kittler, Freidrich. *Gramophone, Film, Typewriter*. Trans. Geoffrey Winthrop-Young and Michael Wutz. Stanford: Stanford University Press, 1999. Print.

Klein, Herman. *Herman Klein and the Gramophone*. Ed. William R. Moran. Portland, OR: Amadeus 1990. Print.

Knight, Douglas M. *Balasaraswati: Her Art and Life*. Middletown, CT: Wesleyan University Press, 2010. Print.

Krishnan, Hari. "Inscribing Practice: Reconfigurations and Textualizations of Devadasi Repertoire in Nineteenth and Early Twentieth Century South India." *Performing Pasts: Reinventing the Arts in Modern South India*. Eds. Indira Vishwanathan Peterson and Davesh Soneji. New Delhi: Oxford University Press, 2008: 71–89. Print.

Krishnaswamy, Arvindh. "Application of Pitch Tracking to South Indian Classical Music." *IEEE ICASSP (*2003): n.p. Web. 14 March 2015.

———. "Pitch Measurements versus Perception of South Indian Classical Music." *Proceedings of the Stockholm Music Acoustics Conference* (2003): n.p. Web. 26 March 2015.

Kruse, Holly. "Early Audio Technology a Domestic Space." *Stanford Humanities Review* 3 (1993): 1–14. Print.

Kvale, S. *InterViews: An introduction to qualitative research interviewing*. Thousand Oaks, CA: Sage Publications, 1996. Print.

———. "Dominance through Interviews and Dialogue." *Qualitative Inquiry* 12.3 (2006): 480–500.

Kvale, S. and Brinkman, S. *InterViews. Learning the Craft of Qualitative Research Interviewing*. Thousand Oaks, CA: Sage Publications, 2009. Print.

Kwan, K. M. K. and Tsang, E. W. "Realism and Constructivism in Strategy Research: A Critical Realist Response to Mir and Watson." *Strategic Management Journal* 22.12 (2001): 1163–1168. Print.

L'Epplatenier, Barbara. "Opinion: An Argument for Archival Research Methods: Thinking Beyond Methodology." *College English* 72.1 (2009): 67–79. Print.

Ledrahl, Fred and Raj Jackendoff. *A Generative Theory of Tonal Music*. Cambridge: MIT Press, 1983. Print.

Lee, Leo Ou-Fan. *Shanghai Modern: The Flowering of a New Urban Culture in China, 1930–1945*. Cambridge, MA: Harvard University Press, 1999.

Leech-Wilkinson, Daniel. "Expressive Gesture in Schubert Singing on Record." *Nordisk Estetisk Tidskrift [Nordic Journal of Aesthetics]*. 33 (2006): 50–70. Print.

———. "Recordings and Histories of Performance Style."Ed. Nicholas Cook et al. *Cambridge Companion to Recorded Music*. Cambridge: Cambridge University Press. 2009. Print.

Legge, Walter. "The Maharaja of Mysore." *Walter Legge: Words and Music*. Ed. Alan Sanders. London: Duckworth, 1998. 186–92. Print.

Lelyveld, David. "Transmitters and Culture: The Colonial Roots of Indian Broadcasting." *South Asia Research* 10.1 (1990): 41–52. Print.

———. "Upon the Subdominant: Administering Music on All-India Radio." *Social Text* 39 (1994): 111–127. Web 11 August 2017.

Leppert, Richard. *The Sight of Sound: Music, Representation and the History of the Body*. Berkeley, CA: University of California Press, 1993. Print.

Lerdahl, Fred. "Cognitive Constraints on Compositional Systems." Ed. John Sloboda. *Generative Processes in Music: The Psychology of Performance, Improvisation and Composition.* Oxford: Oxford University Press, 1988. 231–59. Print.

Lester, Joel. "Performance and Analysis: Interaction and Interpretation." *The Practice of Performance: Studies in Musical Interpretation.* Ed. J. Rink. Cambridge: Cambridge University Press, 1995. 197–216. Print.

Letts, R. "The Protection and Promotion of Musical Diversity". UNESCO(2006). Web. 10 March 2017.

Levin, Thomas. "For the Record: Adorno on Music in the Age of its Reproducibility." *October* 55 (1990): 23–47. Print.

Leucci, Tiziana. *Devadasi e Bayaderes: tra stroia e leggenda*, Bologna: Cooperativa Libraria Universitaria Editrice Bologna, 2005. Print.

Levy, Mark. *Intonation in North Indian Music: A Select Comparison of Theories with Contemporary Practice.* New Delhi: Biblia Impex Private Limited, 1982. Print.

Lichtman, M. *Qualitative Research in Education: A Users Guide.* London: Sage, 2006. Print.

Lincoln, Y. S. and Guba, E. G. "Paradigmatic controversies, contradictions, and emerging confluences." *Handbook of Qualitative Research* (2nd ed.) Eds. N.K. Denzin and Y. S. Lincoln. Thousand Oaks, CA: Sage, 2005. 191–215. Print.

Locher, B. and Prügl, E. "Feminism and constructivism: Worlds Apart or Sharing the Middle Ground?" *International Studies Quarterly* 45.1 (2001). Print.

Loomis, O.H. *Cultural Conservation: The Protection of Heritage in the United States.* Washington, DC: Library of Congress, 1983. Print.

Lvale, Steinar. *Interviews: An Introduction to Qualitative Research Interviewing.* New Delhi: Sage Publications Pvt Ltd, 1996. Print.

Madurai Mudaliar, K. *Gramophone Sangeetha Keerthanamirdam.* Madras: Shanmukhananda Book Depot, 1930. Print.

Madurai Mudaliar, K. *Gramophone Sangeetha Keerthanaamirtham.* Madras: Shanmukhananda Book Depot, 1929–1931. Print.

Malone, Dennis L. "The In-Between People: Language and Culture Maintenance and Mother-Tongue Education." *Highlands of Papua New Guinea.* Dallas, Texas: SIL International, 2004. Print.

Manuel, Peter. *Thumri in Historical and Stylistic Perspectives.* New Delhi: Motilal Banarsidas Publishers Private Limited, 1989. Print.

———. "Popular Music in India: 1901–86". *Popular Music* 7.2 (1993): 157–76.

———. *Cassette Culture: Popular Music and Technology in North India.* Chicago: University of Chicago Press, 1993.

Maciszewski, Amelia. "North Indian Women Musicians and their Words". *Music and Modernity— North Indian Classical Music in an Age of Mechanical Reproduction.* Kolkata: Thema, 2007. Print.

Magriel, Nicolas and Lalita du Perron. *The Songs of Khayal.* New Delhi: Manohar Publishers, 2013. Print.

Marglin, Frederique Apffel. *Wives of the God-King: the Rituals of the Devadasis of Puri.* 1985. Reprint, New Delhi: Oxford University Press, 1989. Print.

———. "Female Sexuality in the Hindu World."*Immaculate and Powerful: The Female in Sacred Image and Social Reality*, Eds. Clarissa W. Atkinson et al. Boston: Beacon Press, 1985a. 39–59. Print.

———. "Types of Oppositions in Hindu Culture." *Purity and Auspiciousness in Indian Society,* Eds. John B. Carman and Frederique Apffel Marglin. Leiden: Brill, 1985b. 65–83. Print.

"Marris College of Music, Lucknow." *Sangeeta: A Quarterly Journal of Hindustani Music* 1.1 (1930): 47–53. Print.

Mark, Katz. *Capturing Sound: How Technology has Changed Music.* Berkeley, CA, University of California Press, 2004. Print.

Mayer, Geeta. "Homage to Bhatkhande." *NCPA Periodical* 9.3. (1980): 31–40. Print.

McCormick, L. "Music as Social Performance." *Myth, Meaning, and Performance: Toward a New Cultural Sociology of the Arts.* Eds. R. Eyerman and L. McCormick. Boulder: Paradigm Publishers, 2006. 121–144. Print.

Meduri, Avanthi. "Western Feminist Theory, Asian Indian Performance, and a Notion of Agency." *Women and Performance* 5.2 (1992): 90–103. Print.

Meer, W. van der. "Theory and Practice of Intonation in Hindusthani Music." *The Ratio Book.* Ed. C. Barlow. Köln: Feedback Papers, 2000: 50–71. Web 14 August 2017.

Melba, Nellie. *Melodies and Memories 1926;* repr. New York: AMS Press 1971: 252–253. Print.

Menon, Indira. *The Madras Quartet: Women in Karnatak Music.* New Delhi: Lotus Collection, Roli Books, 1999. Print.

Menon, Narayana. "The Impact of Western Technology on Indian Music". *Bulletin of the Institute of Traditional Cultures, Madras* (1957): 70–80. Print.

Menuhin, Yehudi. *Unfinished Journey: Twenty Years Later.* London: Fromm International 1997.

Mehta, R.C. *Eminent Musicians of Yesteryears: Short bios of 766 Hindustani Musicians.* Baroda: SRM and SHIKM Trust, 2007. Print.

Merriam, Alan P. "Ethnomusicology—Discussion and Definition of the Field." *Ethnomusicology* 4.3 (1960). Print.

Meyers, Diana T. *Self, Society, and Personal Choice.* New York: Columbia University Press, 1989. Print.

———. *Subjection and Subjectivity.* New York: Routledge, 1994. Print.

Meyers, Diana Tietjens. Ed. *Feminist Social Thought: A Reader.* New York: Routledge, 1997. Print.

Millard, Andre. *America on Record.* Cambridge: Cambridge University Press, 1995. Print.

Miller, Thomas P. "Teaching Histories of Rhetoric as a Social Praxis." *Rhetoric Review* 12.1 (1993): 70–82. Print.

Mir, R. and Watson, A. "Strategic Management and the Philosophy of Science: The case for a Constructivist Methodology." *Strategic Management Journal* 21.9 (2000): 941–953. Print.

Misra, Susheela. *Some Immortals of Hindustani Music.* New Delhi: Harman Publishing House, 1990. Print.

———. *Musical Heritage of Lucknow.* New Delhi: Harman Publishing House, 1991. Print.

Modak, H. "Propriety of Dividing an Octave into Twenty-Two Shrutis." *Journal of the Music Academy of Madras* 38 (1967): 151–59. Web 20 August 2017.

Moore, Jerrold Northrop. *A Voice in Time: The Gramophone of Fred Gaisberg: 1873–1951.* London: Hamilton, 1976. Print.

Morrow, S. "Quality and Trustworthiness in Qualitative Research in Counselling Psychology." *Journal of Counselling Psychology* 52.2 (2005): 25–260.

Morton, Dave. "Recording History: The History of Recording Technology". *History of Sound Recording Technology*. (2014): n.p. Web. 29 November 2015.

Moustakas, C. *Phenomenological Research Methods*. Thousand Oaks, CA: Sage, 1994. Print.

Muddupalani. *The Appeasement of Radhika: Radhika Santawanam*. Trans.by Sandhya Mulchandani. New Delhi: Penguin, 2011. Print.

Mukherji, Kumar Prasad. *The Lost World of Hindustani Music*. New Delhi: Penguin Books, 2006. Print.

Mutatkar, Sumati. "Alladiya Khan Gharana and Kesarbai Kerkar." *NCPA Periodical* 1.1 (1972): 2–7. Print.

Nag, Dipali. *Ustad Faiyaz Khan*. New Delhi: Sangeet Natak Akademi, 1985. Print.

Nagar, Amritlal. *Yeh Kothewaaliyaan*. Allahabad: Lokbharati Prakashan, 2001. Print.

Nagarathnamma, Bangalore. *Radhika Santwanamu*. Madras: Vavilla Ramaswami Sastrulu and Sons, 1910.

Naidu, Tirumalayya. 1912. "Music and the Anti-Nautch Movement." Repr. *Sruti*, E. Krishna Iyer Centenary Issue (1997): 6. Print.

Naidu, Venkataratnam R. 1901. "Social Purity and the Anti-Nautch Movement." *Indian Social Reform*. Ed. C. Yajneswara Chintamani. Madras: Thompson & Co.: 249–281.

Nair, Janaki. "The Devadasi, Dharma, and the State." *Economic and Political Weekly*, (10 December 1994): 3157–67. *JSTOR* Web January 11 2016.

———. *Women and Law in Colonial India: A Social History*. New Delhi: Kali for Women, 1996. Print.

Narasimhan, Sakuntala. *The Splendour of Rampur-Sahaswan Gharana*. Bangalore: Veenapani Centre for Arts, 2006. Print.

Narayanaswami, Dr. P.P. and Vidya Jayaraman. *Sangita Sampradaya Pradarshini of Subbarama Dikshitar*. English Edition. 2008: n.p. Web. 14 February 2015.

Narmour, Eugene. "On the Relationship of Analytical Theory to Performance and Interpretation." *Explorations in Music, the Arts, and Ideas: Essays in Honour of Leonard B. Meyer*. Eds. Narmour and Ruth Solie. Stuyvesant, NY, 1988. Print.

Nayar, Sobhana. *Bhatkhande's Contribution to Music*. Bombay: Popular Prakashan, 1989. Print.

Nettl, Bruno. *The Study of Ethnomusicology: Thirty-one Issues and Concepts*. Urbana, IL: University of Illinois Press, 2005. Print.

Neuman, Daniel M. *The Life of Music in North India: the Organization of an Artistic Tradition*. Chicago: University of Chicago Press, 1980. Print.

———. "Indian Music and the English Language Fifty Years Later". *International Seminar on 'Creating & Teaching Music Patterns'*. Kolkata: Department of Instrumental Music, Rabindra Bharati University, 2013. 15–34. Print.

Nevile, Pran. *Nautch Girls of the Raj*. New Delhi: Penguin Books, 2009. Print.

New York Times. "The Phonograph." 7 November 1877. Print.

Noble, Theobald, T.J. *The Talking Machine News and Side Lines*. 8.10. London, British Library (October 1912): 331–334.

———. *Talking Machine World*. London, British Library (15 May 1913): 48–49.

Nooshin, L. *The Ethnomusicology of Western Art Music*. London: Routledge, 2014. Print.

O'Connell, Roxanne M. "Critical Essay—Your Granny's Gramophone: The Cultural Impact of 78 rpm Recordings on Ireland and Irish America". *Technoculture* 3 (2013): n.p. Web. 1 Jan. 2016

Oldenburg, Veena Talwar. *The Making of Colonial Lucknow: 1856–1877.* New Delhi: Oxford University Press, 1990a. Print.

———. "Lifestyle as Resistance: The Case of the Courtesans of Lucknow, India." *Feminist Studies* 16.2 (1990b): 259–288. Print.

Opinions on the Nautch Question: Collected and Published by the Punjab Purity Association. Lahore: New Lyall Press, 1894. Print.

Owen, I. R. "Applying Social Constructionism to Psychotherapy." *Counselling Psychology Quarterly* 5.4 (1992): 385–402. Print.

Pandither, A. *Karunamirtha Sagaram on Shrutis,* 1917. New Delhi: Asian Educational Services, 1984. Print.

Parker, Kunal M. "A Corporation of Superior Prostitutes: Anglo-Indian Legal Conceptions of Temple Dancing Girls, 1800–1914." *Modern Asian Studies* 32. 3 (1998): 559–633. Print.

Parthasarathi, Vibodh. *Media and Mediation Volume 1.* New Delhi: Sage Publications, 2006. Print.

Pasler, Jann *Western Music and its Others: Difference, Representation, and Appropriation in Music.* Berkeley, CA: University of California Press, 2000. 103. Print.

———. *Writing through Music: Essays on Music, Culture, and Politics.* Cary, NC: Oxford University Press, 2007. Print.

Pedelty, M. *Ecomusicology.* Philadelphia, PA: Temple University Press, 2012. Print.

Perkins, John F., Alan Kelly and John Ward. "On Gramophone Company Matrix Numbers, 1898–1921." *Record Collector* 23 (3–4) (1976): 51–90. Print.

Petersen, Richard. *Creating Country Music: Fabricating Authenticity.* Chicago: University of Chicago Press, 1997. Print.

Peterson, Indira Vishwanathan and Davesh Soneji. *In Performing Pasts: Reinventing the Arts in Modern South India.* New Delhi: Oxford University Press, 2008. Print.

Philip, Robert. *Early Recordings and Musical Style: Changing Tastes in Instrumental Performance, 1900–1950.* Cambridge: Cambridge University Press, 1992. Print.

Pickett, S.T.A. and Cadenasso, M.L. "The Ecosystem as a Multidimensional Concept: Meaning, Model, and Metaphor". *Ecosystems.* 5 (2002): 1–10. Web. 12 March 2017.

Piper, Adrian M.S. "Higher-Order Discrimination." *Identity, Character and Morality.* Eds. Owen Flanagan and Amelie Okensberg Rorty. Cambridge: MIT Press, 1990. Print.

Polkinghorne, D. *Narrative Knowing and the Human Sciences.* Albany, NY: State University of New York Press, 1988. Print.

Post, Jennifer. "Professional Women in Indian Music: The Death of the Courtesan Tradition." *Women and Music in Cross-Cultural Perspective.* Ed. Ellen Koskoff. New York: Greenwood Press, 1989. 97–109. Print.

Powers, Harold S. "Theory and Practice in the Study of Indian Music." *Ethnomusicology* (1962). Web. 17 June 2016.

Prabhakar, Sukanya. *Karnataka Sangeethakke Sri Jayachamaraja Wodeyar avara Koduge.* Mysore: D.V.K. Murthy, 2005.

Pranesh, Meera Rajaram. *Musical Compositions during the Wodeyar Dynasty.* Bangalore: Vee Emm Publications, 2003. Print.

Prasad, A.K. *Devadasi System in Ancient India: A Study of Temple Dancing Girls of South India.* New Delhi: H.K. Publishers and Distributors, 1990. Print.

Price, Pamela. *Kingship and Political Practice in Colonial India.* Cambridge: Cambridge University Press, 1996. Print.

QCRC (Queensland Conservatorium Research Centre). "Sustainable Futures: Towards an Ecology of Musical Diversity." 2013. Web. 20 March 2017.

Qureshi, Regula. "How does Music mean? Embodied Memories and the Politics of Affect in the Indian Sarangi." *American Ethnologist* 27.4 (2000): 805–38. Print.

———. In Search of Begum Akhtar: Patriarchy, Poetry and Twentieth Century Indian Music. *World of Music* 43.1 (2001): 97–137. *JSTOR* Web. 13 February 2016.

Qureshi, Regula Burckhardt. "Female Agency and Patrilineal Constraints: Situating Courtesans in the Twentieth Century India." *The Courtesan's Arts: Cross-Cultural Perspectives.* Eds. Martha Feldman and Bonnie Gordon. 312–31. New York: Oxford University Press, 2006.

Racy, Ali Jihad. "Recording Industry and Egyptian Traditional Music: 1904–1932." *Ethnomusicology* 20.1(1976): 23–48. *JSTOR* Web. 29 May 2015.

Raghavan, V. *Collected Writings on Indian Music*, 3 Vols. Chennai: Dr Raghavan Centre for Performing Arts in association with Sangeet Natak Akademi, 2007. Print.

———. *The Sarvadevavilasa.* Adyar Library Bulletin, Madras. 22 (1–2) (1958): 45–118. Print.

Rahaim, Matthew. *Musicking Bodies: Gesture and Voice in Hindustani Music.* Middletown, CT: Wesleyan University Press, 2012. Print.

Raj, Sundara. *Prostitution in Madras: A Study in Historical Perspective.* New Delhi: Konark Publications, 1993. Print.

Raja, Deepak. *Hindustani Music: A Tradition in Transition, New Vistas in Indian Performing Arts.* New Delhi: D.K. Printworld, 2005. Print.

———. *Khayal Vocalism: Continuity with Change, New Vistas in Indian Performing Arts.* New Delhi: D.K. Printworld, 2009. Print.

Ramachendrier, C. 1892. *Collection of the Decisions of the High Courts and the Privy Council on the Law of Succession, Maintenance, & ac. Applicable to Dancing Girls and Their Issues, Prostitutes Not Belonging to Dancing Girls' Community, Illegitimate Sons and Bastards, and Illatom Affiliation Up to December 1891.* Madras: V. Kalyanaram Iyer. Print.

Ramakrishna, V. *Social Reform in Andhra (1848–1919).* New Delhi: Vikas Publishing House, 1983. Print.

Ramanujachari, C. *The Spiritual Heritage of Thyagaraja.* Madras: Ramakrishna Mission, 1957. Print.

Ramanujan, A.K., Velcheru Narayana Rao and David Shulman. *When God Is a Customer: Telugu Courtesan Songs by Kshetrayya and Others.* Berkeley, CA: University of California Press, 1994. Print.

Ramnarine, T.K. *Ilmater's Inspiration: Nationalism, Globalization and the Changing Soundscapes of Finnish Folk Music.* Chicago, IL: University of Chicago Press, 2003. Print.

Ramesh, Asha. *Impact of Legislative Prohibition of the Devadasi Practice in Karnataka: A Study.* New Delhi: Joint Women's Programme, 1992. Print.

Ramsey, Alexis et al. Eds. *Working in the Archives: Practical Research Methods for Rhetoric and Composition.* Carbondale: Southern Illinois UP, 2010.

Ranade, Ashok. D. *Some Hindustani Musicians, they lit the way.* New Delhi: Promilla & Co, 2011. Print.

Rani, Sandhya. *Uttar Pradesh ke Rohilkand Kshetra ki Sangeeth Parampara: Ek Vivechanaatmak Adhyayan.* Rampur Raza Library, 2005. Print.

Rao, Suvarnalata. "Aesthetics of Hindustani Music: An Acoustical Study." *Acts of Colloque International Musique et Assistance Informatique*, Marseille (1990): 81–108. Web 14 August 2017.

———. *Acoustical Perspective on Raga-Rasa Theory*. New Delhi: Munshiram Manoharlal Publishers Pvt Ltd., 2000. Print.

Rao, Suvarnalata and van der Meer, W. *"Music in Motion: The Automated Transcription for Indian Music"*, 2013. Web 15 August 2017.

Read, Oliver and Walter Welch. *From Tin Foil to Stereo*. Indianapolis: Howard Sams, 1976. Print.

Rao, T.K. Govinda. *Compositions of Mudduswami Dikshitar*. Chennai: Ganamandir Publications, 1997. Print.

Rao, Vidya. "Thumri as Feminine Voice." *Economic and Political Weekly*. (April 28 1990): 31–39. Web. *JSTOR* 20 August 2015.

———. "Thumri and Thumri Singers: Changes in Style and Life-style." *Cultural Reorientation in India*. Eds. Indu Banga and Jaidev. IIAS: Shimla, 1996.

Ray, Bharati. *Women of India: Colonial and Post-Colonial Periods and Colonial Politics*. Kolkata: SAGE Publications, 2005. Print.

Read, Oliver and Walter L. Welch. *From Tin Foil to Stereo* (2nd ed.). Indianapolis: Sams.,1976.

Reddy, S. Muthulakshmi. *Why Should the Devadasi Institution in the Hindu Temple Be Abolished?* Chintadripet: Central Co-operative Printing Works Ltd., 1927. Print.

———. *The Awakening: Demand for Devadasi Legislation*. Madras: Madras Printing Co., 1928. Print.

Report. 1916. *First All-India Music Conference*. Baroda: Baroda Printing Works. Print.

Report. 2 vols. 1918.*Second All-India Music Conference*. Delhi. Print.

Report. 2 vols. 1919.*Third All-India Music Conference*. Banaras. Print.

Report. 1925.*Fourth All-India Music Conference*. Lucknow: Taluqdar Press. Print.

Report. 1926.*Fifth All-India Music Conference*. Lucknow: Taluqdar Press. Print.

Richardson, L. "Writing: A Method of Inquiry." *Handbook of Qualitative Research* (2nd ed.). Eds. N. Denzin and Y. Lincoln. Thousand Oaks, CA: Sage, 2000. Print.

Rothenbuhler, Eric W. and John Durham Peters. "Defining Phonography: An Experiment in Theory." *Musical Quarterly* 81 (1997): 242–64. Print.

Ryan, C. "An Alternative Scientist." *The Uncertainty Principle*. Ed. R. Williams. Crows Nest: ABC Enterprises, 1991. Print.

Rice, Timothy. *Ethnomusicology: A Very Short Introduction*. New York: Oxford University Press. 2014. Print.

Richardson, V. "Constructivist Pedagogy." *Teachers College Record*. 105. 9. (2003): 1623–1640. Print.

Ritter, Kelly. "Archival Research in Composition Studies: Re-Imagining the Historian's Role." *Rhetoric Review*. 31.4 (2012): 461–78. Print.

Ross, Alex. "The Record Effect: How Technology has Transformed the Sound of Music." *New Yorker* 6 June 2005: n. p. Web. 1 Jan. 2016.

Russell, R.V. *The Tribes and Castes of the Central Provinces of India*. London: Macmillan and Co., Limited, 1916. Print.

Ruswa, Mirza Muhammad Hadi. *Umrao Jaan Ada*. The Courtesan of Lucknow: Umrao Jan Ada. Trans. Khushwant Singh and M.A. Husaini. New Delhi: Orient Paperback, 1970. Print.

Sambamoorthy, P. "Madras as a Seat of Musical Learning." *The Madras Tercentenary Volume*. London: Humphrey Milford and Oxford University Press, 1939. Print.

———. *History of South Indian Music*, 6 vols. Madras: Indian Music Publishing House, 1952. Print.

———.*Dictionary of South Indian Music and Musicians*, 3 vols. Madras: Indian Music Publishing House, 1955. Print.

———.*Great Musicians*. Madras: Indian Music Publishing House, 1959. Print.

———.*The Teaching of Music*. Madras: Indian Music Publishing House, 1966. Print.

Sampath, Vikram. *Splendours of Royal Mysore: The Untold Story Of The Wodeyars*. New Delhi: Rupa & Co. 2008. Print.

———. *My Name Is Gauhar Jaan: the Life and Times of a Musician*. New Delhi: Rupa & Co, 2010. Print.

———.*Voice of the Veena: S. Balachander, a biography*. New Delhi: Rupa & Co, 2012. Print.

———. "The Voice of Salem Godavari." *The Hindu* 14 August 2014. Web. 19 October 2016.

Sankaran, T. *Isai Medaikal*. Chennai: Tamizh Isai Sangham, 1962.

———. "Dharmapuri Subbarayar." *Glimpses of Indian Music*, Eds. Gowry Kuppuswamy and M. Hariharan, 23–25. New Delhi: Sundeep Prakashan, 1982: 23–25. Print.

———. *Bangalore Nagaratnammal: A Devadasi True*. Chennai: *Sruti* 4 (January/February 1984). Print.

———. *Kanchipuram Dhanakoti Ammal*. Chennai: *Sruti* 11 (September 1984): 31–32. Print.

———."Women Singers": *Kalakshetra Quarterly* 8.1–2 (1986): 58–65. Print.

Saunders, M., Lewis, P. and Thornhill, A. *Research Methods for Business Students*. 4th ed. Harlow: Prentice Hall Financial Times, 2007. Print.

Saurman, Todd. "Singing for Survival in the Highlands of Cambodia: Tampuan Revitalization of Music as Cultural Reflexivity." *Music and Minorities in Ethnomusicology: Challenges and Discourses from Three Continents*. Ed. Ursula Hemetek, 2012. Web. 16 March 2017. Print.

Schippers, H. *Facing the music: Global Perspectives on Learning and Teaching Music*. New York, NY: Oxford University Press, 2010. Print.

———. Applied Ethnomusicology and Intangible Cultural Heritage: Understanding "Ecosystems" of Music as a Tool for Sustainability. Eds. S. Pettan and J.T. Titon. *Oxford Handbook of Applied Ethnomusicology*. New York, NY: Oxford University Press, 2015. Print.

Schippers, Huib and Catherine Grant. Eds. *Sustainable Futures for Music Cultures: An Ecological Perspective*. Oxford University Press, 2016. Print.

Schmalfeldt, J. "On the Relation of Analysis to Performance: Beethoven's Bagatelles Op. 126, Nos. 2 and 5." *Journal of Music Theory* 29.1 (1985): 1–31. Print.

Schofield, Katherine Butler. "The Courtesan Tale: Female Musicians and Dancers in Mughal Historical Chronicles, c. 1556–1748." *Gender and History* 24.1 (2012): 150–171. Web 12 August 2017.

Schulz-Kohn, Dietrich. *Die Schallplatte auf dem Weltmarkt*. Berlin: Reher, 1940. Print

Schwandt, T. A. "Three Epistemological Stances for Qualitative Inquiry: Interpretivism, Hermeneutics, and Social Constructionism". *Handbook of*

Qualitative Research (2nd ed.). Eds. N. Denzin, and Y. Lincoln. 189–214. Thousand Oaks, CA: Sage Publications, 2000. Print.

Seeger, Anthony. 2009. "Lessons Learned from the ICTM (NGO) Evaluation of Nominations for the UNESCO Masterpieces of the Oral and Intangible Heritage of Humanity, 2001– 5." *Intangible Heritage.* Eds. Laurajane Smith and Natsuko Akagawa. 112–18. London: Routledge, 2009. Print.

Seetha, S. *Tanjore as a Seat of Music, during the 17th, 18th and 19th Centuries.* Madras: University of Madras, 1981. Print.

Seidman, I. *Interviewing as Qualitative Research: A Guide for Researchers in Education and the Social Sciences* (2nd ed.) New York, NY: Teachers College Press, 2006. Print.

Seroussi, Edwin. "The Growth of the Judeo-Spanish Folksong Repertory in the 20th Century." *Proceedings of the Tenth World Congress of Jewish Studies, Division D. 2.* Jerusalem: World Union of Jewish Studies (1990): 173–80. Print.

Shaffer, Henry and Neil Todd. "The Interpretive Component in Musical Performance." *Musical Perceptions.* Ed. Rita Aiello. New York, 1984. Print.

Shah, Hasan. *The Nautch Girl.* Trans. by Qurratulain Hyder. New Delhi: Sterling Publications, 1992. Print.

Shankar, Jogan. *Devadasi Cult: A Sociological Analysis.* New Delhi: Ashish Publishing House, 1994. Print.

Sharar, Abdul Halim. *Lucknow: The Last Phase of an Oriental Culture.* New Delhi: Oxford University Press, 2000. Print.

Sharngadeva. *Sangit Ratnakara.* Trans. R. Shringy and P. Sharma, 2 Vols. New Delhi: Munshiram Manoharlal, 1996. Print.

Sharma, A.N. *Bajanaama: A study of early Indian Gramophone Records.* Lucknow: Kathachitra Prakashan, 2012. Print.

Sheehy, D. "A Few Notions about Philosophy and Strategy in Applied Ethnomusicology." *Ethnomusicology* 36.3(1992): 3–7. Web. 15 March 2017.

———. *Mariachi Music in America: Experiencing Music, Expressing Culture,* New York, NY: Oxford University Press, 2006. Print.

Shklar, J. "Squaring the Hermeneutic Circle." *Social Research* 71.3 (1986): 655–678. Print.

Shukla, Shatrughna. *Thumri Ki Utpatti, Vikas aur Shailiyaan.* New Delhi: Delhi University, 1983. Print.

Silverman, D. *Interpreting Qualitative Data.* Thousand Oaks, CA: Sage, 1993. Print.

Singh, Jaideva. "The Evolution of Khyal" *Commemorative Volume in honour of Dr. S.N. Ratanjankar.* Bombay: K.C. Ginde, 1961. Print.

———. "The Evolution of the Thumri." *National Centre for the Performing Arts* 5.2 (1976): 10–15. Print.

Sinha, Mrinhalini. "Gender in the Critiques of Colonialism and Nationalism: Locating the "Indian Woman." *Feminism and History.* Ed. Joan Scott. New York: Oxford University Press, 1996. 477–504. Print.

Slobin, M. Ed. *Returning Culture: Musical Changes in Central and Eastern Europe.* Durham, NC: Duke University Press, 1996. Print.

Small, C. *Musicking: The Meanings of Performing and Listening.* Hanover: Wesleyan University Press, 1998. Print.

Soobrayan, V. "Ethics, Truth and Politics in Constructivist Qualitative Research." *Westminster Studies in Education* 26.2 (2003): 107–123. Print.

Soneji, Davesh. *Unfinished Gestures: Devadasis, Memory and Modernity in South India*. Ranikhet: Permanent Black, 2012. Print.

Spivak, Gayatri. "Can the Subaltern Speak?" *Marxism and the Interpretation of Culture*. Eds. Cary Nelson and Lawrence Grossberg, 271–313. Urbana: University of Illinois Press, 1998: 271–313. Print.

Srinivasan, Amrit. "Reform and Revival: The Devadasi and her Dance." *Economic and Political Weekly* (1985): 1869–1876. Web. *JSTOR* 18 July 2015.

Sriram, V. *The Devadasi and the Saint: the Life and Times of Bangalore Nagarathnamma*. Chennai: East-West Books [Madras] Pvt. Ltd, 2007. Print.

Stake, R. E. *The art of case study research*. Thousand Oaks, CA: Sage Publications, 1995. Print.

Stock, Jonathan P.J. "Documenting the Musical Event: Observation, Participation, Representation." *Empirical Musicology: Aims, Methods, Prospects*. Eds. Eric Clarke and Nicholas Cook. Oxford: OUP, 2004. Print.

Steiner, John V. *Notebooks of the Mind: Explorations of Thinking* (Revised ed.). New York, NY: Oxford University Press, 1997. Print.

Subramanian, Lakshmi. *From the Tanjore Court to the Madras Music Academy: A Social History of Music in South India*. New Delhi: Oxford University Press, 2006. Print.

Subramanian, M. *Carnatic Ragam Thodi: Pitch Analysis of Notes and Gamakams*. 2000. Raga Gaayaka Shishya: Software for Carnatic Music. December 2013: n.p. Web. 17 October 2015.

Sud, Anil. "Gramco: A Voice in Time". *IFPI News* 9 (1980): 10. Print.

Suisman. David. "Sound, Knowledge, and the 'Immanence of Human Failure': Rethinking Musical Mechanization through the Phonograph, the Player-Piano, and the Piano." *Social Text*. Duke University Press, 102.28 (2010). Print.

Sullivan, Shannon. *Living Across and Through Skins: Transactional Bodies, Pragmatism, and Feminism*. Bloomington: Indian University Press, 2001. Print.

Sundaram, Tanjavur B.M. *Marabu Thantha MaanikkangaL*. Chennai: Dr. V. Raghavan Centre for Performing Arts (Regd.), 2003. Print.

Tan, S. B. "Activism in Southeast Asian Ethnomusicology: Empowering Youths to Revitalize Traditions and Bridge Cultural Barriers." *Musicological Annual* 44.1(2008): 69–83. Print.

Taruskin, Richard. *Text and Act: Essays on Music and Performance*. New York/ Oxford: Oxford University Press, 1995. Print.

Taylor, Timothy D. *Strange Sounds: Music, Technology, and Culture*. New York/ London: Routledge, 2001. Print.

Tembe, Govinda Sadashiva. *Maazha Sangeeth Vyaasanga*. Pune: Mauj Prakashan. 1988. Print.

Temperley, D. "Empirical Musicology: Aims, Methods, Prospects: Empirical Musicology: Aims, Methods, Prospects." *Music Perception* 23 (2005): 191–96. Print.

Temperley, D. and Sleator, D. "Modeling Meter and Harmony: A Preference Approach". *Computer Music Journal*. 23 (1999): 10–27. Print.

Tenney, J. "Temporal Gestalt Perception in Music." *Journal of Music Theory* 24 (1980): 205–241. Print.

Tharu, Susie and K. Lalita. "Empire, Nation and the Literary Text." *Interrogating Modernity: Culture and Colonialism in India*. Eds. Tejaswini Niranjana, P. Sudhir, and Vivek Dhareshwar. Calcutta: Seagull, 1993. 199–219. Print.

The Record News. 1(January 1991); 2 (April 1991); 3 (July 1991); 4 (October 1991); 5 (January 1992); 6 (April 1992); 7 (July 1992); 8 (October 1992); 9 (January 1993); 10 (April 1993); 11 (July 1993); 12 (October 1993); 13 (January 1994); 14 (April 1994); 15 (July 1994); 16 (October 1994); 17 (January 1995); 18 (April 1995); 19 (July 1995); 20 (October 1995); 21 (January 1996); 22 (April 1996); 23 (July 1996); 24 (October 1996); 25 (January 1997); 26 (April 1997); 27 (July 1997), 28 (October 1997) and 29 (January 1999). Bombay: Society of Indian Record Collectors.

The Talking Machine World (1905–1929). Internet Archive. Web. 12 April 2014.

Theberge, Paul. *Any Sound you can Imagine: Making Music, Consuming Technology.* Hanover, N.H.: University Press of New England, 1995. Print.

Thomas, Pradip Ninan and Elske van de Fliert. *Interrogating the Theory and Practice of Communication for Social Change: The Basis For a Renewal.* Hampshire: Palgrave Macmillan, 2014. Ebook UQ Library. Web. 08 May. 2016

Thurston, Edgar, and K. Rangachari. *Castes and Tribes of Southern India, 7 vols.* Madras: Government Press, 1909. Print.

Titon, Jeff Todd. "Introduction". *World of Music.* 51.1 (2009a): 7–13. Print.

———. "Music and Sustainability: An Ecological Viewpoint." *World of Music* 51.1 (2009b): 119–37. Print.

Tomlinson, G. "Musicology, Anthropology, History". Eds. M. Clayton, T. Herbert and R. Middleton. *The Cultural Study of Music: A Critical Introduction.* New York: Routledge, 2003: 31–44. Print.

Tracy, S. J. "Qualitative Quality: Eight 'Big-Tent' Criteria for Excellent Qualitative Research." *Qualitative Inquiry* 16 (2010): 837.

UNESCO. "Declaration on the Promotion of Cultural Diversity". 2001. Web. 25 March 2017.

———. "Convention for the Safeguarding of Intangible Cultural Heritage". 2003. Web. 25 March 2017.

———. "Convention on the Protection and Promotion of the Diversity of Cultural Expressions". 2005. Web. 25 March 2017.

United Nations High Commission for Human Rights. "Declaration on the Rights of Indigenous Peoples". 2007. Web. 25 March 2017.

Valian, Virginia. *Why So Slow? The Advancement of Women.* Cambridge: MIT Press, 1998. Print.

Vasudevacharya, Mysore. *Naa Kanda Kalaavidaru.* Trans. S. Krishnamurthy as *With Masters of Melody.* Bangalore: Ananya GML Cultural Academy, 1999. Print.

Vedavalli, M.B. *Mysore as a Seat of Music.* Trivandrum: CBH Publications, 1992. Print.

Velankar, Ramesh Makarand and Hari V. Sahasrabuddhe. "Exploring Data Analysis in Music Using Tool Praat." *First International Conference on Emerging Trends in Engineering and Technology. ICETET* (2008): 508–509. Web. *JSTOR* 1 February 2015.

Vijaisri, Priyadarshini. *Recasting the Devadasi: Patterns of Sacred Prostitution in Colonial South India.* New Delhi: Kanishka Publishers, 2004. Print.

Vishwanathan, Lakshmi. *Women of Pride: The Devadasi Heritage.* New Delhi: Roli Books, 2008. Print.

Vishwanathan, T. "The Analysis of Raga Alapana in South Indian Music," *Asian Music* 9.1 (1977). Print.

von Glasersfeld, E. 1984. "An Introduction to Radical Constructivism." *The Invented Reality: How Do We Know What We Believe We Know? (Contributions to Constructivism).* Ed. P. Watzlawick. New York: Norton, 1984. 17–40. Print.

von Foerster. 1984. "On Constructing a Reality." *The Invented Reality: How Do We Know That We Believe We Know? (Contributions to Constructivism).* Ed. P. Watzlawick. New York: Norton, 1984. 41–61. Print.

Wade, Bonnie. *Music in India: The Classical Traditions.* Cambridge: Cambridge University Press, 1979. Print.

———. *Khyal: Creativity within North India's Classical Music Tradition.* Cambridge: Cambridge University Press, 1984. Print.

Walkowitz, Judith. *Prostitution and Victorian Society: Women, Class and State.* Cambridge University Press, 1980. Print.

Watzlawick, P. Ed. *The Invented Reality: How Do We Know What We Believe We Know?* New York: W.W. Norton, 1984. Print.

Weidmann, Amanda J. *Singing the Classical, Voicing the Modern: the Post-Colonial Politics of Music in South India.* Kolkata: Seagull Books Pvt. Ltd., 2006. Print.

West, C. and D.H. Zimmerman. "Doing Gender." *Gender and Society* 1.2 (1987): 125–151. Print.

West, Richard L. and Lynn H. Turner. *Introducing Communication Theory: Analysis and Application.* 5th ed. Boston: McGraw-Hill, 2010. Print.

Wheeler, George. *The Visit of the Prince of Wales: A Chronicle of His Royal Higness' Journeyings in India, Ceylon, Spain and Portugal.* London: Chapman and Hall, 1876. Print.

———. *Early Records in India: a History of English Settlements in India.* London: Trübner, 1878. Print.

Willard, N. Augustus. *A Treatise on the Music of Hindoostan: Comprising a Detail of the Ancient Theory and Modern Practice.* Calcutta: Baptist Mission Press, 1834. Print.

Willis, K. (2006). "Analysing Qualitative Data." *Social Research Methods: An Australian Perspective.* Ed. M. Walter. South Melbourne: Oxford University Press, 2006: 257–279.

Willis, P. *Profane culture.* Oxford: Blackwells, 1978. Print.

Winograd, T. "Linguistics and the Computer Analysis of Tonal Harmony". *Journal of Music Theory.* 12 (1968): 2–49. Print.

Wolcott, H. "On Seeking – and Rejecting – Validity in Qualitative Research." *Qualitative Inquiry in Education: The Continuing Debate.* Eds. E. Eisner and A. Peshkin. New York, NY: Teachers College, 1990. 178–192. Print.

Young, Iris Marion. *Stretching Out.* Bloomington: Indiana University Press, 1990. Print.

Yow, V.R. *Recording Oral History.* Thousand Oaks, CA: Sage, 1994. Print.

Yin, R. *Case Study Methods Revised Draft.* Cosmos Corporation, 2004. Print.

Zagorski-Thomas, S. "The Musicology of Record Production, 20th Century" *Music* 4.2 (2008). Print.

———. "Real and Unreal Performances."*Rhythm In The Age of Digital Reproduction.* Ed. A. Danielsen. Ashgate Press, 2010. Print.

———. "Musical Meaning and the Musicology of Record Production". *Beitraege zur Popularmusikforschung* 38 (2012). Bielefeld. Print.

———."Sonic Cartoons."*Sound as Popular Culture.* Eds. M. Hanáček, H. Schulze, and J. Papenburg. MIT Press, 2016. Print.

Zagorski-Thomas, S. and Frith, S. Eds. *The Art of Record Production: an Introductory Reader for a New Academic Field.* Ashgate Press, 2012. Print.

———. *The Musicology of Record Production*. Cambridge: Cambridge University Press, 2014. Print.

Zhang, Yingjin. *Cinema and Urban Culture in Shanghai, 1922–1943*. Stanford, CA: Stanford University Press, 1999.

Unpublished Dissertations/Works

Foreman, Ronald. "Jazz and Race Records, 1920–1932." Ph.D. diss. University of Illinois 1968. Print.

Gopalrao Kelkar, Rajesh. *"Agra Gharane ka Bharatiya Sangeet Mein Srujanatmak Yogdaan: Agra Gharana's Creative Contribution to Indian Music"*. Diss. University of Maharaja Sayajirao Baroda, 2015. Print.

Jafa, Navina. *"Changing Economic and Patronage Patterns influencing Performing Arts. Case Study: Kathak Dance and related art forms in Delhi, Lucknow, Banares, Raigarh and Rampur (1800–1945.)"* Diss. University of Jamia Milia Islamia, 1998. Print.

Rapmund, V. J. "Enhancing Students' Personal Resources through Narrative." Diss. University of South Africa, Pretoria, 2000. Print.

Sachdeva, Shweta. *"In Search of the Tawaif in History: Courtesans, Nautch Girls and Celebrity Entertainers in India (1720s–1920s)."* Diss. University of London, 2008. Print.

Archival Sources

Andhra Pradesh State Gazetteers, *A Manual of the Kurnool District in the Presidency of Madras*, (Hyderabad: the State Editor, District Gazettteers, 1922), Originally published in 1886.

Brackenbury, C.F., *Madras District Gazetteers, Cuddapah*, Madras Government Press, 1915.

Census of India, 1881–1951, Reports relating to Madras Presidency; H.E.H Nizam's Dominions, Hyderabad; Bombay Presidency and Mysore State.

Grihalakshmi January 1910 edition page 19.

Files related to the visiting musicians to the Palace under H.H. the Maharaja of Mysore, Mysore Palace Archives.

Legislative Assembly Debates of Madras, 1924–1946.

Legislative Assembly Debates of Bombay, 1926–1947.

Muzrai Department, Karnataka State Archives, Bangalore

Proceedings of Governments of Madras, Bombay and Mysore, Andhra Pradesh State Archives, Hyderabad; Tamil Nadu State Archives, Chennai; Karnataka State Archives, Bangalore and National Archives of India, New Delhi (of Home Department, Home Political, Education Department, Public and Law Departments and Judicial Department).

Vernacular Newspapers: *Andhra Patrika, Deshabhimani, Gruhalakshmi, Arya Janapriyan, Karnataka Vaibhav, Sanmarga Bodhini, Swadesamitran, Swarajya, Vrittanta Chintamani, Young India*, and *South Indian Mitran*.

S. Muthulakshmi Reddy Papers, 1915–58, NMML, New Delhi.

Annexure to letter from Telugu translator to Government to Chief Secretary, Tamil Nadu Archives: 4 February 1911.

Tamil Nadu Archives; GO 348, Judicial; 4 March 1912; p. 7 of Notes.
Tamil Nadu Archives; GO 348, Judicial; 4 March 1912; Minutes of Dissent to the Report of the Registrar of Books and the Chairman of the Telugu Board of Studies; 15 December 1911; p. 17.
Tamil Nadu Archives; notes to GO No 348: Judicial; 4 March 1912, p. 14.
Tamil Nadu Archives GO 348; Judicial; 4 March 1912; Enclosure to letter from F Armitage, Commissioner of Police to Chief Secretary, Government of Madras 1911; p 6
Tamil Nadu Archives GO 348; Judicial; 4 March 1912;Official Memorandum No 4370–1: Judicial; 27 September 1911; p. 9.
The Archives of The Hindu newspaper, Chennai; correspondences of 1910–1930
The Archives of The Hindu newspaper, Chennai; correspondences of 1930–1940
T. Duraikkannu, handbill, dated 1927, the Muthulakshmi Reddi Papers, Nehru Memorial Museum and Library, New Delhi, subject file II (part II), p. 72.
EMI Music Archives, London, Indian correspondence, 13 January 1900
EMI Music Archives, London, Indian Correspondence, 29 August 1901.
EMI Music Archives, London, Indian Correspondence, 1 January 1902
EMI Music Archives, London, Indian Correspondence, 3 June 1902.
EMI Music Archives, London, Indian Records catalogues, 1902
EMI Music Archives, London, Indian correspondence, 23 December 1903
EMI Music Archives, London, Indian Correspondence, 23 December 1904.
"Report on Future Prospects of the Entire General Business of the Gramophone Company," EMI, 1921. Collected from the EMI Archives London.
Compagnie Frangaise du Gramophone Past History, 7 Feb. 1921; File: France, Portugal, Switzerland, Algeria, EMI.
The Voice of the Victor (1906–20). British Library, London. Print.
The Columbia Record (1903–16), British Library, London. Print.
Edison Phonography Monthly(1903–1920). British Library, London. Print.

Newspapers Consulted

Fitna, 8 January 1911, National Archives of India, New Delhi.
Leader, 21 January 1911, National Archives of India, New Delhi.
Musafir, 27 January 1911, National Archives of India, New Delhi.
Abhyudaya, 9 February 1911, National Archives of India, New Delhi.
Hindustani, 20 February 1911, National Archives of India, New Delhi.

Notes

1 Published Books, Journals, Articles, and Web resources (in English, Hindi, Bengali, Tamil, Kannada, Urdu, Marathi, and Telugu languages).
2 Significant content for Chapter 4 has been drawn from a series of articles written by the author himself for a news portal *ThePrint*. Readers who wish to delve deeper into the lives of these artists and also hear their recorded music may do so by visiting the following pages:
https://theprint.in/opinion/treasured-tunes/gauhar-jaan-indias-first-record-artist-took-rs-3000-a-session-threw-party-for-her-cat/230906/
https://theprint.in/opinion/treasured-tunes/salem-godavari-the-carnatic-vocalist-fought-superstitions-to-record-erotic-compositions/233481/

https://theprint.in/opinion/treasured-tunes/bangalore-nagarathnamma-the-singer-who-took-to-sanskrit-and-feminism-in-19th-century-india/240743/
https://theprint.in/opinion/treasured-tunes/janki-bai-singer-disfigured-by-56-stab-wounds-sold-more-records-than-her-contemporaries/243124/
https://theprint.in/opinion/treasured-tunes/coimbatore-thayi-the-carnatic-singer-who-struck-a-chord-in-paris-but-is-unknown-in-india/247641/
https://theprint.in/opinion/treasured-tunes/sundarabai-the-versatile-singer-actor-who-helped-women-musicians-herself-died-unsung-poor/250586/
https://theprint.in/opinion/treasured-tunes/kesarbai-kerkar-the-indian-voice-that-made-it-to-nasas-voyager-mission/256137/
https://theprint.in/opinion/treasured-tunes/from-mahatma-gandhi-to-nehru-everyone-was-an-ms-subbulakshmi-fan/259757/
https://theprint.in/opinion/treasured-tunes/indias-shy-classical-musicians-made-way-for-theatres-entry-into-gramophone-record-books/262495/
https://theprint.in/opinion/treasured-tunes/when-vande-mataram-inspired-many-recording-artistes-to-join-indias-freedom-movement/264966/

Index

Note: Page references in *italics* denote figures, in **bold** tables and with "n" endnotes.

For Product Safety Concerns and Information please contact our EU
representative GPSR@taylorandfrancis.com
Taylor & Francis Verlag GmbH, Kaufingerstraße 24, 80331 München, Germany

www.ingramcontent.com/pod-product-compliance
Lightning Source LLC
Chambersburg PA
CBHW071239050326
40690CB00011B/2180